SOCIAL SCIENCE
AS CIVIC DISCOURSE

SOCIAL SCIENCE
AS CIVIC DISCOURSE

Essays on the Invention, Legitimation,
and Uses of Social Theory

Richard Harvey Brown

The University of Chicago Press ■ Chicago and London

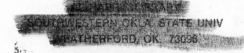

Richard Harvey Brown, professor of sociology at the
University of Maryland, is the author of *Society
as Text* and *A Poetic for Sociology*, both published
by the University of Chicago Press.

The University of Chicago Press, Chicago 60637
The University of Chicago Press, Ltd., London
© 1989 by The University of Chicago
All rights reserved. Published 1989
Printed in the United States of America
98 97 96 95 94 93 92 91 90 89   5 4 3 2 1

Library of Congress Cataloging-in-Publication Data
Brown, Richard Harvey.
    Social science as civic discourse : essays on the invention,
legitimation, and uses of social theory / Richard Harvey Brown.
        p.   cm.
    Bibliography: p.
    Includes index.
    1. Social sciences—Philosophy. 2. Languages—Philosophy.
3. Social change. 4. Social sciences and history.   I. Title.
H61.B6793 1989
300'.1—dc20   89-34221
ISBN 0-226-07624-5 (alk. paper)   CIP

⊗ The paper used in this publication meets the minimum requirements of the
American National Standard for Information Sciences—Permanence of Paper for
Printed Library Materials, ANSI Z39.48-1984

For my son,

RAMIRO BROWN Y BABEL

> May he create harmony
> from the discords
> of his several worlds

CONTENTS

PREFACE

THROUGH WHAT discourse might society enact its own emancipation? Social science is a candidate for this project. In the twentieth century, sociology, history, and their sister disciplines have become major languages through which peoples define and justify themselves and their affairs. But to a great extent the discourse of social science is technocratic, denuded of intersubjective meanings, devoid of categories through which moral agency might be articulated within public life. Social science provides a language for our bureaucratic and market systems, but it largely fails as a discourse for moral agency and political obligation. By contrast, the discourse of romanticism and humanism describes subjective feelings and moral obligations, but seems unable to integrate these with the knowledge necessary to effectively guide our states and markets. Our task, then, is not merely to reject the positivism of conventional social science in favor of romantic alternatives. Instead, we need to criticize both positivism *and* romanticism, and to conjoin them in a more comprehensive language of public life that respects systems efficiency as well as moral agency, and thereby allows persons to act responsibly as citizens governing their polities.

In the spirit of this task, the present volume attempts to reorient the language and thus the practices of the social sciences so that they might become an agency for the empowerment of citizens. Thus this work is part of a larger project that has occupied many scholars of our time—to transform the human sciences into a fully democratic civic discourse. Ideas alone, no matter how eloquently formed, cannot by themselves redirect the language and the mission of the social sciences towards politically enlightened ends. Obviously, this is truer still of any single work. Disciplines are sedimented structures that do not yield easily to arguments about their social responsibilities.

Positivist bashing has been a minor industry for over a generation now, and there are few true blue, or black and blue, worshippers of A. J. Ayer left. Most remotely conscious social scientists have heard of Popper and Kuhn and will admit to at least some relevance of their method and findings. For all that, most social scientists eschew reflection in order to do their jobs and solve their puzzles. To a degree this is properly so. A narrowly technical orientation to research is often appropriate to narrowly technical questions, and even narrow findings are sometimes useful for larger social and intellectual ends. The problem, however, is that the technicist language of puzzle solving has insinuated itself into almost all domains of civic life, so that there is little public space for moral civic discourse based on reason. Thus in public life we tend to have either the technical analyses of experts or the moralistic exhortations of politicians, with no meta-discourse to criticize and overcome their inadequacies.

At the same time, however, the features of partisanship and interest-dependency, which weaken the claims of social science to represent objective truth, can also be made to liberate and transform the discourse of social science into a language for a humane civic practice. My criticisms of narrow scientism and moralistic humanism therefore are not gestures of dismissal but efforts at transformation.

How might the argumentation for such a project unfold? A first step would be to find a language in which object-oriented and agent-oriented forms of social thought would be subsumed under a common meta-discourse. Most social science imitates physics or biology, eschews conceptions of human agency as explanatory variables, and justifies itself in terms of a positivist epistemology. In contrast, humanistic social inquiry seems truer to lived experience, but it appears to operate in the realm of intuition, to be a matter of artistic interpretation more than of scientific truth. My earlier book, *A Poetic for Sociology: Toward a Logic of Discovery for the Human Sciences* (1989 [1977]) suggests "cognitive aesthetics" or "symbolic realism" as a vocabulary to critically reformulate and dialectically sublate the traditions of both positivism and romanticism within the social sciences. Using the symbolic realist perspective, interpretive procedures may be justified as a rigorous way of knowing, and positive science can be shown to be itself a thoroughly interpretive procedure.

A second step in transforming the social sciences into a humane civic discourse would be to develop new metaphors and methods for a social science now understood to be a poetical and rhetorical practice. One such metaphor is elaborated in my *Society as Text: Essays on Reason, Rhetoric, and Reality* (1987). While preserving a sensitivity to mechanisms of structural causation, a humane civic discourse must provide a principal role of human agents in shaping their social realities. But if society is a text authored by men and women, it must not only be "observed" but also "read" by social scientists. How might this be properly done? And what relations will different social scientific readings have with alternate forms of moral political action?

These questions, raised in *Society as Text*, are explored more fully in the present volume. In this treatise I invoke several additional argumentative moves. First, I describe how the positivist habitus embraces epistemology, social theory, and social practice in a way that depowers ordinary citizens in the name of efficiency and expertise. Then, I critically assess the romantic, anti-positivist, alternative to reveal that it too shares many traits of positivism—foundationalism, inadequate critical awareness, and failure to describe a humane civic practice. Symbolic realism, a concept outlined in *A Poetic* and developed in *Society as Text*, is introduced again as a vocabulary for assessing the competing claims and objectives of disciplinary inquiry—at least as these might impinge on the arena of civic issues and disputations.

How might such a vocabulary help revise our understanding and practice of social science in relation to society and history? In a further rhetorical move, I address this question by considering existential phenomenology and French structuralism as examples respectively of an agent-centered and an object-centered discourse, and I suggest how these might be dialectically joined to yield a richer and more humane understanding of self and social structure. I then show that all historical representations are forms of linguistic figuration—that is, that the alternative ways of representing our pasts (and hence, ourselves) are encoded in four root metaphors that correspond to the four major linguistic tropes. In this fashion I show that human experience gains its status as a real historical past through alternative forms of symbolic representation. Once fully appreciated, this revised understanding of the social and historical sciences offers a critical rhetorical opening for a humanized civic discourse. In a final argumentative step, I try to demonstrate this by reformulating in symbolic realist terms two usually reified domains of public life—"organizational behavior" and "social planning."

This logical development also may be stated as a topical preview of the present volume. I begin in chapter 1 with an overview of the general problematic along the lines discussed above. Chapter 2 sets up the first moment in may dialectic by outlining the nature of positivism on the levels of metaphysics, social theory, and social control. I argue that positivist metaphysics—ontology and epistemology—provides a legitimation for much social theory, which in turn legitimates management, expertise, planning, and other forms of societal direction.

The positivist tradition has been challenged not only by reform movements from within but also by a romantic countermovement from without. In chapter 3 I review the philosophic bases of this countermovement, drawing on pragmatism, hermeneutics, existential phenomenology, and especially ordinary language philosophy. These language interpretive theories of conduct are the inverse of positivism, replacing the positivists' foundation of brute facts with

one of brute meanings. In focusing almost exclusively on interpretations of intentional actions by agents, I argue, such discourses can
yield little more than complicitous redescriptions of members' versions of their own conduct and settings. What is thereby omitted is an
account of the structured scarcities of the social system as a whole, as
well as of the *mis*understanding and *false* consciousness of its members. Thus a method is needed that combines an intentional description of conduct with an analysis of structure and scarcity. What would
be the philosophic legitimation for such a method? In what context
could we more securely resolve the debate between the romantic
idealism of consciousness and the scientific realism of structure. Such
a warrant, I argue, is offered by "symbolic realism." In this perspective, science itself is seen as a symbol system and symbols are seen as
the constitutive medium of all human experience. In this view,
symbols make experience real in the sense of rendering it communicable and hence capable of intersubjective validation. Symbolic realism focuses on language and speech as the most universal structure
and use of symbols. For symbolic realists, discourse is the medium
from which both individual consciousness and social systems
emerge.

This argument is continued in chapter 4, in which I focus on the
works of Jean-Paul Sartre and Claude Lévi-Strauss in an effort to fuse
positivist and romantic forms of description. I argue for a dialectical
relationship between agency and order or, in this instance, between
existentialism and structuralism. Such a dialectic, I suggest, would
provide a discourse the envisions persons as moral agents, but that
would do so in the context of largely predetermined social structures.
In so conjoining structure and agency, such a discourse would invite
us to speak not merely of micro processes and macro structures, but
of citizens governing their polities.

This argument is extended in chapter 5, in which I illustrate more
precisely how symbolic realism might inform our self-understanding
as social thinkers. I do this by expanding on my earlier works on
metaphor and on historical consciousness (Brown 1989 [1977], 1987).
I show how the explanatory power of the two major approaches to
historical science—functionalist evolutionism and experimental
empiricism—derive their power from language, from their deployment of two different metaphors—the organism and the machine.
Taking their cues from the biological thinking of Aristotle, organicists
conceive of change as slow, continuous, and teleological, a steady
movement of Society through a homogeneous Time. By contrast, in
the spirit of Newton and Hobbes, mechanists see change as occurring
through discrete events that impacted on other discrete events

according to general causal laws. Each school sees its own formulations as literal descriptions of an available past, while each school
accuses the other of error. Yet, seen in a symbolic realist perspective,
each approach is both metaphorical *and* true. Each is founded in
language and each underwrites its truth claims by respecting the rules
of its own linguistic practice. Poesis and noesis are joined in the logos;
both creativity and knowledge emerge from language.

This contention is broadened in chapter 6, where I discuss two
other root metaphors of historical figuration—context and form—as
these are developed in two additional approaches to historical science, French structuralism and existential phenomenology. This
discussion builds on the earlier one concerning Claude Lévi-Strauss
and Jean-Paul Sartre, but now it is placed in the general perspective of
symbolic realism and focused on the specific disciplinary area of
historical science. I argue that the structuralist project—as in the
works of Louis Althusser and the *Annales* school of *histoire des
mentalités*, is an elaboration of the root metaphor of context. Similarly,
I describe a social phenomenology, based on the root metaphor of
form, that provides a method for decoding the historicity of praxis,
both of historians and of historical actors past and present. In a final
section I return to the linguistic model of the previous chapter and
relate the four root metaphors of historical science—organism, mechanism, context, and form—to the four tropes of linguistic figuration—
synechdoche, metonymy, metaphor, and irony. I conclude that the
deployment of one or another of these metaphors and tropes is
ineliminable in any linguistic representation of reality and that,
therefore, the determinate scientific and the creative artistic dimensions of the social-historical sciences are separated only in error or bad
faith.

If this symbolic realist conception of what we do as social thinkers
is accepted, how might it change our theoretical practice? My answer
is that the understanding that all human activity, including theory making, is communicative behavior invites a more catholic, dialectical, and
integrative discourse on social process. This is shown in chapter 7,
which focuses on theories of bureaucracy and formal organization, perhaps sociology's richest area of empirically grounded generalizations.
Conceiving organizations as communicative behavior, I inquire how
they are engendered and constrained by the grammar of the larger social structure and how they in turn constitute and are constituted by
the speech acts that go on within them. To develop this argument I first
discuss the basic orientations of Marx, Weber, and Durkheim as these
have informed contemporary theory of organizations. I then invoke the
work of Harold Garfinkel and others to demystify the Weberian mys-

tique of organizational rationality, showing how rationality is itself a social symbolic construction. I also reformulate Marx's concepts of labor and ideology to refer to the construction of both social structure and forms of consciousness out of everyday interactions. Finally, having "Marxized" Garfinkel and "phenomenologized" Marx, I fuse these new alloys both with each other and with neo-Weberian organizational theory. The result is an incipient political symbology of formal organizations that encompasses politics at the structural level as well as moral consciousness in the lifeworld.

Does all this bring us closer to our original goal—a discourse that provides for the predictability and control necessary for systems management, yet one that emerges from human experience and ethical accountability? Put slightly differently, even if we could envision a liberated society on the level of theory, by what methods might such a liberated society be achieved? On the one hand, the manipulativeness of technicist means for effecting social change tends to negate our humanistic ends. On the other hand, in accepting the romantic critique of positivist social planning we appear to consign ourselves to contemplative passivity. What method of societal self-direction would overcome this apparent choice between amoral activism and passive moralism? In the final chapter 8, I explore the implications of a symbolic realist perspective for social planning. Such an approach does not reject positivist or romantic ideas out of hand, but seeks to transform them. Drawing on the work of Merleau-Ponty, I discuss social planning as a mode of reality construction. Under the aegis of this conception, I shift the positivist ideal of elitest planning to a post-positivist, post-romantic one of mutual learning. I also move the concept of ultimate perfection to that of excellence by stages, a move from a product toward a process orientation. Similarly, I decenter the concept of making intelligent decisions to include negotiating frameworks of intelligibility. Finally, I argue that fantasy as well as rationality are essential ingredients in an emancipatory approach to societal self-direction. I conclude with remarks on relations between the social thinker and political praxis.

ACKNOWLEDGMENTS

MANY PERSONS have helped shape the spirit and substance of this work. My brother, Jason Brown, encouraged me by the purity of his commitment to the life of the mind. My wife, Nathalie Babel, nourished me by her daily example of the moral use of reason. My parents, Samuel and Sylvia Brown, have been a constant source of support. I am greatly inspired also by my friends in Colombia, South America, who risk their lives to seek and speak the truth.

Robert Brulle, Fred Dallmayr, Joseph Gusfield, Michael Overington, George Ritzer, Manfred Stanley, and Trutz von Trotha were generous with suggestions on the manuscript as a whole. Thomas Farrell made critical remarks of immense value, many of which were incorporated into the text without explicit acknowledgement. Randall Collins and Jack Douglas offered critical comments on chapter 2. Robert Brulle, Herbert Simons, and Manfred Stanley gave editorial and substantive help with chapter 3. My mentors in historical sociology prepared me over many years to compose chapters 5 and 6. They include Kenneth Bock who introduced me to evolutionism and its empiricist alternative; Stanford Lyman who suggested the anti-positivist, phenomenological critique; Carl Schorske and the late Cesar Graña who taught me the historicity of ideas; Herbert Passin and the late Benjamin Nelson who instructed me in the comparative study of social structures and structures of consciousness; Sigmund Diamond who guided me in my efforts at historical research; and Rudolf Makkreel who introduced me to the philosophy of history. My discussion of the logico-meaningful method in chapter 5 reflects extensive conversations with Stanford Lyman. Chapter 8 benefited from the advice of Robert Brulle, Kurt Finsterbusch, and Jacqueline Wasilewski. This chapter also incorporates insights provided by Ana Cristina Gardano, Stanford Lyman, D. Sam Scheele, and Manfred Stanley.

Thanks is also due to Geraldine Todd and the staff of the sociology department at the University of Maryland, and to my research assistant, Zhao Shanyang, for preparing this manuscript for press.

My graduate students and many colleagues at the University created the agonistic environment from which dialectical thought might arise. Of these I especially thank the members of my seminar on the rhetoric of the social sciences, the participants in the faculty seminar on narrative, and Michael Agar, Fred Alford, Remi Clignet, Barbara Finkelstein, Kurt Finsterbusch, Jerald Hage, James Glass, James Klumpp, George Ritzer, and John Robinson.

To all these persons I owe a profound debt. I cannot hope to acquit it with thanks, but wish to acknowledge it here with heartfelt gratitude.

Parts of this volume have appeared in earlier versions. Much of chapter 1 was published as "Utopia, Praxis y los trajabos de la verdad social," in the *Revista Colombiana de Sociologia* 4, 1 (Mayo 1986):107–113. Several paragraphs of chapters 2 and 3 are taken from my *A Poetic for Sociology*, Cambridge University Press, 1977, reprinted by University of Chicago Press, 1989, and from "Philosophical Perspectives on Positivist and Humanist Forms of Social Theory," in *The Emergence of Existential Thought*, edited by Jack D. Douglas and John M. Johnson, Cambridge University Press, 1977, pp. 77–100. Parts of chapter 3 also appear as "Critical Rhetoric and the Dualism of the Human Sciences: Toward a Reformulation of the Debate between Positivism and Romanticism," in *Case Studies in the Rhetoric of the Human Sciences*, edited by Herbert W. Simons, University of Chicago Press, 1989. Versions of chapter 4 were published variously as "Dialectica y estructura en la teoría sociológica: La búsqueda de un método lógico," in the *Revista Española de Investigaciones Sociológicas* 37 (Enero–Marzo 1987), and the *Revista Paraguaya de Sociologia* 23, 65 (Enero–Abril 1986). Other parts of what became chapter 4 appeared as "Dialectic and Structure in Jean-Paul Sartre and Claude Lévi-Strauss," published in *Internationale Zeitschrift für Philosophie der Erkenntnis* 32, 2 (1978): 164–184, and in *Human Studies* 2, 1 (January 1979):1–19. An earlier version of chapter 5 was published as "Metaphor and Historical Consciousness: Organicism and Mechanism in the Study of Social Change," in *Cognition and Symbolic Structures: The Psychology of Metaphoric Transformations*, edited by Robert E. Haskell, Ablex 1987. Several paragraphs of chapter 5 also are adapted from my discussions of metaphor in *A Poetic for Sociology*, University of Chicago Press, 1989 [1977], and in *Society as Text*, University of Chicago Press, 1987. Parts of chapters 5 and 6 were published as "Historical Science as Linguistic Figuration," *Theory and Society* 14, 5 (September 1985): 677–703. An earlier version of chapter 7 was published as "Bureacracy as Praxis: Toward a Political Phenomenology of Formal Organizations," *Administrative*

Sciences Quarterly 23, 3 (September 1978): 365–382. Much of chapter 8 appeared as "Social Planning as Symbolic Practice: Toward a Liberating Discourse for Societal Self-Direction," *International Journal of Sociology and Social Policy* 7, 1 (1987): 13–37, 1987.

ONE

INTRODUCTION
Civic Discourse and the Travails of Social Truth

> Words, those guardians of meanings, are not immortal, invulnerable. Like men, words also suffer. . . . Some can survive, others are incurable. . . . In the night everything gets confused, there are no more names, no more shapes.
>
> Adamov (1938)

> If names be not correct, language is not in accordance with the truth of things. If language be not in accordance with the truth of things, affairs cannot be carried on to success. . . . Therefore, a superior man considers it necessary that the names he uses may be spoken appropriately, and also that what he speaks may be carried out appropriately. What the superior man requires is just that in his words there may be nothing incorrect.
>
> Confucius, *Analects*

WHY SHOULD the social theorist continue to theorize? That is the question. Social science in its value-neutral guise has become a component of technocratic domination. And in its guise as one of the humanities it is largely irrelevant. In either aspect, social science is inadequate to the moral and political requirements of our age. A generation after Americans liberated Paris from Nazi occupation, the countrymen of Madison and Jefferson were occupying Vietnam. The CIA intellectuals of Harvard and Columbia found their research techniques well suited to programs of "disinformation." And social thinkers of a more humanistic persuasion saw their former students dropping napalm on villagers or acid on their brains. Though Gulag and Auschwitz are the archetypal symbols of modern evil, even in their more ordinary forms deceit and cruelty seem not merely impervious to the constraints of reason but in fact a by-product of the hyperrationalization of the modern world, a rationalization that science serves and the humanities ignore.

We can no longer theorize as if no vital change had occurred in our sense of the human possibility, as if the organized extermination of

tens of millions of people had not altered, profoundly, the quality of
our awareness. We cannot pretend that such events do not affect the
obligations of thought and the responsible life of the imagination.
"What man has inflicted on man, in very recent time, has affected the
writer's primary material—the sum and potential of human
behavior—and it presses on the brain with a new darkness" (Steiner
1974, 4). The human studies in Europe did little to warn us against
totalitarianism. And in America, young men conscripted to fight
fascism wound up largely as creatures of the corporate state. Many
economists, political scientists, historians, and sociologists who ad-
vised on the victory of democracy in Europe were soon advising on
the suppression of democracy in Brazil, in Indonesia, in Chile, in all
those countries that required what is called a stable political climate
for investment. With even more tragic irony, in communist societies
Marx's theories of the social bases for human liberation were transformed into an ideology of total domination. Moreover, in Asia, Africa,
and Latin America, the realization of an Enlightenment vision of
national liberation has not brought an end to despotism, nor has the
application of rationalistic economic theories much diminished poverty and injustice. All this casts doubt on the efficacy of social theory
as a humanizing social force. In such circumstances is not the life of
the mind a vanity? Is not reflective consciousness an extravagance in
a world dominated by falsehood and cruelty, a world in which pain
has become the universal language and torture is practiced by all
peoples because it is the one code which everyone understands?

Another curious feature of the postwar era has been the "demo-
cratization" of what used to be called higher learning and, with this,
the fragmentation of knowledge. Knowledge itself has been redefined
from an end to a means. Universities have largely become factories
dedicated to producing trained graduates and research reports,
whereas formerly, ideally, they consecrated themselves to cultivating
citizens and seeking truth. In becoming a professional the new man
of science has to "exchange general citizenship in society for membership in the community of the competent. Within his field of
expertise, the worth of his opinions henceforth would be judged not
by open competition with all who cared to challenge him, but by the
close evaluation of his professional colleagues" (Haskell 1977, 67).
Professional enrichment, public impoverishment. The division of
labor between and within departments, the status insecurity and
careerism of both students and teachers, the rise of "applied social
science" that is neither scientific nor applied, all contribute to the
uneasy feeling that professors no longer have anything to profess.
Like the man who came to know more and more about less and less,

our knowledge has been trivialized with the growth of our expertise. With the separation of scientific and existential vocabularies of understanding, the more we have scientific explanations, the less ground we have for dignity and freedom. And so the thoughtful social scientist finds himself in much the same position as Samuel Beckett. When asked, "With your despair about language and the human condition, why do you keep on writing?" Beckett responded, "That's what I'm trying to find out" (Strong 1978, 253).

The challenge of such questions has driven many social scientists into silence. This refusal of the word is not a protest against the age in which public relations, image-making, and lies govern the norms of public speech (Jung 1982, 57). Instead, the silence of social scientists is complicitous with modern evil. By breaking our understanding of ourselves into the parochial specialties of particular disciplines, and by conceptualizing society as the aggregate of tiny factors, positive social science fractionates our attention, directs awareness away from our political economy and collective psychology, and prepares us for a thunderous silence on the morally and politically significant issues of our age. "By thus leaving the job of worrying to the powers that be, sociologists have implicitly recognized the legitimacy of these powers; their disengagement has turned out to be engagement—however involuntary—on the side of the status quo" (Dahrendorf 1968, 123).

These remarks are not meant to diminish the value of advanced statistical techniques, large date bases, sophisticated mathematical models, or the use of social science to inform social movements or form policies of the state. Yet if social science pursues such activities to the exclusion of broad theoretical inquiry, these activities themselves become vacuous and ideological. Without a reflective theoretical framework, such activities do not draw on the reservoir of concepts that provide a critical distance from the ahistorical common sense of ordinary members or elites. And since policy-oriented research rarely is directed toward intellectual much less theoretical or scholarly concerns, researchers are routinely co-opted by the immediate utilitarian interests of the powers whom they serve (Goldfarb 1970, 16–17).

The corruption of the word by the world is as old as the search for political community. In this search, reasoned public persuasion has always had a central role to play. Thucydides' analysis of the rhetoric[1] used by Athenians at the end of the Peloponesian War, for example, is infused with a religious sense of the *logos*. But the collapse of the *polis* was accompanied by a breach in the lived connection between political discourse and public life, between *theoria* and *praxis*, with nothing at hand to replace it. Eventually the Christian idea of community reintroduced a relation of significance between politics and persons. But now this bond too has collapsed. And since few modern thinkers would pretend to play the role of Paul or Jesus, what means of recreating political and moral community are left to us today? Perhaps all that is permitted us is to try to speak the truth, to be sure that in our words "there may be nothing incorrect." Yet, how is this to be done when our very language is permeated with lies, when our words are exhausted from the burdens of deceit they already carry?

In and through all this, the social sciences and humanities remain a theology for the twentieth century and, as such, they retain an implicit critical potential. Despite their travails, they still provide the vocabularies through which we express our ultimate concerns and thus articulate standards against which contemporary society might be judged. In the Middle Ages theological language was used by people who sought a definition of the world and their place in it, a theory of origins, nature, and destiny, an agenda of problems to address or sufferings to accept. Contemporary persons asking similar questions use the language of the human sciences, whose vocabularies serve today as instruments for articulating and responding to basic human and societal interests. Our collective self-definitions as well as our personal identities are articulated through the languages of sociology, anthropology, economics, psychology, and history. In this sense social science is a theodicy of the twentieth century. Why do just men suffer?, one formerly asked the rabbi. Because of structural unemployment, today answers the economist. Why does evil go unpunished?, one used to ask the priest. Because in market-oriented societies we have restorative law rather than retributive justice, today answers the criminologist. When will my troubles be over, dear Lord? Once you become adjusted, says the psychologist. The theological language of sin and redemption has been replaced by the scientific language of disequilibrium and adjustment.

Because the pressing questions of the modern era are formulated in the terms of the secular human studies, social science involves more than academic research. It also provides an implicit philosophical anthropology and social ontology. By using the language of social science to speak of our own and other human conditions, we thereby posit a definition of the nature of the human and the social. But if the human sciences provide a privileged discourse for addressing fundamental questions, they do not permit us to address them any way we choose. Like theology in former times, the social sciences today have their own rules of proper discourse. These rules must be respected if one is to use the language as a member. Syntactic or semantic incompetence in social science marks one as illiterate in a major language of personal self-definition and collective self-direction.

A reformulation of the language of the social sciences is thus a reformulation of the means for our collective public discourse. In an important sense, our lives are at stake in the debates over the social sciences. Our conscious awareness of our shared existence, and the very character of our being human, are shaped by these modes of symbolization. Social science "realizes" the world. Those who control this discourse thus control a principal means for publicly defining reality. As the "real-ization" of experience, social science denotes not only what is to be taken as normal, legitimate, or rational, but also what is to be taken as reality itself. To alter the rules for sociological truth-telling is thus to influence the ways by which we come to know both who we are and what we might become. In this sense sociology is inevitably normative: It is always ideological and value-laden even while being objective or value-free. There is a political morality of thought just as there is a socio-logic of action. To deny the political and ethical implications of our forms of theorizing is to engage in civic inauthenticity and intellectual bad faith.

Social thought is a symbolic expression of the culture from which it springs. Whatever its pretensions, social thought is not a hermetic system isolated from its engendering context. Instead, it always emerges from and helps to shape culture and society. For example, most of the concepts that serve as icons for modern consciousness are also central to formal social theory. Such terms as citizen, ideology, bureaucracy, intellectual, revolution, alienation, and industry were first used in their modern sense only at the time of the French and the industrial revolutions as part of a renewed movement in systematic social analysis. "Industry" once meant the virtue of hard work and diligence, but it has assumed a very different meaning since 1800. Similarly, "revolution" used to mean a turning, a going back to origins, but the content of the phonetic sign changed as its context altered. Terms such as industry, revolution, bureaucracy, or alienation as we understand them today are central to social analysis, but before the mutual advent of social science and modernity these concepts were not available to us as instruments of collective self-awareness.

Though drawing on and clarifying ideas that are broadly shared in modern cultures, however, sociology and other disciplines are not merely a science of unreflective common sense. Instead, the particularly modern quality of social science is its reflexiveness. It does not simply use common sense as a resource for understanding. It also makes "common sense" a topic of investigation. Sociology, for example, provides methodological tools for reflecting critically upon what members of a society take for granted in their everyday views of the world. How such a taken-for-granted, shared natural reality comes to exist, how it changes or is sustained, are prime topics for sociological analysis. Common sense, by itself, lacks cognitive tools for such reflexivity. The human studies thus provide representations of and for a society by which it can link itself with a civilizational tradition. As formal articulations of sentiments and sensibilities, social theories infuse everyday life with a universal dimension and thereby are a means by which peoples can transcend mundance consciousness and come to know themselves.

In this sense, the crises within the human sciences are inextricably related to crises within our culture as a whole. With the collapse of tradition and revelation as sources of epistemological and political justifications, social science emerged as the main mode of social truth. This has proved a shallow well for those thirsting for firm knowledge and direction, however, since the human studies have internalized the very crises and conflicts they sought to describe. The separation of individual from society, reason from emotions, facts from values, objective knowledge from subjective opinion, are taken for granted as much by social scientists as by anyone else. These bifurcations all represent cognitive crises not only in our general culture, but also within the human studies. Such antimonies must be overcome if the social sciences are to advance their own agendas, yet they cannot be overcome by mere reforms in these disciplines alone.

The human sciences cannot solve their own problems unless and until the crises in our culture as a whole find resolution. The struggle of these disciplines to address their own contradictions, however, can itself be a prime resource for engaging the larger issues of our times. Social thought is both a mirror and a lamp, both legitimation and critique. It reflects the evident facts of society and also lights up its darker workings. But social theory can be our mirror and our lamp in a more profound and existential sense, for the social sciences reflect in their own praxis the contradictions of society as a whole, and reveal, by their own hopes and illuminations, not only what society is, but also what it might become.

A century ago, before the social sciences became "mature," this was still clearly understood. Since their inception the human studies have been a collective *cri de coeur*, an appeal in secular language for ontological redemption. The theories of Comte, Tocqueville, Marx, Weber, Durkheim, or Mead all envisioned a nature of man and society and implied a utopia against which history and present practice might be assessed. Durkheim, for example, understood society as a moral reality in the sense that social order involved the unity of personal identity and social collectivity through systems of moral meaning. Durkheim was as much a social psychologist as a structural sociologist in his view of social systems as symbolic orders that give ethical and practical significance to the life worlds of their members. It is through such systems of interpretation that identities are stabilized, the performance of roles is insured, and social order is maintained. On the one hand, these systems are radical in promising a truth or meaning to human existence and implying that this truth must be redeemed. On the other hand, such systems of interpretation are conservative in providing a consolation, a reason for bearing what otherwise could not be borne. Durkheim sought to make such systems of meaning self-reflective and available to the consciousness of members of modern societies. Today social science itself serves as a collective representation, but it is often less self-reflective than primitive religion. Social science has become technocratic, spiritually denuded, lacking the courage to acknowledge its normative presuppositions.

Social theory since the eighteenth century was born of the attempt to understand the modernization of society and the crises of emergent liberal institutions. To the master social theorists—Tocqueville, Marx, Durkheim, Weber, Simmel, and others—industrial civilization was characterized simultaneously by unregulated concentrations of vast power and a radical individualism and value segmentation arising from the social division of labor. In this historical and intellectual context, social theory became "a language whose primary mission is to articulate the quest for a specifically modern understanding of the ancient notion that man is a social being" (Stanley 1978, 20). Moreover, classical thinkers such as Comte or Marx hoped that social theory would convert popular consciousness to new modes of historically redemptive thought. This more synoptic view-at once philosophical, historical, and sociological-characterized the makers of modern social thought. Today narrowly professional social scientists seem both incapable and uninterested in this classical pursuit. In order to reappropriate this larger, classical view "we must try to restore the idea of social science as public philosophy" (Bellah et al. 1985, 298; see Bellah 1983; Gellner 1965, 34).

There are reasons for the demise of social science as a moral public discourse. Our age of progress and enlightenment is also an age of darkness and despair (Hawthorne 1976). The collapse of the French Revolution, the failure of industrialism to overcome existential scarcities, the debasement of socialist hopes in totalitarianism, the great and ever more deadly wars, all seem to justify an abandonment of faith in the meliorative power of ideas. Reason in the world seems largely to have become the application of instrumental rationality to all of human relations, even to the extent that persons could be treated solely as the objects of other people's calculations.

In such a dystopian vision, whether already upon us or merely a potential, what is the place for moral agency and ethics, for personal dignity and freedom? Indeed, is there not a fundamental conflict between scientism and humanism, between rational calculation and humane values? On one hand, our manipulative means for affecting social change tend to negate our humanistic ends. On the other hand, in accepting the romantics' criticisms of positivist techniques we appear to consign ourselves either to mindless activism or to contemplative passivity in the face of genuine social crises. In such a context the debate between technicists and their humanistic critics grows sterile. Instead, it becomes vital to question the basic terms of discourse about the relations between scientific and humanistic forms of theory, as well as between such theories and their implicit praxes. We need new ways of symbolizing present conditions and conceptualizing alternative social orders. And we need new methods of social transformation that do not of their nature violate humane intentions.

Put slightly differently, the crises of our culture, and the framework of our task, manifest themselves on three levels: the philosophical, the social theoretical, and the political. The *philosopher* is concerned with the nature of reality, how it can be known, and what it should become. The social *theorist* is interested in describing that which is, its origins, causes, and functions, its scarcities and potentials. The *activist* focuses on how we are to move from the theorists' "is" to the philosopher's "ought."

These issues are the context for my treatise. I launch a philosophic critique of social theory and a practical critique of philosophy. As domains of discourse, philosophy, theory, and practice all exist through language and, indeed, language is my leitmotiv throughout. By so constituting my topic, I invite the construction of a science of human authorship of the world. Such a social science has a cognitive interest in human dignity because it presupposes persons to be moral agents, albeit operating within a text that is prescribed by others past and present. To the extent that derivatives of such a science become a common discourse in the broader culture, it would provide a barrier against technocratic and bureaucratic dehumanization. This, at least, is the utopia implicit in my own rhetorical strategy and the telos of this book.

Two

THE POSITIVIST HABIT OF MIND
Metaphysics, Social Theory, and
Social Control

There is no second power in our modern world that may be compared with scientific thought. [Science has become] the summit and consummation of all our human activities, the last chapter in the history of mankind, and the most important subject of a philosophy of man. . . . We may dispute concerning the results of science or its first principles, but its general function seems to be unquestionable. It is science that gives us assurance of a common world.

Ernst Cassirer

If you want to know the nature of a given philosophy (its concept of reality or truth) you must know what sort of world would have to exist for that philosophy to coherently unite thought and experience.

Richard Rorty

THE CONCEPT *habitus mentalis*, of habit of mind, embraces philosophic, theoretical, and practical dimensions of human reality. It refers to those societal or epochal structures of consciousness that provide the ordering principles for accounts in everyday life. A habitus mentalis is constituted of a people's usual way of thinking and conducting themselves, their dominant collective paradigm, their way of seeing that defines them *as* a people. The habitus provides the means by which persons regularly connect observations with intentions and link values with methods in order to produce and justify the choices and actions that make up their scenes and social structures. By using such a concept I hope to describe the implicit styles of thought, preconscious background assumptions, root metaphors, and rules of reason by which we have come to define ourselves in our particular way and by which we legitimize and guide our action.

The dominant habitus mentalis of modern Western societies has been "positivism"—the world vision that by and large has accorded with and supported the rise of industrial capitalism and the nation state.[1] Positivism draws sustenance from the practical experiments of Bacon and the mathematical deductions of Descartes. It takes physical science as its model and assumes a natural standpoint in which reality is strictly distinguished from the symbols that represent it. From this position the meaning of a word or expression is the thing or behavior to which it refers. Statements that are true are those that correspond to objectively verified facts or conditions. Moreover, for positivists such objective, law-like statements can provide the bases for a scientific management and politics.

The contrast to this view has been expressed by "romanticism"— the world vision that opposes the rationalization of life. Unlike positivists who believed in progress and modernity, romantics have tended, as reactionaries, to hark back to preindustrial times or, as radicals, to envision a future post-bourgeois social order. Inspired by (and partly distorting) Vico and Hegel, romanticism crystalized as an opposition ideology in the nineteenth century. Romantic philosophers and poets defended art as representing various truths higher than those of science. "We have Beauty" as Nietzsche put it, "in order to preserve us from Truth." Such thinking fostered interpretive methods in the human studies and diverse antirationalistic tendencies in politics.

In the positivist view, the human sciences were to imitate physics, in the romantic view they were to emulate art. But the human studies are akin both to science *and* to art. Their explanations seek the empirical rigor that we imagine of physics, but they also require motivational insight in the manner of a poem. While many analysts have noted hese conflicts—between positivism and romanticism, hard and soft methods, objectivity and subjectivity, value freedom and commitment—we do not yet know how these opposites can be contained within a general theoretical approach that would account for both structural determinism as well as conscious intention, and that would be consistent in its epistemology yet humanizing in its practice. Such a post-positivist, post-romantic discourse would enable persons to articulate their personal agency through actions in social institutions as citizens governing their polity.

The Absolutist Metaphysic

Systematic rationality had been pursued in classical times and in the medieval period, but no one thought it could yield absolute certainties about human affairs. Science in the Greek world concerned that which showed permanence or regularity of occurrence (Aristotle *Physics* 2.8; *Metaphysics*, 11.8). By contrast, human conduct reflected the inconstant appetites and will, as well as reason. Scientific truth (*episteme*) took as its form and contents mathematics, astronomy, and, later, Scripture. Knowledge of the social world *(phronesis)* was a practical wisdom, sagacity gained through experience, travel, or responsible participation in civic life.

Though mystical rationalists like Plato were suspicious of poetry, most Westerners appreciated the evocative power of language in public discourse. Roman jurists did try to purify language into an instrument for precise replicability of reasoning in cases as did certain theologians, but their efforts never set the dominant tone in classical or medieval culture. Instead, rhetoric—the skilled deployment of anecdote, irony, metaphor, and the other resources of language—was respected by philosophers, statesmen, clerics, academics, and lay people alike (Levine 1985).

In the seventeenth and eighteenth centuries, however, certain protocols of reason crystallized to provide new definitions of the nature of knowledge and society. The world had been rediscovered in the Renaissance through the revival of Greek science and by the great explorations, and it had been made rationally calculable through the use of Arabic mathematical techniques. Philosophers, scientists, and statesmen came to believe that laws governing the universe could be discovered and exploited. The goal of controlling a population by means of an absolute state was paralleled by the hope of controlling nature through knowledge of absolute laws. Clear and distinct ideas found their counterparts in the concept of the clear and distinct individual that developed in Protestant belief and in new statues that were codified to replace traditional communal law.

The plain language of Puritan aescetics extended also to philosophy and statecraft. New techniques of warfare, production, and commerce encouraged greater use of money and a shift in the mode of interaction from relations of personal honor and obligation to ones of commodity exchange. The new market economy made every individual appear to be the autonomous source of his decisions and contracts, just as the new philosophies made him the ultimate arbiter of his knowledge and actions. The emergence of individual volition in regulating production and distribution was matched by the emergence of individual reason as the supreme cognitive authority (Goldmann 1973, 20). Perspective became the mode of visual representation, to be read off serially by the eye just as the new progressive conception of time was to be read off linearly by the mind. Practical and abstract knowledge was organized into the encyclopedia. Machine parts became interchangeable; weights and measures were standardized; Linnaeus ordered the species and, later, Mendeleev arranged the elements; the factory system regulated tasks; social statistics were used politically; and stained glass windows were covered by the bourgeoisie's mechanical clocks. By the end of the eighteenth century Mary had been dethroned, and Reason had taken her seat in the Cathedral of Notre Dame de Paris.

The Cartesian notion of pure mathematical laws governing the universe, and the Baconian dictum that knowledge is power, together sum up the epistemology associated with these practical developments. Westerners had "agreed" that they could achieve mastery of their world by understanding the natural forces, the facts and laws that existed out there apart from either God or man.[2]

In many expositions of the philosophic speculation of this period, two broad trends are seen as discrete and competing—the speculative, mathematical, logical-deductive tradition inspired by Descartes, and the more empirical, inductive, research- and fact-oriented tradition heralded by Bacon. This distinction is useful for some purposes, but it describes a family squabble compared to the war *both* these schools were waging against the older theological habitus. Cartesian rationalism and Baconian empiricism both are mechanistic and deterministic, both sought absolute truth about reality.

This absolutism is illustrated by the conflict between Galileo and the Church. The bishops were prepared to let Galileo publish his research if only he would state in the preface that his conclusions were hypothetical, for only theological knowledge could be absolute. Whereas Galileo pretended to capitulate, Newton expressed his Protestant independence by asserting *"Hypothesi non fingo,"* I do not feign hypotheses. Newton thereby made explicit the absolutist assumptions of both his own speculative theories as well as the experimentalism of Galileo.[3] In this sense, early modern science and philosophy remained close to medieval conceptions, though it transferred these to the natural and human realms.

The epistemology of early modern science as developed from Bacon and Descartes served as the go-between for the marriage of medieval metaphysics and positivist theories of society. Both idealists and empiricists in this broad tradition shared the same vision of the world as a machine. The influence flowed back and forth across the English Channel. For example, Harvey's discovery of the circulation of the blood, and his characterization of the heart as a pumping machine, suggested to Descartes that the entire animal-human organism could be treated as a mechanical contrivance. Whereas Harvey still considered the blood to be the seat of a soul, Descartes eschewed this residual animism. But Descartes, as a Catholic, was still inclined to build bridges between the old organic and craft images of the world and the new mechanistic one. By contrast, Hobbes extended Descartes' own logic and dismissed as absurd any use of reason that went beyond the stuff of observable experience. (Tönnies 1974, 20, 33; Hobbes 1957 [1651], 2:65).

This empiricist vision of the world as a machine was passed to John Stuart Mill by his father James, who taught him logic with part 1 of Hobbes's *De corpore* as a text. Evidence, said John Stuart, is not "that which the mind does or must yield to, but that which it *ought* to yield to, namely, that, by yielding to which, its belief is kept in conformable to fact". Mill gave this view of knowledge its classical expression in his treatise *On the Logic of the Moral Sciences*:

> There are a set of alternative hypotheses (H_1, H_2, H_3) concerning the possible determining observed conditions $(C_1, C_2, C_3,$ etc.) of a phenomenon, P.
>
> It is possible to eliminate some or all of these alternative hypotheses if they are not in accord with the experimental evidence.
>
> The elimination of alternative hypotheses, combined with an inability to eliminate a given hypothesis, makes it preferable to its rivals. (Mill 1965 [1843], bk. 3, chap. 8–10)

To understand human action mechanically thus is to understand it in terms of antecedent conditions taken as efficient causes. Explanations must take the form of law-like generalizations, for to explain something in terms of causes is to cite a necessary or sufficient condition or a necessary *and* sufficient condition of the behavior to be explained. Causes therefore were to be universal within a precisely specifiable scope, Newton's laws of motion being the exemplar. If such generalizations were to be taken as true, they should be true not only for all relevant evidence presently observed, but also for all evidence that may be observed from the past or into the future. Given the concepts of strictly objective knowledge, of universal causal laws, and of predictive certainty, a superhuman intelligence theoretically could, in the words of Laplace, "embrace in the same formula the movements of the largest bodies and those of the lightest atom: nothing would be uncertain for it, and the future like the past, would be present to its eyes" (quoted in Polanyi 1958, 140).

This ideal of mechanical explanation was transferred from physics to biology to the study of human conduct in the seventeenth and eighteenth centuries, and it emerged as the various behavioral and social sciences of the twentieth. It was only in this last period, and largely unbeknown to social scientists themselves, that reservations concerning the precise requirements of such an enterprise would be laid out (see MacIntyre 1981, 80; Quine 1960, chap. 6). Thus, for more recent generations of positivists, Mill's formulation left several questions unanswered: What is the justification of the logical canons themselves? How can the ideal character of mathematics and logic (Descartes) be reconciled with the empiricist doctrine that all intelligible propositions are based on perception (Bacon)? Moreover, when we speak of "verification by experience" we refer to mental states (e.g., consciousness of certain perceptions) that each of us experiences individually. Thus further questions arise: What is it that is to be expressed linguistically in an objective fashion? How can language accurately represent experience in consciousness?

Confronted with such difficulties, neopositivists and critical rationalists have modified or reformulated the earlier positivist approach. For example, the idea of causality was qualified by theories of probability; the canons of proof and verifiability were largely replaced by those of disproof and falsifiability. Carnap (1963) limited the task of inductive logic to testing hypotheses rather than discovering them. Weyl (1949) noted that only the subjective is absolute, the objective being relative to rules of observation and verification that, as rules, presuppose a shared community of discourse. Karl Popper allowed that the foundations of science are less bedrock than swamp.

> Science is like a building erected on piles. These piles are driven down from above into the swamp, but not down to any natural or 'given' base; and when we cease our attempts to drive our piles into a deeper layer, it is not because we have reached firm ground. We simply stop when we are satisfied that they are firm enough to carry the structure, at least for the time being. (1957, 111)

In a similar vein, Thomas Kuhn, distinguished the neopositivist position from the traditional one:

> While we both insist that scientists may properly aim to invent theories that *explain* observed phenomena and that they do so in terms of *real* objects, Sir Karl and I are united in opposition to a number of classical positivism's most characteristic theses. We both emphasize, for example, the intimate and inevitable intanglement of scientific observation with scientific theory; we are correspondingly skeptical of efforts to produce any neutral language of observation. (1970, 2)

With respect to understanding people and society, then, we can sum up the positivist approach as having two principal components: a Baconian one dealing with "objective facts," and a Cartesian principle of "causal laws" that explain them. Accordingly, we are enjoined to seek out the verifiable units of data hidden behind the surface meanings of conduct, discard unverifiable (non-sensical) assertions, and explain what is left as expressions of the operative factors, variables, causes, or laws. Knowledge about ourselves and society, to this way of thinking, is constituted ideally of explanations that are

Objective. That is, based on observation that is independent of the biases of the observer and verifiable by anyone at any time. The facts themselves have to speak independently of the particular voice of the observer or of the particularities of any observational setting. Moreover, such explanations must be . . .

Causal. That is, the variegated and contextually embedded world of language and experience must be abstracted into a controllable number of functions or variables that can be interpreted and codified into mathematical formulas or some similar law-like construction.

Positivist Social Theory

The opposition between truth *(episteme)* and opinion *(doxa)* is as old as analytic reasoning itself, but only in the seventeenth century was this dichotomy linked with that between subject and object, between the *res cogitans* and the *res extensa*. The implicit pathos of this bifurcation was developed a century later by Immanuel Kant: Modern persons live in a moral world as free and active subjects, not the natural world as passive and determined objects. Yet subjects seem capable only of opinion, whereas truth apparently is reserved to the world of objects (Nelson 1983).

For positivists the Platonic distinction between knowledge and opinion, and between reality and appearance, was given a new embodiment in the image of the knower as a Newtonian physical scientist. The access to nature that physical science had provided was taken as a model for establishing social, political, and economic theories and institutions in accordance with the laws of nature. "Man exists in Nature", said Holbach, "He is submitted to her laws. He cannot deliver himself from them. . . . The universe. . . . presents only matter and motion. . . . an uninterrupted succession of causes and effects" (1957, see Naville 1943). In this spirit of mechanism, the study of politics became "political science" and natural philosophy became "social science." The scientist of society claimed authority to know, and thence to shape, human nature based on the power of Newtonian physics to explain physical nature. Positive social science became a new alchemy, able to transform personal experience into objective facts and collective beliefs into universal truths.

Founders of this new science, such as Saint-Simon and his disciple Auguste Comte, believed that Newton's "universal gravity is the sole cause of all physical and moral phenomena" (Comte 1887). Concurrently in Britain, Mill and Bentham articulated a stimulus-response psychology to be used as a yardstick for legislative decisions. In Bentham's Felicific Calculus, happiness was simply the outcome of various needs and forces. William Graham Sumner, an exponent of Spencer and the leading American social Darwinist, stated this idea succinctly:

> We are convinced that this way of looking at things frees our treatment from a current tendency, which we regard as confusing and unproductive, to refer societal results to conscious, reasoned, and purposeful action on the part of the individual. (1883)

A similar sentiment was expressed by the Austrian sociologist Ludwig Gumplowicz:

> The great error of individual psychology is the supposition that man thinks. . . . A chain of errors; for it is not man himself who thinks but his social community. . . . The individual simply plays the part of the prism which receives the rays, dissolves them according to fixed laws, and let them pass out again in a predetermined direction and with a predetermined color.

Even dialecticians such as Marx and Engels did not escape the deterministic imagery of positivism. Engels repeatedly asserted that "Marxian dialectics is nothing more than the science of the general laws of motion and development of Nature, human society, and thought". Marx himself invoked the model of physics, insisting that "it is the ultimate aim of this work to lay bare the laws of motion of modern society". In the first preface to *Capital* (1967, 1:15), Marx warned that "here individuals are dealt with *only in so far* as they are personifications of economic categories, embodiments of particular class relations and class interests."

If determination by natural law was the Cartesian side of positivism, its Baconian side was the gathering of social statistical facts. This tension within positivism was relfected in the oscillation between data-free theory and theory-free research. Such statistical research appeared in the West during the Renaissance, when Italian city-states began using quantitative comparisons of social groups to assess political and military strength (Nef 1960). In England, John Graunt's *Natural and Political Observations* (1662) and William Petty's *Several Essays in Political Arithmetic* (1682) initiated a tradition of statistical analysis of social rates that was inherited and continued by King, Davenant, Wallace, Derham, Maitland, Smart, Simpson, Hodgson, Short, and others. Government commissions and private reform groups also contributed to the gathering of social facts, especially after the inquiries into factory conditions in the 1830s.[4]

In Germany, Conring, Achenwall, and Sussmilch argued that statistical analysis must be *the* basic knowledge of the state. Such thinking, called *Staatswissenschaft* since the eighteenth century, became prominent after 1872 through the efforts of welfare-oriented professors and administrators who grouped themselves into the *Verein für Sozialpolitik*.

In the French-speaking world, Laplace, De Guerry, and Quételet undertook moral-statistical research that influenced Durkheim profoundly. In his *Suicide* and *Rules of Sociological Method*, Durkheim argued that social facts exist as a reality sui generis and that individual behavior can be explained as a consequence of the push and pull of societal forces that operate independently of individual volition. Durkheim's statement "We must gave either God or society" goes beyond even medieval absolutism, which at least had allowed the individual the moral choice of loving and following the Lord. Durkheim's affirmation of the power and value of science took the form of an attack on rhetoric and a strict segregation of scientific and ordinary speech. "The words of everyday language, like the concepts they express, are always susceptible to more than one meaning, and the scholar employing them . . . risk[s] distinguishing what should be combined, or combining what should be distinguished, thus mistaking the real affinities of things, and accordingly misapprehending their nature." By contrast, science uses univocal language; it therefore "is the highest grade of knowledge and there is nothing beyond it" (quoted by Levin 1983: 2–3).

In the spirit of Durkheim's urgings, discussions of human mind, behavior, and social relations departed from the evolutionary philosophies of the early nineteenth century and came more to resemble the discourse of the sciences of nature. This shift is notable in the growth of specialized journals whose prose narrows the meanings of terms originating in normal educated speech and uses more specialized words, some of which are themselves replaced with acronyms or abbreviations.

Sociology had come of age, declared Albion Small (1916, 748), when it began to meet the "expansion of DEMAND FOR OBJECTIV- ITY." This hope was vindicated in America in the 1930s when the quasi-ethnographic style of the Chicago School was displaced by mathematical models and statistical methods after the image of natural science. The new mathematical formulas were to be made empirical through carefully defined sampling procedures, controlled observation, quantification, and experimentation. Texts and articles on research methods by Chapin, Festinger, Lazarsfeld, Lundberg, Zetterberg, and others explained how such a transfer of methods from physics and chemistry was to be achieved. Through operation- alization, abstract or ideal concepts are translated into discrete units of data. The subject and object both are collapsed into the operations of measurement. The recipe, in effect, defines the cake, regardless of who baked it and how it might taste (Lundberg, Shrag, and Larsen 1954, 34). Thus Binet defined intelligence as what is measured by intelligence tests, Chapin operationally defined social status in terms of a social status scale, and Riley (1594, 7) saw scales as providing "empirical representations of certain sociological concepts." Similar operational instruments are Bogardus's social distance scale, Thurst- one's social attitude scale, Guttman's scalogram analysis, and the various ordinal measuring devices invented by Stevens and Coombs, Guttman, and Lazarsfeld (Jack D. Douglas 1971; Gabaglio 1888, 1–36; Sjoberg 1959, 606; and Thurstone and Chave 1929).

In applying this style of thinking to "Total Society," perhaps the most articulate spokesman of the positivist-functionalist position was Talcott Parsons, chair of the Department of Social Relations at Harvard. Structural-functionalism is characterized, on the one hand, by an or- ganic or mechanical model of society as a structured system and, on the other, by a logic and technique of inquiry which assumes that this functional structure can be revealed through the statistical analysis of aggregated data about behavior (Gouldner 1970, chaps. 1–3). In this view the "personalities of the members" are outside of or "exogenous to the social system" (Parsons 1970, 87). Individuals composing the so- ciety or group became carriers of forces and variables. Instead of serving as descriptions or general conceptions of action, however, such vari- ables are seen to lie beneath or behind social action, which is presumed to be a manifestation or product of them.

The thought of Talcott Parsons, like that of other positivist-func- tionalists, reflects the cognitive bias that has dominated Western thought since Bacon and Descartes: that the only valid knowledge is that based on objective facts formulated into general laws. The task then with respect to understanding human conduct is to discover

the falsifiable propositions hidden within it, discard unverifiable
assertions (the symbolic or metaphorical guise of behavior), and
explain what is left as expressions of the operative factors, variables,
or causes. Since Parsons, "the bulk of younger sociologists [have
focussed on] 'operational,' 'quantitative,' 'experimental,' 'precise'
research of specialized problems . . . methods and techniques . . .
and they are trying to build a 'natural-science sociology' as a replica
of a physical science" (Symposiasts 1956).

Similar tendencies have dominated other disciplines as well.
Charles Darwin (1896, 87) disingenuously renounced his own imagination, claiming that he had "worked on true Baconian principles,
and without any theory collected facts on a wholesale scale." In 1936
the economist Edward A. Ross announced his pursuit of the research
program contained in "that majestic phrase, *wissenschaftlicht Objektiv-
itat*." The political scientist David Easton (1953, 221) insisted that
"values can ultimately be reduced to emotional responses. . . . Facts
and values are logically heterogenous. The factual aspects of a
proposition refers to a part of reality. . . . The moral aspect of a
proposition, however, expresses only the emotional responses of an
individual." Arthur Lovejoy (1917, 163) urged that philosophy become like the natural sciences and adopt an empirical methodology
that seeks objective, verifiable, and clearly communicable truths.
Likewise, the goal of Freud's early "Project for a Scientific Psychology" (1954, 355) was "to furnish us with a psychology which shall be
a natural science; . . . to present psychical processes as quantitatively
determined states of specifiable material particles and so to make
them plain and void of contradiction." Similarly, behavioral psychol-
ogists such as John B. Watson, B. F. Skinner, and the Pavlovians held
that "the hypothesis that man is not free is essential to the application
of scientific method to the study of human behavior" (Skinner 1953,
447).[5] Similarly, Watson (quoted by Woodward 1965, 215) declared
that,

> The duty of the behaviorist is to describe behavior in exactly the same
> way as the physicist describes the movement of a machine. . . . This
> human machine behaves in a certain way because environmental
> stimulation has forced him to do so. If we are to use the methods of
> science in human affairs we must assume that behavior is lawful and
> determined—that what a man does is the result of specifiable condi-
> tions and that once these conditions have been discovered, we can
> anticipate and to some extent determine his actions.

The positivist spirit penetrated even into history, which in the
nineteenth century had still been closer to literature than to science.

"The historian's vocation," wrote Oscar Handlin, "depends on this minimal operational article of faith: Truth is absolute; it is absolute as the world is real. . . . Historians who cut loose from this faith do so at the peril of their discipline" (quoted by Gordon Wood 1982, 59).

The antirhetorical rhetoric of positivist social science casts the reader in a special role. No longer a collaborator in pursuasive discourse, she is now to be *convinced* by the *force* of facts and logic. Readers of objectivist sociology, psychology, economics, or history are not presumed to be people trying to understand something. Instead, they are thought to be looking for additional bits of definitive information to fit with their previous bits. "In this world", as Bazerman (1984, 35–36) wrote, 'individuals do pieces, follow rules, check each other out, add their pieces to an encyclopedia of behavior of subjects without subjectivity. There is not much room for thinking or venturing here, but much for behaving and adhering to prescriptions."

The Positivist Approach to Social Control

The same type of thinking about the world and human nature was carried into a third aspect of the industrial habitus; societal direction—how people plan, manage, and get things done. Absolutist conceptions of truth had counterparts not only in positive science, but also in tools, practices, and organizational forms. Saint-Simon and Auguste Comte, for example, asserted that in the industrial age those with the competence and license to guide would be scientists, engineers, and planners, rather than the nobles, warriors, or priests of earlier times. "Scientific men ought in our day to elevate politics to the rank of a science of observation" (Comte 1877, 4:547). Having abolished politics as an activity for mere citizens, the new elite would organize society in a rational, positive manner according to function and capacity. Under a new "religion of Newton . . . the real noblemen would be industrial chiefs and the real priests would be scientists."

By end of the nineteenth century Saint-Simonism was being put into practice by "captains of industry like Ferdinand de Lesseps, railway promoters, and great financiers like the brothers Emile and Isaac Perière, who named one of the first ships of the Compagnie Générale Transatlantique the *Saint-Simon*. We can find the tradition carried on directly today in the American ideology of the 'managerial' society. This was promoted by Edward Bellamy (author of *Looking Backward: 2000–1887*, published in 1888); later by Thorstein Veblen, and by Technocracy Inc., the engineers movement of the 1930s; and finally by James Burnham in the *Managerial Revolution* (1941)" (Benthall 1976, 40).

It was not writers and scholars, however, but an engineer, Frederick W. Taylor, who did most to translate Saint-Simonism into the actual practices of industry. Taylor is justly called the father of scientific management. His work in industry suffused by emulation into public administration and national planning, scientific marketing, and later into institutionalized research and development. In a series of practical experiments, public addresses, and publications around the turn of the century, Taylor and his associates advanced "a complete mental revolution, both on the part of the management and of the men", for enhancing the profit efficiency of human, physical, and financial resources (Taylor 1947).

Taylor's whole system, like that of Comte or Bentham before him and like management science ever since, was a search for a technology for getting people to do things that are intrinsically unpleasant to do. In this system there was no place for rewarding activities or relations, but only for rewards *for* activities, and relations that dish out rewards (Skillen 1978, 146). And given the values of determinism and objectivity that he shared with other positivists, Taylor did not view himself as arbitrary or self-interested. Instead, he felt his right to direct others was based on his knowledge of human nature's pre-existing laws. Similarly, he thought workers owed managers obedience because the managers were themselves obedient to the laws of human nature.

In Taylor's system any goals other than production and efficiency were either nonexistent or valueless. Human agency was reduced to strictly economic calculations, though later "motivation'" would be included as an additional factor of production. Man disappeared, and all that remained were "hands" and "things" organized in the most efficient manner by the benevolent despotism of the managerial elite.

The broad preconditions of the development and spread of Taylorism were the ideological predominance of the Protestant ethic and social Darwinism, the pervasive positivist habitus, and the social and economic movement after the American Civil War from a craft tradition to the specialization of the industrial factory system. Men and women coming from a rural background balked at their new work situations and rhythms. Similarly, the industrial capitalists had little knowledge of the effects of fatigue, tempo, sequence, and methods of work on their employees and their productivity. The role of management had not developed sufficiently to fully exploit the possibilities of the new factory system.

At the same time, an ethic of hard work and the survival of the fittest encouraged early industrialists to view workers as interchangeable economic parts. To the extent that the question of incentives to labor was raised at all, workers were thought to be motivated by a just wage scientifically deduced, by the paternalism of their betters, and by their pride in contributing to more efficient production (this last being a cornerstone in the mercantile conception of national loyalty).

With the rise of the labor movement and the growth in complexity of technology and organizations in the twentieth century, the early concepts of scientific management have been refined. Elton Mayo's famous Hawthorne experiments at Western Electric in the late 1920s demonstrated "scientifically" for the first time the relationship between productivity and the employees' informal subgroups and attitudes. Mayo's work, along with that of Kurt Lewin in the 1930s, introduced the human or group dimension to models and practices of planning and management. Later, in the 1940s, led by the National Training Laboratories, sensitivity training was developed as an instrument for attitudinal adjustment and organizational change.

Concurrently as it was made more "humane", the formal technical aspects of scientific management were deepened and extended. The widespread expansion of Saint-Simonist social engineering included the collaboration, on the one hand, between managers and politicians interested in rational policy control and, on the other, thinkers convinced of the possibility of a "policy science" to guide social planning, decision making, and problem solving. The offspring of this union between intellectuals and technocrats were "intellectual technologies" that replaced intuitive judgments with decision algorithms, that is, rules and procedures for solving problems. Examples are game theory, simulation, cybernetics, decision theory, utility theory, and operations research. Such intellectual technologies responded to a widely felt need for techniques to manage large, complex organizations ranging from business corporations and government agencies to whole societies. Operations research emerged as a tool for making decisions during the Battle of Britain in World War II. Mathematical modeling, optimization, linear and dynamic programming, gaming, simulation, and sequencing and replacement were developed for military as well as commercial applications. Other new tools for programming activities and controlling people included PERT, CPM, PPBS, MIS, ISM, and other network systems.

The use of techniques for social control expanded internationally and into virtually all sectors of society. In Europe, Karol Adamiecki, Henri Fayol, and Oliver Sheldon were writing at about the same time as Taylor and saying similar things. They and other leaders converged

in 1934 under the Comité Internationale de l'Organisation Scientifique, established in Geneva by Herbert Hoover and Thomas Masaryk
with affiliates in thirty-seven countries. Since then, local counterparts
such as the Society for the Advancement of Management or the
American Management Association have sprung up in virtually all
nations that are seeking to industrialize along Western capitalist lines.

A scientific approach also found its way into public administration
and social planning. In public administration the cry for greater
efficiency was coupled with the plea for political reform. The reform-
ists generally advocated the professionalization of the civil service
and the contracting out of routine functions to the private sector. This
bent was expressed in Gulick and Lyndall's (1937) advocacy of public
administration as a way to scientifically bypass politics, as well as in
Simon's plea (1964) for "a pure science of administration."

As the government has come to absorb formerly autonomous areas
of life, many practices previously considered matters of civic judgment have since become matters of scientific public policy. One sign
of this is the shift from the "well-educated generalist" to the "technically trained expert" as a leader or advisor. Positivist theories of
science and management, and the policy and administrative expertise
that these theories create, appeared for example in the sphere of
public education. Schooling was to be removed from the irrationalities of politics and placed in the hands of scientific administrators.
Thus, Nicholas Murray Butler could confidently assert that he should

> as soon think of talking about the democratization of the treatment of
> appendicitis [as to speak of the] democratization of the schools. The
> fundamental confusion is this: Democracy is a principle of govern-
> ment; the schools belong to the administration; and a democracy is as
> much entitled as a monarchy to have its business well done. (Tyack
> 1974)

In urban planning, this professional, scientific style was first
concretely formulated by Bettman in 1928. "A city plan is a master
design," he wrote, and urban form had to be disciplined by that
design, much as the construction of a building had to be guided by
the blueprint. This elitist, comprehensive approach to urban design
continues to dominate graduate schools of planning, architectural
firms, and city planning commissions today, and it has been canon-
ized in federal legislation. The Housing Act of 1961, for example,
required that a comprehensive metropolitan plan must be submitted
before federal funds can be released. Similarly, the Federal Highway
Act of 1967 demanded comformity to a master plan for "orderly

metropolitan growth" as a prerequisite to aid. The technical requirements of these plans, as stated in the respective federal grant
manuals, include the measurement of facts and the prediction of
probable causal effects of the program. Their political implications are
bureaucratic and technical-elitist.

The extension of formal city-planning activities has reached both
rural and recreational areas. Ideas of "development standards" such
as sidewalks, street lighting, lot size, setbacks, and so forth are
rigorously enforced without regard for the quality of local development they foster. Notions of symmetry (balanced and equivalent
services provided equally to every place), comprehensiveness (a
planned place for everything) and zoning (everything in its place),
have institutionalized mediocrity. Building codes and other restrictions literally set the past in concrete and, through the prevailing
positivist concept of planning, impose it on the future. Agencies that
were established to deal with new environmental concerns also are
adopting these techniques and publishing standards and guidelines
to be ubiquitously applied. The Army Corps of Engineers, U.S.
Bureau of Reclamation, and National Parks Service have undertaken
similar predictive-prescriptive planning for recreation areas. That the
future belongs to the past may soon be not merely one possibility, but
a fait accompli.

All these approaches to societal and organizational direction can be
seen as extensions and applications of the earlier positivist ideals of
strictly objective knowledge, universal general laws, predictive certainty, and operational control. Statistical analyses of cost-benefit
alternatives are thought to provide the objective bases for rational
decisions. Models of rational decision making are used to enumerate
the processes of setting goals, identifying obstacles, developing
alternatives, designing and implementing selected programs, and
feeding program evaluations back into the planing cycle. The method
assumes that its objects can be positively known and the causal
factors identified and manipulated. Neither of these assumptions
resorts to interpretive procedures on the level of meaning nor,
indeed, do they even require the notion of an intending consciousness (except that of the manager-analyst herself).

Though criticism of positivist management and planning began
almost from the day Taylor and others expounded them, this opposition rarely challenges the fundamental epistemological and social-
theoretical assumptions of the positivist approach. For example,
Charles Lindblom attacked the classical decision model from the
standpoint of marginal economic analysis; yet modern exponents of
classical decision theory can counter Lindblom by dropping "pure
rationality" as the criterion for relating means to ends, and instead

substituting the notions of bounded rationality and "satisficing." Similarly, Lindblom was himself criticized by scholars such as Dror and Etzioni for neglecting the need for changes in the institutional parameters of social action. Yet, like Lindblom's, their critique does not get to the logical heart of the positivist habitus. Instead, these and other contemporary critics continue to focus on decisions and the conditions that would ensure their rationality, rather than on "extrarational" modes of societal and organizational conduct.

All of these developments have changed the nature of policy itself. Following Manfred Stanley's seminal work, this shift can be expressed as a series of oppositions and questions.[6]

Citizens versus experts. The positivist separation of fact and value, objectivity and subjectivity, and means and ends, has a parallel in the distinction between the proper roles of experts and citizens. In the imagery of positivists, experts are thought to deal objectively with facts and citizens are seen to act on the basis of values, opinions, and interests. Citizens set the "ends" of government politically, whereas experts direct the administrative "means" for their efficient achievement. But what are the implications of this division for ideals and practices of democratic self-direction? And for the role of reason as a ground for democratic ends or values?

Technical Rationality versus Social Rationality. Given the instrumentalist conception of knowledge in positivism, policies are often viewed as technical responses to problems that have a technical solution. But is it always appropriate to conceive of public policies as pragmatic technical responses to specific issues? Technical policies are regarded by their designers as scientifically valid means for achieving a finite, specifiable end. By contrast, social rationality questions the circumstances called "problems" and how they are generated by society as a whole. Such theories may suggest activities that will refine people's capacity for self-direction, but they also show that many situations cannot fully be specified as problems having adequate technical responses and that societal outcomes are often unamenable to even the most carefully calculated interventions. Technical rationality also eschews radical institutional changes. Technicists assess "costs" and "benefits" of alternate responses to conflicting needs in a culture that validates the claims of diverse interest groups. In such a context, radical initiatives or social proposals, however necessary they may be for social transformation, seem implausible and indefinable because their "risks" always outweigh their "benefits".

Social Policies versus Cultural Policies. Public policy may be of many types. Social policies are those intended to affect institutional or distributive arrangements such as employment rates, economic growth, or levels of educational attainment. Cultural policies are those designed to affect the concepts and symbols that are embodied in social institutions and public discourse, and that justify social practices. Most Americans regard the formation of systematic, domestic cultural policy by government as illegitimate. Yet there are many examples of cultural policies emanating from both government and private souces. Given the materialistic, reductivistic, and literalist bias of positivist thought, however, such policy actions, though potent and consequential, become hard to discern and even harder to discuss. How then might citizens become more aware and self-directing concerning those cultural policies that profoundly affect their society's entire symbolic order?

Public Policies versus State Policies. "Policy" has come to be thought of as something that the state does. But is it always appropriate to regard public policies as synonymous with actions sponsored by the government? Should certain policies—for example those regarding religious belief—never become issues for state intervention? Is not the public distinguishable from the state, and might there not be some policies important to public welfare but detrimental to the interests of government bureaus? Yet how can these issues be addressed in a vocabulary that equates "public policy" with government intervention? Conversely, how might we develop a language that presupposes the privileged response of citizens?

I believe that such questions cannot be adequately addressed by either positivism or romanticism. The first openly eschews moral reflection, the second implicitly rejects public policy analyses. Yet the language of structural causation and the language of moral agency both must infuse policies formed by a democratic public. This of course presupposes that the dichotomies of positivism and romanticism can be overcome.

IN THE PAST three hundred years positive science emerged in the West as a new rhetoric for describing man and nature. This new rhetoric of reason eschewed belief in saints and elfs and spirits in stones. At first positive science was allied with humanism because both sought to extend the knowledge and powers of man. But as positivism penetrated more and more into social relations it changed its character and meaning. Soon societies, institutions, and people also were seen as secular, mundane, purely empirical things, and social relations became organized according to profit efficiency or *raison d'État.* As people came to be the objects of impersonal scientific calculation, the earlier marriage of science and humanism began to dissolve, and humanism came to be opposed to scientism.

Harvey's and Newton's mechanical universe presaged an incipient commercial and industrial economy. By the close of the nineteenth century, when this economic revolution had been largely accomplished in core states, the Cartesian-Baconian view had become a definition of rationality itself. We have moved from the seventeenth century revolution in philosophy and science, through the eighteenth century ideal of a science of behavior modeled after Newtonian physics, to the aspirations of the nineteenth century prophets of social transformation, and have arrived at the practices of contemporary managers, civil servants, and techno-administrators, and the legitimation of these practices in positivist social theories.

When the exploratory spirit of science was combined with utopian social energies, many interesting experiments were launched in the interest, or at least in the name, of human betterment. But just when science was shown to be epistemologically relative, its social dominion grew more absolute. With the exhaustion of utopian energies, truly experimental applications of social science were replaced by the drudgery of scientistic expertise wedded to a depoliticized corporate state. The history of these developments is different in each country. But the rise of corporate and bureaucratic expertise is everywhere the same, and in each case positive science is invoked as both the theoretical basis of such expertise as well as its moral justification in the form of efficiency, objectivity, and value-neutrality (MacIntyre 1981, 83). Social science and social life of the current era turn out to be an ironic enactment of the natural science and philosophy of the Enlightenment, only now more as a form of domination than of liberation.

THREE

THE ROMANTIC ALTERNATIVE AND ITS LIMITS
A Rhetorical Reformulation of the Debate between Positivism and Romanticism

> The problem is overwhelmingly real, and not simply theoretical. Briefly, it could be summarized as the incompatibility of cognition and identity. . . . The price of genuine, powerful, technically enriching science is that its style of explanation ruthlessly destroys those very notions in terms of which we identify ourselves. . . . The world we live in and the world of [scientific] thought are not the same. The *Lebenswelt* loses its status; though we must need go on living in it, for we have no other, it becomes devalued, and we cannot treat it seriously.
>
> Ernest Gellner (1974)

RHETORICIANS OF the human sciences investigate how language is used to gain knowledge of human experience. Why choose language as a key? Partly from despair, partly as an affirmation. The despair is for apodictic truth, revealed as an impossibility through reflection on the relativity of our ways of knowing. The hope, the affirmation, is for a renewed humanism that transcends both positivist nominalism and romantic idealism even while affirming reason and freedom.

A rhetorical approach also transvalues positivist and romantic theories of language. The positivist sees language as a copy of facts or things, the romantic sees it as an expression of thoughts or feelings. Each is the other's mirror twin, each blind in one eye. One twin opens the door with his right hand, the other closes it with his left. Through this unwilling cooperation a whole movement is formed. But neither twin speaks to his brother and neither sees that they pass through an illusory portal. For language is not something one passes through to another side, whether that other side be the world of facts and things or the world of insights and feelings. Instead, these worlds and all others do not become real for us outside of language but through it.

The one-eyed positivist twin, call him Ayer (1946), says that language is nonsense if it does not stand for facts or for logical relations between such facts. And so he is blind to any practical wisdom, aesthetic knowledge, or even his own metaphysics. By contrast, the one-eyed romantic, who could be Hirsch, sees language as an instrument for expressing a prior intention, thought, or psychic state. And so he not only is distracted from the truth as it manifests itself in language; he also cannot find the subjectivity behind language that he seeks. When he does recover a meaning or intention in the text or conduct, the claim that this represents an "expression of mind" (Hirsch 1976) or "mentalities" (Quentin Skinner 1969) that are prior to language is at best redundant (see Gadamer 1975).

This debate between positivists and romantics has grown sterile. Adequate social theory, like effective social policy, must be both objectively valid and subjectively meaningful; it must yield understanding of persons' agency as well as explanations of social forces beyond their control. Yet in terms of the debate between positivists and romantics such theory would appear to be methodologically impossible. Each side cherishes different assumptions concerning the nature of social reality and how we can know it. Yet each position presupposes and completes the other, and each is self-refuting if it stands alone. For example, a behaviorist such as B. F. Skinner (1971, 77–92, 99, 191–192, 195) cannot with consistency defend his position with good reasons since, as such reasons appear in *consciousness*, these by definition are inadmissable in the behaviorist's analysis. The behaviorist presumably has considered the views against which he is arguing and has chosen environmental determinism as the superior position, a position which, however, he has refuted in the course of choosing it. If the possibility of determinism's being false is not a real possibility for Skinner, then he cannot claim for it scientific truth. Yet if falsification is really possible, he is free (Marsh 1983, 482).

The opposite position, of complete indeterminism and freedom, is equally self-refuting. A world with no prior determination comes to appear arbitrary, meaningless, and absurd. As Sartre (1967, 418) put it, there are only two alternatives: "Either man is wholly determined . . . or else man is wholly free." Yet Sartre's arguments that man is condemned to freedom contradict his premises, for why should freedom, good faith, or reason be preferred, or even believed, in a world that is totally absurd? Sartre's freedom turns out to be a freedom that is humane and honest, has positive content, and is delimited by certain structures (Marsh 1983, 485).

Thus both positivist and romantic absolutisms are solipsistic. The assumption of a totally determined world that permits total agreement is self-refuting. The assumption of total personal freedom that engenders total dissimilarity of viewpoints leads to absolute relativism, with no shared criteria for truth or even intelligibility (Wright 1977a, 1977b). The paradox, however, is that although the aspiration for total freedom is logically incoherent, it underlies all our notions of personal responsibility and moral judgement.

The intensification of this polarization would be catastrophic for the prospects of a truly humane culture in a science-oriented society. As we have seen, this polarization takes an epistemological form. On one side are the gatekeeper philosophers who name what may enter the kingdom of science and consign all else to the purgatories of superstition, emotive expression, or unfounded opinion. These gatekeepers—the hydra-headed dogs of positivism—assert that knowledge is science, that science is knowledge, and that there is no other. Their advocacy helped clear space for a new interpretation of nature in part by establishing from the outset a strict separation of object and subject, body and mind, nature and culture. But positivist epistemologies are not descriptions of what scientists do or how science works. Instead, they are normative; they idealize and justify a certain form of knowing (Gellner 1975). And as scientific thinking is basic to modern civilization, say neopositivists, our very survival depends on the preservation of the scientific worldview.

On the other side of the polarity are open-admission philosophers of the romantic tradition who seek to dethrone positivism and provide an epistemological warrant for human self-understanding. Romantic thinkers, as I am using this term, take artistic interpretation rather than mechanistic explanation as their model. They are sympathetic with Novalis's dictum (1953–1957) that "poets know nature better than scientists," or Coleridge's (1956, 39–40) statement that "the true naturalist is a dramatic poet." Such anti-positivists relativize science. They argue that it is a social, historical, and political practice, but that, unlike poets, scientists deny the origin of their works in language. Thus, whereas the problem for positivist thinkers has been to keep narrow and straight the gates to knowledge, for romantic critics it has been to open them wider.

It could well be argued that the opposition I have defined between positivism and romanticism is already outdated, and that few sophisticated thinkers today accept the image held by both positivists and romantics of a solid foundation for knowledge. Yet such an argument would be only partly correct. Most practicing researchers in most disciplines still accept the foundation metaphor as does the public at large. Moreover, a surprising number of leading philosophers—such as Derrida, Gadamer, Gellner, Habermas, and Winch—presuppose this bifurcation as the bases of their theories of knowledge. And others, like Searle, are highly ambivalent.

As an example of the continuity of this opposition we might compare Peter Winch's subjective idealist position to Durkheim's supposedly objective conception of social facts: Winch and Durkheim both assume a strict, even absolute, separation between interpretive and causal ways of knowing. Winch cited Durkheim as stating that "social life should be explained, not by the notions of those who participate in it, but by more profound causes which are unperceived by consciousness." Then Winch proceeded to elaborate an alternative romantic epistemology that is an intaglio of Durkheim's positivism. Similarly, Feyerabend (1978, 385) assumed that scientific method must be constrictive and absolutist, and so he advocated an epistemological anarchy in which "what remains are aesthetic judgments, judgments of taste, metaphysical prejudices, religious desires, in short, *what remains are our subjective wishes.*"

Such ambivalence is also illustrated by John Searle's critique of Jacques Derrida. In remarks to literary scholars Searle moved beyond the positivist-romantic debate (Searle 1983, 78–79). Yet elsewhere he committed the very positivist crimes of which he accused the literati.

> When I have lectured to audiences of literary critics, I have found two pervasive philosophic presuppositions in the discussion of literary theory, both oddly enough derived from logical positivism. First there is the assumption that unless a distinction can be made rigorous and precise it isn't a distinction at all. . . . People who hold the assumption that genuine distinctions must be made rigid are ripe for Derrida's attempt to undermine all such distinctions. . . . Second, and equally positivistic, is the insistence that concepts that apply to language and literature, if they are to be truly valid, must admit of some mechanical procedure of verification. . . . The crude positivism of these assumptions . . . is of a piece with Derrida's assumption that without foundations we are left with nothing but the free play of signifiers.

Nonetheless, Searle's (1970) own theory of speech acts is quasi-positivistic in its insistence on univocality of meaning and its recourse to unequivocal "literal" meanings of verbal expressions. "[In literal speech,] sentences are precisely the realization of intentions" (Searle 1977, 202). This is a kind of verbal factism. It may tell us how speech acts must be viewed by members, but it begs the question of how intersubjective comprehension of intentions actually is realized. If we wish to discover and account for the coming to be of shared meanings, we may assume that *members* must behave as if differences of perception and interpretation of communicants are negligible. But the *researcher* is not required to make such an assumption. Instead, to acknowledge an "as if" quality in the structure of human intersubjectivity is also to recognize that reciprocity is a member's idealization (Schutz 1962, 32) and that there is a measure of illusion, of fiction, in all human interaction, a fiction that sometimes intensifies to paradox (Wright 1983, 394–397).

The indeterminism of both positivist and romantic paradigms has been attributed to the nature of reality of the lack of fit between theories and evidence. But it is much more useful to construe this indeterminism rhetorically as a feature of language itself, for language is the medium through which we constitute reality as an object of experience and by which we shape both theories and data. The "advancement of science" depends on the imprecision and multivalence of language. Even the willfully denotative language of science must preserve sufficient ambiguity and incompleteness to leave room for stating later what one at the moment does not know. Garfinkel (1967, 28) made this point empirically by showing how openness to future possible meanings is a precondition of the intelligibility of even the most precise communications:

> No matter how specific the terms of common understanding may be—a contract may be considered the prototype—they attain the status of agreement for persons only insofar as the stipulated conditions carry along an unspoken but understood *et cetera* clause.

It is essential to science, as well as to law and other domains of discourse, that one be able to say *something* without knowing everything (Bondi 1967, 10). If language were able to precisely exhaust any matter at hand it would not be polysemous and malleable. And therefore we would not be able to speak at all since intersubjectivity would not be possible between persons in different particular settings. To be at all determinate, language (or theory or facts, etc.) must also be partly indeterminate. If reality for us were wholly determinate, sane persons in the "same" situation would never disagree with others and, hence, would never know that they ever agreed. And if others did not disagree with us about the way the world is, we could not know either them or the world to be real.

Positivism *and* romanticism must be reformulated and sublated into an ontology and epistemology that encompass both scientific and artistic modes of representation. As Randall Collins (1975, 28, 34) said, "Positivism needs to be purged. Romanticism needs to be borrowed from. It is the combination of determinism and freedom, after all, that constitutes the greatest art; advances in scientific sociology can move its aesthetics beyond a tired romanticism, hopefully into something greater."

Epistemology helps us to effect such transformations. It is maeutic, a midwife between different forms of imagination and belief. We use epistemology to name the conditions for possible kinds of knowledge and so ease ourselves into new conceptual experience. By advocating certain procedures as correct and certain statements as true, we invite and legitimate belief in a certain (version of the) world. What then are the epistemologies most useful in legitimating different conceptual and preconceptual worlds? What rhetoric of reason would most support the telos of human emancipation?

Criticisms of Positivist Epistemology

The positivist approach to knowledge and society has been criticized by neo-positivist sociologists and philosophers themselves. For example, Karl Popper and other critical rationalists modified some of the basic assumptions of earlier positivist thought: The idea of causality was qualified by theories of probability, and canons of proof and verifiability were largely replaced by those of disproof and falsifiability. Likewise, Thomas Kuhn stressed the communal aspects of scientific activity and the consensual character of scientific truth.

Such circumspection would seem to safeguard contemporary positivists against criticisms from non-positivist points of view. Other thinkers, however, have challenged the foundationalist assumptions of the positivist method and metaphysic. These critics have argued that the subject matter of social science—human conduct—cannot as such be known through purely objectivist methods and that the more objective our observations, the further we are from what we want to know. The views of humans as objects, and of statistical experimentalism, deductive functionalism, or structural linguistics as explanatory ideals, say these critics, beg the very questions that the human studies should address. Having begun with Vico's rebuttal of Descartes, these anti-positivist epistemologies today include pragmatism, the analysis of ordinary language, existentialism, hermeneutics, phenomenology, the philosophic history and sociology of science, and neo-Marxist critical theory. Though often antagonistic to each other, the basic complementarity of these approaches has encouraged the emergence of a human-centered science of knowledge and conduct.

Philosophers as diverse as Dewey, Wittgenstein, Dilthey, Husserl, and Polanyi took the commonsense understanding of experience as the framework within which all inquiry must begin and to which it must return. Dewey spoke of this framework as the social matrix within which emerge unclarified situations that may then be transformed by science into justifiable assertions. Wittgenstein referred to knowledge as a "form of life." Husserl wrote of the "life-world" within which all scientific and even logical concepts originate. Alfred Schutz, speaking on "The Basic Subject Matter of Sociology," summed up a perspective common to all these thinkers:

> Any knowledge of the world, in common sense thinking as well as in science, involves mental constructs, syntheses, generalizations, formalizations, idealizations specific to the respective level of thought organization. The concept of Nature, for instance, with which the natural sciences have to deal is, as Husserl has shown, an idealizing abstraction from the *Lebenswelt*.

Schutz then drew the implication of such thinking for the social sciences: "Exactly this layer of the *Lebenswelt*, however, from which the natural sciences have to abstract, is the social reality which the social sciences have to investigate" (1970, 272).

The philosophic opposition between positivists and romantics also can be seen through ordinary language philosophy which, like Schutz's phenomenology, takes as its starting point the clash between the scientific or mechanistic image of persons and the image that is manifested in everyday life (Sellars 1963). This manifest image is expressed most directly when we observe everyday accounts of behavior: "Why does she study hard?" "Because she wants to get into college." "Why does he walk that way?" "He's trying to look cool" (see Lyman and Scott 1970, 11–44). In the positivist view, however, such accounts of behavior couched in ordinary language can never be granted the status of knowledge. Instead, they represent an obstacle to the acquisition of empirically grounded explanations because they refer to mentalistic concepts (e.g., wanting, trying). The job of philosophy for positivists is to purge language, at least scientific language, of such usage. Language must be made objective, the word must refer to the thing or to the specifiable relation between things, preferably in an operationalized form.

Difficulties emerge when one attempts to put this principle into effect. A basic problem occurs for positivists when they confuse motion with action, reflex with conduct (Urmson 1956). For example, a woman holding her arm out, palm forward, might be warding off a mugger, drying her nail polish, hailing a cab, or admiring a ring. Yet if mind is reduced to body, there is no way to distinguish these actions. Instead, say ordinary language philosophers, the above instances must be seen as acts, not motions, and hence they cannot be explained in terms of causes. Indeed, the terms of the thing-world of cause and effect do not allow us to know or even name what these actions are and mean. Because actions are essentially normative and bounded by rules in contexts, it is logically impossible to explain human conduct if we restrict ourselves to the vocabulary of physical science. There is no way of deducing from physiology whether an extended arm is a sign for traffic to halt or for Nazis to salute. Instead of having the character of self-evident physical facts (whatever these may be), action must be understood in terms of reasons, rules, and projects which themselves are problematic constructions. For example, whether a case is to be one of "suicide" of "accidental death" depends upon the reconstruction of a context of meaning and the attribution of an intention (Jack D. Douglas 1967). Thus the very possibility of a social *science*, at least on the positivists' model of physical science, is called into question (Winch 1958; Louch 1966; Richard Taylor 1966, 39; Charles Taylor 1964, 33).

In contrast to the positivist model, then, philosophers in the romantic tradition insist that a sufficient explanation of action must include the

> notion of consciousness, in the sense of intentionality. To speak of an "intentional description" of something is to speak not just of any description which this thing bears, but of the description which it bears for a certain person, the description under which it is subsumed by him. Now the notion of an action as directed behavior involves that of an intentional description. (Strasser 1964, 58; see 1962, 3)

If we allow that intentional description is essential to the understanding of action, it becomes questionable whether positivists, because they disavow the concepts of agency and intentionality, are able to account for human conduct at all. R. S. Peters stated that "human actions cannot be sufficiently explained in terms of causal concepts," and Louch insisted that in their efforts to imitate the natural sciences, "most of psychological and sociological inquiry . . . has been vitiated by methodological concerns that have no bearing upon the puzzles and problems that arise within a view of man as an agent" (1966, 237–238). Whether we put ourselves into the role of the spectator or of the agent, then, what behavior is *as an act* emerges only from "the description which it bears for a certain person, the description under which it is subsumed by him."

In response to these criticisms, neo-positivists have insisted that, even if we grant the presence and structure of the purposive image of humans, such an image is not necessarily true. None would deny that a persistent strain in philosophy since Kant has sought to identify the basic categories of thought. Yet all these efforts have focused on the purposive or manifest image of persons. This image is radically different from, and not reduceable to, the scientific image of man. Instead of insuring the truth of the purposive model, however, these very differences guarantee its falsity. The purposive image may be perhaps an accurate account of our *beliefs*, say neo-positivists, but it is a false picture of the way things really are. The debate surrounding ordinary language philosophy thus reflects the older anti-thesis of intentional understanding versus causal-mechanical explanation, with each paradigm claiming priority over the other.

At stake here are our root images of the person, social action, and our knowledge about them. The early positivists not only wanted explanatory laws that everyone must accept, but also insisted that these laws correspond to a purely material world. They denied all subjective reality, even that of their own theories. Neo-positivists modified this. They still sought lawlike generalizations about real objects, but they allowed that these objects could never be directly known and that their theories could never be justified absolutely by either physical facts or mathematical truths. In contrast to both early and later positivists, however, romantic critics have suggested that if we were to conceive of the actor as a conscious agent, rather than as an object, we would not seek causes of behavioral events but reasons for meaningfully intended conduct. This requires us to impute awareness and choice to actors and to imaginatively reconstruct the meanings they give to their situations and the processes by which they decide or justify the courses they pursue. Thus, where the positivist seeks causes and lawlike constructs, the romantic seeks grounds and consequences. For the one the explanatory terms are external forces, for the other they are the actors' conceptions of meaning and value (Fite 1930, 34).

The Critical Theorists' View of Science as Ideology[1]

Other thinkers in the romantic tradition have attacked the relation of positivism to practice. In the view of critical theorists such as Max Horkheimer, Theodor Adorno, Herbert Marcuse, Jürgens Habermas, Manfred Stanley and their followers, positivist philosophy and social theory support instrumental approaches to politics and public actions. Indeed, for these thinkers the most striking aspect of the positivist habitus is not the development of science and technology as such, but the effort to apply them to society. Especially since World War II, modern states increasingly expect civil and military payoffs from the "disinterested" pursuit of knowledge, and governments invest heavily in R&D that involves little scholarly research and much technical development. More subtle but equally powerful are the pressures toward cognitive styles appropriate to technoadministrative control. For example, the uncritically quantitative bent of social science and the naive oppositions between rational versus intuitive, scientific versus metaphysical, and empirical versus evaluative, all encourage a conceptualization of the person and society as objects of instrumental calculation.

To the degree that a positivist theory of scientific knowledge has become the criterion for all knowledge, moral insights and political commitments have been delegitimized as irrational and reduced to mere subjective inclination. Ethical judgment is now thought of as personal opinion, a category error if we claim that it emerged from rational discourse. Like beauty, human values for the positivist are in the eye of the beholder. Unlike scientific knowledge, reasoning from moral rules is not considered objective, falsifiable, or empirically grounded. Hence, in this view, ethical political discourse lacks epistemological status and thus can have no legitimate claim on public credence. A. J. Ayer (1946, 170–171) put this succinctly:

> Our conclusions about the nature of ethics [are that] ethical terms . . . are employed . . . simply to express certain feelings and evoke certain responses. . . . In ethics there is . . . no sense in attributing objective validity to . . . judgments, and no possibility of arguing about questions of fact. [Ethical] criticism purposes not to give knowledge but to communicate emotions.

Critics of logical positivism have argued that this type of thinking also contains a contradiction, for the very assertions of facticity, causality, and procedures of verification are themselves criteria of value and validity. Scientific inquiry, like moral conduct, rests not on self-given facts, but on rules of procedure and structural coherence. These rules are themselves values, and they are not located in facts or direct intuitions, nor are they mere behavioral indicators of emotion. Rather, in science as in ethics, values are the principles by which facts and intuitions are organized, interpreted, and apprehended.

Liberal positivists insist that the scientific rationalization of society is good because it enables us to pursue more efficiently our humanistic values. Such a defense of technique assumes that the functional rationalization of means can in principle heighten our capacity to achieve ethically rational ends. The goal of optimizing social utilities requires a systematic, cost-benefit approach to organizing the means, they say, and such organizing leaves open the question of what constitutes utility. Indeed, for liberal positivists utility is taken to include humanistic values themselves.

By contrast, critical theorists argue that the technological use of knowledge from the human sciences is not comparable with such use of the natural sciences. They note for example, that the positivists' division between means and ends and between facts and values are themselves value positions which are philosophically unjustified and alienating in principle. Carried to its ultimate application, rationalization or technical efficiency involves the instrumental use not only of tools but also of persons. Moreover, argue critical theorists, rational-ization as a social process creates its own constituency, a new class of managers, owners, and technicians. For such persons the process of rationalization is a value in that it represents and advances their interests. And as a value, rationalization competes with other values. For example, when deception is more useful than truth, truth may be subordinated to utility. Similarly, though instrumental rationality is said to serve humane purposes, it may be more efficient in the service of those purposes to treat some people as means. Even in democratic societies the manipulation of persons for "historical necessity" or "their own good" can easily become a habit of rationalistic thought, with science and humanism serving as the legitimating rhetoric for this dehumanizing practice.

In such a dystopian social order, rather than the social machine serving values, values would be invoked instrumentally to serve the self-generated ends of the rationalized state. Indeed, the very vocab-ulary by which social values could be discussed would either be absorbed upwards by the state or reduced downwards to the sphere of personal opinion. Objectivity and reason would be conceived in terms of cost effectiveness for systems maintenance, whereas feelings and values would be relegated to the private realm. Moral language would be considered subjective and private, and would therefore cease to exist as a public discourse. In such a circumstance it would be impossible to express values as the measure of social policies or, indeed, to act publically as a moral agent. The application of scientific methods to the management of society would have brought with it an epochal change in our conception of citizenship and polity, of personal dignity and political obligation.

Coleridge said that "reality flouresces in the light of a rhetoric." A rhetoric in this sense refers to the conceptual vocabulary, models and metaphors, the stylistic tropes and devices through which experience is construed. So understood, the rhetoric of the policy sciences not only describes the social choices before us, it also creates both the choices and the background against which these choices are assessed. Thus, for its critics, the positivistic language of the policy sciences is not a neutral carrier of meanings or facts. Instead, it helps create what it describes. For if positive science seeks predictability and control, does it not encourage those conditions that permit this type of knowledge—a stable, technically manipulable social and political order? And are not the contents of theories that are derived from this method in fact largely technocratic, inviting elitest management of society or, at their most generous, participation through top-down liberal reform?

In this sense, say critical theorists, the political use of behavioral science has made positivism into a legitimating ideology of dominant groups. Despite the objections of many behavioral scientists themselves, their logic of method has been used as "the doctrine that social order can be consciously adopted to the requirements of contemporary science and technology" (Habermas in Adorno el al. 1976). Ironically, value-freedom itself has come to provide an ethic for calculated bureaucratic control. Calculative rationality, once a heuristic analytic model, has been largely realized, either normatively through the "scientization" of public discourse, or practically through the rationalization of social relations. Critical theorists thus blame positivism not only for its political prejudices but also for its attempts to mask them under the alibi of objectivity. Science, by virtue of its success as a value-free mode of inquiry, has become an instrument of domination. But in whose interest and for what principles and values? By its own admission, cultural meanings and forms of consciousness, including justice and freedom, are not accessible to positive science. The very ascendancy of such a science thus has engendered a crisis that science itself is incapable of solving.

Limits of the Hermeneutic Critique

Many critics of positivism are themselves vulnerable to attack, for in some ways their theories are reverse images of what they scorn. For example, in place of positivism's brute facts as a foundational datum for the human sciences, hermeneutic thought posits brute interpretations. Just as the epistemology of positivists cannot explain their intellectual practice, so the conception of self-contained language games renders ordinary language philosophers incapable of explaining either their own philosophic anthropology or, indeed, any social science. Social historians of knowledge have linked science to communitarian practices, but they have tended to see this scientific community as abstracted and disconnected from a larger political economic context, much as positivists view science itself. In place of Descartes' a priori cogito of the individual, pragmatists, ordinary language philosophers, and social historians of science posit an a priori collective cogito of the community of investigators.

How might these limitations be overcome and not merely reproduced in contrasting forms? How might we preserve the cognitive power and critical insight of both positivist as well as romantic rhetorics of reason? Such a task bristles with difficulties. Consider, for example, the trajectory of Peirce's original semiotic project: His heirs divided his pragmatist theory of signs into either structuralist reifications of language or hermeneutic reductions of meaning. On the one hand Peirce's semiotics was mediated by Charles Morris and conflated with the linguistics of Ferdinand de Saussure and his followers, issuing into the linguistic determinism of structuralist thinkers such as Claude Lévi-Strauss and Louis Althusser. On the other hand, certain neo-Peirceans held that social reality is uniquely and wholly constituted of interpretations. In this view, what is both human and social about human society is the actor's interpretations. Social reality, in effect, was reduced to the members' versions of it.

Neither of these forms of thought—structuralist reification or hermeneutic reduction—encourages critical reflection. In the case of Lévi-Strauss this is explicit (1969, 12). In the case of reductive hermeneutics, no exterior viewpoint is provided for critically assessing the account of agents. Such a hermeneutics can treat understanding and meaning, but it cannot distinguish *mis*understandings, *non*comprehensions, and *false* meanings from correct ones.

It thus appears that human works, taken by Vico as *the* content for the human sciences, share the same difficulty as the apodictic cogito posited by Descartes for the study of nature: Neither works nor mind can provide their own epistemological guarantees. For the cogito to initiate its axiomatic play, Descartes had to supply some content that was not itself rationally warranted in his system. And this prior content, which the cogito cannot demonstrate but must presuppose to do its proofs, of this it must remain uncertain. Similarly, for man to make his works, Vico (and later Dilthey and others) must supply a pre-existent something from which they can be made. And this prior something, which man himself did not make, of this he has no privileged understanding (Bhaskar 1982, 289–290; Gödel 1962).

With the revival of Vichian thought in the human sciences, Interpreting Man is replacing Explanatory Man. The categories have been recut to show persons as self-interpreting and self-motivating creatures of language. Thus the would-be explanatory scientist now faces her subject matter as "already preinterpreted, as linguistically and cognitively 'done' as it were, prior to any scientific investigation of it. These preinterpretations are *not* externally related and contingently conjoined to what happens in social life, but internally related and constitutive of it" (Bhaskar 1982, 289; see Charles Taylor 1971).

Given this view of persons as interpreting animals, it was natural to assume that such interpretations, beliefs, or works could provide a foundation for the human studies. This was true whether the hermeneutic foundation was viewed as finished products, as in early symbolic interactionism or functionalist anthropology, or conceived dialogically as emerging from cultural practices, as in ethnomethodology or cognitive anthropology. In its weaker form the hermeneutic foundation metaphor holds that knowledge is rooted in, and therefore must not be inconsistent with, members' self-interpretations. In its stronger form it assumes that social knowledge is exhausted by the intentions and meanings of members. But either way the foundation metaphor sheds its positivist garb, it reappears in hermeneutic drag.

Subjective idealist hermeneutics shows that absolute objectivity in positive social science is a fiction. But it also interprets conduct in terms of motives that are identical with the subjects' own assessments of the situation. In this subjectivist approach, meanings become equivalent to the linguistically articulated meaning, that is, they are assumed to be isomorphic with the verbal statements by which the actors orient themselves. But as ordinary language analysts themselves have shown, explanation in terms of motive is not the same as explanation in terms of cause. Motives or intentions do not cause actions; instead they provide a teleological account for them. Ordinary language philosophers have demonstrated that intentional action is relatively autonomous of nonintentional natural constraints, and that it must be accounted for by rules rather than by laws. Yet the question remains, Whence come these rules? And it is here that a *critical* hermeneutic can show that purely language-interpretive approaches are themselves a kind of myth, in that they posit as their subject matter a hermetic world of language outside of time or space (Wellmer 1971).

A dialectical, critical hermeneutic reveals the factual limits of subjective idealist social science. Society is not only praxis, but also practico-inert. It is in part like nature. To the extent that society is the product of conscious human intentions, hermeneutics better encompasses what is salient. But history also is made behind the backs and against the wills of even powerful persons. More important, history—especially history of the *longue durée*—is also made before the eyes but below the awareness and intentions of virtually everyone. Language-interpretive social theory does capture what is or can be communicated. But much, perhaps most, of what goes on is not and cannot be stated, and at least part of what is stated misinterprets this unstated and often unmentionable domain.

It is a disavowal of critical reflection to deny that a social structural or naturalistic level of reality enables and emerges from a communicative one. To accept all forms of consciousness as, in their ways, true is to eschew analysis of forms of consciousness that are false. Such a forfeiture is displayed in Peter Winch's essay, "Understanding a Primitive Society" (1970), in which Winch virtually precluded the possibility of cross-cultural anthropological comparison. In treating

Azande culture and its magic as a fully coherent web of ideas and practices, Winch thereby ascribed to contingent empirical "forms of life" or "language games" a rationality and intelligibility that logically could be possible only on the plane of wholly nondistorted communication. But for Winch various language games are self-justifying, because in his linguistic philosophy all interpretations are equally valid within the limits of the theory that warrants the given rules of speaking.[2]

Even if we were to accept Winch's hermeneutic reduction as internally consistent, it still leaves out a lot. His model permits us to say little or nothing about deviance, social change, domination, ideology, or cross-cultural understanding or analysis. Winch's proposed method enables us to address what people *do* but not what they *are* or *suffer.* "But social scientists are concerned with the causes and effects of being unemployed, having kin relations of a particular kind, rates of population change, and a myriad of conditions of individuals and societies, the descriptions of which have a logical character other than that of action descriptions. None of this appears in Winch's account" (MacIntyre 1978, 222, see 219). If we were to accept Winch's argument and prohibit causal or functional analyses of rule-governed action, then we could not distinguish the degree to which social structure controls or constrains individuals, nor could we identify cases in which the members' intentions or accounts are partial, inadequate, or misleading. For example, the taboo of many groups against postpartum sexual relations may be explained satisfactorily, perhaps more satisfactorily, by functionalist arguments than by members' accounts. Members might likely report that such relations are immoral or disgusting, whereas the functionalist or social ecologist might refer to the taboo's role in extending the infant's nursing period or defending it and the mother against infection.

Members' versions of these realities are shaped to perpetuate, not to explain, social phenomena. To say that all social realities are intersubjective constructions masks the role and extent of *precon*scious actions and begs the question of why so many social outcomes differ from individual intentions. The corrective to this difficulty is not simply to be found in a faulty, objectivist methodology. The *un*awareness and *mis*comprehension of members involves their failure to recognize their activities as the organizing of which their organizations are made, the habits of deference through which their hierarchies are lived, the processes by which their culture and social institutions are transformed into nature. But positivism has even less access to this on-going practical level of reality than does subjective romanticism.

The doctrine that all language games are equally valid and self-justifying also confuses the transcendence of particular language games with the transcendence of everything (Gellner 1975). The clarification of language games and the subversion of positivism's absolutist pretentions were achievements of ordinary language philosophy. But to show that there are no absolute ultimate grounds for knowledge is not to show that there are no relative penultimate ones. Epistemological transcendence of self-endorsing parochial visions—whether positivistic *or* romantic—need not be a transcendence to some absolute first sensa or meanings. Instead it can be a trancendence to a more cogent, embracing, and comprehensive system of signification.

Language idealists tend to endorse every circle of ideas as unitary, true, and complete, a kind of self-justifying first foundation. "What has to be accepted, the given, is—so one could say—forms of life" (Wittgenstein 1963). But a less absolute idealist look at practical uses and forms of lived speech would reveal them to be anything but self-contained, internally consistent, or simply given. As Evans-Pritchard observed, "Azande themselves say that the authority of their leaders was strengthened by war and the increase in numbers of their followers [that] each new conquest brought them. Another consequence has been ethnic intermingling of great complexity. I have listed over twenty foreign peoples . . . who have contributed to the Zande amalgam. . . . In the Sudan alone, in addition to Zande, there are spoken in Zande country seven or eight different languages. . . . Zande culture is a thing of shreds and patches" (Evans-Pritchard 1965, 105, 106, 110).

The relativism and idealism of other scholars is less radical or idealist than that of Winch, but they too are vulnerable to the same criticisms. "While authors such as Winch seem to have held that sociological explanations are exhausted by actors' explanations in terms of their intentions, the predominant view seems to draw more upon Schutz's two-stage model of sociological methodology. According to this model, actions must first be described, and understood in terms of actors' meanings after which they can be explained by concepts meaningful to the analyst and the audience" (Knorr-Cetina 1981, 18). This approach conceives of social science theories as "constructs of the second degree, that is, constructs of the constructs made by actors on the social scene" (Schutz 1962, 59).[3]

By the same logic, however, if cultures or historical epochs really were as self-contained as Winch's absolutism of language games asserts, they would not be susceptible to interpretation or translation into the idiom of another language, except, as Schutz implies, as a complicitous restatement of that culture's official version of itself.

This would be the reductio ad absurdum of any social science knowledge, since no social understanding or explanation on Winch's (or Schutz's) account is possible other than an inward familiarity with concepts used in a society by its members. The practices of comparative anthropology or historical sociology contradict and are contradicted by the conception of a wholly hermetic and internally self-contained cultural language game (see Winch 1958, 134–136). The solution, however, is not to seek an extralinguistic, positivistic philosophy of science to provide transcultural rules of interpretation, because in such philosophies the subject matter of language games and cultures ceases to exist or is reduced to a set of behavioristic signals.

A non-positivist corrective to Which is provided by Winch himself in an earlier essay on "Nature and Convention."[4] Here the author did not say that standards of truth-telling are culturally variable and self-contained from one language game to another. Instead he adduced belief to be a noncontingent precondition for the operation of any discourse or interaction. Other emergents such as canons of integrity or fair play also are presented in this light. In a similar spirit, Garfinkel (1967) noted that interactions have properties that do not vary and that are presuppositions of any meaningful discourse even though the rules of the interactions may be different in different cultures or settings. As Karl-Otto Apel (1967; see Dallmayr 1981, 151–152) pointed out, arguments and findings of this type imply an ideal language game that is differently distorted as it is incarnated in different particular language praxes. Such an ideal is not an empirical hypothesis that can be tested. Instead it functions as the premise of cross-cultural and historical research and also, though less evidently, of interactions between contemporaries.

The Critical Theorists and Praxis

The alternatives to positivism all help legitimate an emancipatory habitus, for all posit and elaborate the assumption of the human authorship of (knowledge about) reality. As the positivist habitus includes practical activities as well as ideas and concepts, however, we are still left with the question of the relationship of these alternative views to an alternative, emancipatory practice. What are the moral and political implications of these critiques of positivism? Do they encourage a way of knowing that conjoins reason and freedom? And do they thereby provide a warrant in reason for the pretheoretical belief in the telos of human agency and collective self-direction?

Critical theory has been advanced as such a form of rationality. In contrast to the positivists' dictum that "knowledge is power," critical theorists answer that "truth shall make you free." "Knowledge" and "truth" both connote reason, but positivists and critical theorists have different understandings of reason as well as its relation to an intended democratic practice. Whereas positivists have struggled for freedom from values and for a scientific politics, critical theorists have sought to conform reason and freedom. Such a conception would have to separate reason from ideology or passive contemplation on the one hand, and to distinguish freedom from a purely "interior" liberty or a merely procedural democracy on the other.

Critical theorists have looked variously to work, art, and discourse as possible models for an emancipatory reason. Horkheimer and Adorno (1973, 213), for example, sought to derive such a conception of reason from the Marxian category of human work:

> The viewpoints which critical theory draws from historical analysis as the goals of human activity, especially the idea of reasonable organization of society that will meet the needs of the whole community, are immanent in human work, but are not correctly grasped by individuals or by the common mind.

But how is the conception of work as an anticipation of liberation any less ideological than the medieval conception of work as a necessary evil, or the classical idea of work as a distortion of human creative capacity? Moreover, if work as the basis for a liberating reason is "not correctly grasped by individuals or by the common mind," who then will grasp it? The discontented intellectuals? The revolutionary vanguard? And how is such elitism in theories of freedom to avoid becoming unfreedom of the masses in practice?

Another practical source for an immanent emancipatory reason is certain aspects of culture, such as art, especially in its sensuous or even erotic dimensions. According to Marcuse (1978, 72–73),

> Art fights reification by making the petrified world speak, sign, perhaps dance. . . . Art breaks open a dimension inaccessible to other experience, a dimension in which human beings, nature, and things no longer stand under the law of the established reality principle. Subjects and objects encounter the appearance of that autonomy which is denied them in their society.

Marcuse lyrically evoked a romantic conception of art which has little to do with the actual social bases and functions of most forms of art in most times and places of human history (see Brown 1988;

Clignet 1985; Hauser 1958). Art as a separate domain of experience is a modern idea that reflects the compartmentalization of modern experience generally. Marcuse focused only on high culture, and particularly modernist art; he singled out its aspect as protest and suppressed its role in expressing, even reinforcing, the conditions from which it springs; and then he offered this distorted image as *the* aesthetic dimension of all human experience, a harbinger of human emancipation (Marcuse 1978). The problem is not merely that this is transparently ideological, but that Marcuse provided no criteria for distinguishing ideological art from emancipatory art, or for discerning how these two aspects intermingle in any given work or school. Into this lacuna falls his project of establishing reason/art as a liberating social practice.

Another writer who has struggled with the question of emancipatory reason is Jürgen Habermas, the most thorough and sophisticated of the critical theorists. Habermas has sought to establish philosophically an interest of reason in emancipation. His goal has been to link the truth of statements to the intention of the good and true life (Habermas 1968, 301–317).

Thus Habermas asks how a consensus emerging from "discourse" can be distinguished from one that is founded on interests other than truth and justice. How, in other words, can we know when reason is coincident with freedom? The answer, in a somewhat circular fashion, is that truth and freedom are linked when truth is arrived at through a discourse characterized by freedom. What, however, is a situation of "free" communication, of "discourse" in Habermas's sense? It is a situation in which there is no domination, in which there are no power differentials, in which all participants have equal access to all roles in the dialogue, to start or terminate discourse, to raise questions or submit evidence, a discourse in which the "unforced force" of the superior arguments prevails.

Truth, contrary to the positivist conception, cannot in this view be judged independently of its mode of constitution. Of course the ideal conditions of speech rarely if ever exist in reality. But this does not invalidate the ideal discourse as a standard by which to distinguish ideological from nonideological statements, and to link through a body of discourse reason or truth on the one hand, and freedom and justice on the other.

> The ideal speech situation is . . . a reciprocal supposition unavoidable in discourse. This supposition . . . alone is the warrant that permits us to join in an actual attained consensus the claim of a rational consensus. At the same time it is a critical standard against which

every actually realized consensus can be called into question and tested. (Habermas 1973, 258)

A life of freedom and justice is therefore not the goal merely of a critical theory. It also is a telos inherent in the very concept of truth and anticipated in every act of communication (see McCarthy 1973, xviii).

Let me elaborate this way of thinking and connect it with my earlier remarks. Critics of positivism have considered science and magic as simply two different language games. This is fruitful if one's purpose is to delegitimate scientific absolutism and reductivism. By the same token, however, the view that rival epistemologies are mere language games also suggests that any cognitive practice can be evaluated in terms of a telos or existential function, that is, in terms of what that particular game does. Once this shift is made it becomes clear that one may well establish cognitive hierarchies for various purposes in terms of which certain forms of thought will be distinctly superior to others. Formal thought in general has a cognitive superiority over *doxa*. Moreover, specific types of formal thought—principally those that highlight mechanisms and structural properties—tend to be superior at unmasking contradictions, scarcities, miscommunications, and relations of domination that are often disguised in ordinary languages. This seems to be understood implicitly even by microsociologists who ally themselves with Winch's or Schutz's philosophy: In their actual research practice they pursue a more critical agenda. This research shows how actors' meanings are accomplished interactively in contexts, but it makes little use of the actors' avowed intentions, either as explanations themselves or even as a primary resource for explanation generated by the social scientist. Some ethnoscientists even proclaim themselves to be uninterested in actors' intentions, and most give their attention instead to the routine practices of everyday life that apparently are not specifically motivated. By this tactic such researchers construe individually meaningful social action to be derivative rather than constitutive of these situated interactions, speech practices, and larger social structures (Knorr-Cetina 1981, 18; see Menzel 1978). For such researchers, "society" creates "intentions" as much as the reverse.

To put this more precisely, the power to constitute is not merely an abstract quality of language itself, but lies in the speech community that authorizes a language and invests certain users and usages with authority. The hierarchically superior authors of regulations, sermons, five-year plans, orations, constitutions, or vocabularies of lineage and honor are usually able to impose what they state, tacitly demarcate what is thinkable and unthinkable, and thereby fortify the social symbolic order. "Language is real, practical consciousness,"

said Marx in *The German Ideology* (1965), and part of its being real and
practical is that it masks as much as it reveals, suppresses as much as
it expresses, takes as tacit more than it makes explicit. Through
language we distinguish the universe of what can be stated and the
universe of what goes without saying or is unmentionable. This is
why an emancipatory theory of knowing must be critical of both
meaning as well as structure, for only such a critical analysis can
elevate the "return of the repressed" to the level of articulate
consciousness. In Marxian terms, to articulate in a previously unavailable discourse what until then was repressed is to abolish a linguistically encoded false consciousness (Bourdieu 1977, 21, 170). Such a
process is a beginning of political awareness and self-direction.

To see knowledge and experience as symbolically constructed is to
break the spell of the positivist epistemology that is in fact a white
man's magic, a metaphysics of society dressed up in the language of
logic or natural science. But to see knowledge and experience as
exhausted by or necessarily consistent with the speakers' versions of
it, is to invoke another form of magic—hermeneutics as hermeticism
(see Festugière 1950–1954; Yates 1964). Both these magics confer a
perfect coherence on inchoate historical practice. They transform
methodological postulates of Explanatory Man or Understanding
Man into epistemological conclusions. They equate intelligibility with
ontology. Social orders do this. Critical thinkers must avoid it. Instead
of acting like shamans and priests who seek to produce a closed unity
of mental structures and social structures, human scientists can
assume a critical posture by showing how such unities, whether
positivist or hermeneutic, help to naturalize the arbitrariness of any
social order. Such a critical posture also decenters the concept of
emancipation from individual consciousness to collective practice. By
focusing on communicative action as the essence and integument of
both consciousness and social structure, such an approach permits a
dialectical overcoming of many sterile oppositions in social science as
a professional and a public discourse. The importance of Habermas's
Spraketic is that it provides a guide for such a critical practice.

Is this enough? Critical theorists have shown how science and
knowledge, when free of values and removed from moral or political
commitment, actually encourage the redefinition of politics as the
official function of techno-administrative elites. But such critiques, as
well as Habermas's normative ethics of discourse, do not in themselves specify critical theory's relation to praxis, much less suggest a
practical program. Thus to accept the romantic critique of positivism
is not to accept, or even to know, the romantic solution. Critical
thought is a beginning of emancipation, and critical discourse is an

embodiment of intellectual freedom. It is hard to imagine an emancipatory political program emerging from a discourse that was not
critical and self-reflective. Opposition to dogmas, an attitude of
sustained doubt, a willingness to take the viewpoint of the other, a
suspension of intellectual closure, a desire to align concrete instances
with general principles, a love of cogency in thought for its own
sake—all these are convictions of members of the party of truth. No
thinker can revoke this membership without negating what she is.
But such awareness and commitment is not the same thing as a
political agenda, it does not tell us how to move from the sociologist's
"is" toward the philosopher's "ought," nor does it answer the
question of who is to be the historical agent of emancipation.

Symbolic Realism: Beyond
the Positivist-Romantic Debate

To sum up, on the one side is the rhetoric of old-fashioned positivists
who advocate not only explanatory laws to which everyone must agree,
but laws that assume a purely material world and deny all subjective
reality, including that of the theorist. Opposing this is the rhetoric of
subjective romantics who want no laws, but experience and intuitions
that, they claim, are a higher kind of science. Sublating both these views
would be a critical rhetoric of reason that defended generalized explanations of the natural as well as of the human world, including subjectivity, but without a reductive materialist or mechanist bias. This
view finds its justification in a postpositivist, postromantic, dialectical,
symbolic realist theory of knowledge. In such a view, causal, lawlike
explanation is itself an interpretive procedure, and critical interpretation itself can be rigorous way of knowing

Ironically, the earlier positivists' program to reduce our vague
language to instant-by-instant experience is precisely the problem of
setting sociological abstractions on an experiential basis. Only now
this empiricism need not be either objective of subjective, but can be
intersubjective and mediated by a self-conscious critical rhetorical
practice. Informed by continental and pragmatic thought, contemporary empirical research may abandon the idea of a self-subsisting
world-out-there, a world the data of which could speak for themselves before any theorizing. Instead, a critical rhetoric of reason
recognizes that scientific reality is itself symbolic, that validity implies
a fit between our ideas and perceptions, that powerful theories make
things coherent strikingly and economically, that originality involves
ambiguity and difference, and that such diverse criteria can be made
to inform theories through dialectical discourse.

In symbolic realism the subject-object dichotomy of the early positivist-romantic debate also is transformed. For in this view one's own subjective states can be analogic instruments for observing the subjective states of others. Such observations differ only in degree, not in kind, from so-called objective observations; both types of observations are linguistically mediated, both are shaped by their instruments of observation, and both are subject in principle to validation by their coherence with a larger body of data and theory.

In contrast to both scientific realism and subjective or symbolic idealism, symbolic realism seeks a warrant for both scientific *and* ethical judgments, and hence for a public discourse that would be adequate both for moral self-understanding of the lifeworld as well as for management of complex systems. Of help in such a project is Marie Swabey's discussion of logical or postulational systems. Swabey (1961, 17) distinguished postulates *from* which we reason and the principles in accordance *with* which we reason:

> The first, [postulates *from* which we reason], are free assumptions of a point of view, optimal conveniences, differing from one scheme of thought to another, [i.e., they may be scientific or ethical, depending on the appropriateness of either to one's purposes]. The second, [postulates *with* which we reason, are] a group of comprehensive regulations necessary to all systems, the basic logic of sanity and rationality. These later are the principles of consistency and inference. As such they are not factual . . . laws but canons of validity, constituting the comprehensive framework of both thought and things, principles whose certification is discursive in that they are reaffirmed in their very denial.

This distinction is useful in describing normative paradigms in general, whether they be scientific or ethical in starting point or content. In the elaboration of all such paradigms, adherence is required not only to the internal rules of the postulation system chosen, but also to the principles of formal expression in general.

Having noted these features common to both science and ethics, several further comments become possible. It is clear that science and ethics are different in that they assume different postulational systems *from* which to reason—they are different kinds of games. Moreover, since science and ethics are systems not only of action but also for ordering such action, both must presuppose principles of structural cohesion and order—the principles *with* which we reason. To see forms of life for a moment as language games, we may say that such principles are implicit in the relationship between the rules of any game and its moves. This relationship must be maintained regardless of what kind of game is being played or what are the strategies of the players. Without such a relationship, the term "game" (read science, ethics, art,) would have no meaning; likewise, without principles with which we construct relationships between value and conduct, or between theory and data, neither ethics nor science would be intelligible.

Scientific and ethical discourse—that is, forms of talk that presuppose causality or freedom—both are rational in that they presuppose various criteria of economy, congruence, and consistency. Such criteria are those by which we organize experience into formal structures of which "knowing" is constituted. Such a view of knowledge undercuts both scientific *and* moral absolutism: It presupposes that the practice of science itself constitutes a commitment to values such as fitness, consistency, etc., and that conduct becomes amoral and incomprehensible *as* conduct unless conducted in terms of some (rational system of) ethics. This is what Durkheim meant when he said, "Logic is the morality of thought; morality is logic of action." The rightness of this statement hinges on the norms of order and judgment implicit in both thought and action.

The coherence systems of positivism and romanticism obviously are different enough to justify distinction. To borrow the example of languages, French is not Spanish, and even less is it Chinese. Yet linguistics may reveal commonalities among all three, and even show how the particular genius of each lies in the way it solves problems common to all languages. Similarly, the policy sciences are neither social physics nor are they social ethics. Yet as a coherence system or symbolic form, they share features with both science *and* ethics. And, with the fall of absolute distinctions between positivism and romanticism, a possibility is opened for creating a methodology of social and policy analysis that is at once "objective" and "subjective," at once valid scientifically and significantly humane.

In the symbolic realist view, language is not a reflection either of the world or of the mind. Instead, human worlds and minds emerge from the social historical *practice* that is language. Symbols are understood as taking their meanings not from things or intentions, but from socially coordinated actions. Words help constitute and mediate social behaviors, provide legitimating or stigmatizing vocabularies of motive, and mask or reveal structures of domination. Semantical changes express cultural conflicts. "Because . . . words carry meanings by virtue of dominant interpretations placed upon them by social behaviors, . . . we can view language functionally as a system of social control" (Mills 1974, 677; see Brown 1987, 7–9).

The worlds of language are not made from extralinguistic things or ideas. Not from Heraclitus's fire nor from Thales' water. Not from brute facts nor from brute interpretations. There is no foundational stuff out of which worlds can be made because there is neither stuff nor worlds for us without communicative action. Human perception requires conception, and conception presupposes a social symbolic world. Thus facts are entrenched tiny theories, and true theories begin as objects held at arm's length (Hansen 1958; Campbell 1984; Quine 1960). Social facts are things, as Durkheim said, but only to the extent that all things already are social facts. Words are signs for things and facts; things and facts are socially objectified, pragmatically concretized signs for words.

How then are worlds made? They are made from other worlds. And there are no worlds without words or other symbols. Worlds are shaped linguistically through metaphor, beginning much like a dialect or pidgin (Nelson Goodman 1978; Brown 1987). When first created, Swahili and biophysics both were new worlds made from old ones. The search for a universal or necessary beginning of human worlds or of human knowledge—in facts, innate ideas, or meanings—is thus akin to the search for the beginnings of human language popular in the nineteenth century. Anthropology, paleontology, or developmental psychology may study social, protohistorical, or individual comings to be of worlds, but the search for a first world is as misguided as the search for a first moment in time or the search for the last elephant upon which all elephants stand who hold up the earth (actually they stand on a tortoise). Such "investigations" are futile because they mistake a regulative principle for an empirical one. The concept of first origins, like the concept of structure or evolution or causality, is much like a Kantian synthetic a priori. It enables us to organize our perceptions into comprehensible experience, but cannot itself be empirically nor logically grounded.

This is not to say that we should not mind mind, or that matter does not matter. Original thinkers design as much as they discover what they describe. But most science (or art, etc.) is mainly an elaboration of existing modes of representation, and even highly original thinkers cannot design in any way they choose. Unless they respect the regulative principles of their publics they are unlikely to gain credence or even to secure an audience. "While readiness to recognize alternative worlds may be liberating, and suggestive of new avenues of exploration, a willingness to welcome all worlds produces none" (Nelson Goodman 1978, 97). Which worlds are to be accepted as true is both a normative and practical question, both epistemological and political, aesthetic and moral. Yet epistemology and politics, aesthetics and morals, also are symbolic constructions. They are worlds as well. Both the ingredients and the criteria of worlds are rhetorically constructed from (other) worlds.

The universe is always a universe of discourse in the classic sense given by de Morgan in his *Formal Logic*, "a range of ideas which is either expressed or understood as containing the whole matter under discussion" (1847, 41). Such discursive understanding also includes the tacit and necessarily unnoticed realm that is undiscussed, unnamed, and admitted without argument or scrutiny but that is, nevertheless, contained in language, though it may be unstated or expressed only as irony, blasphemy, or euphemism. Symbolic realism thus takes Plato's remark as literal: "The philosopher is a mythologist." But it adds that the philosopher also can be a demythologist.

This critical thrust of symbolic realism also is directed against the radical relativism of purely subjectivist language interpretation. It shows how purely analytical or purely interpretive accounts inevitably miss their target because neither can "bring out the incoherence of a discourse which, springing from underlying mythic or ideological schemes, has the capacity to survive every reductio ad absurdum. Systems of classification which reproduce, in their specific logic, the objective classes (i.e., divisions by sex, age, or position in the relations of production)," contribute to the reproduction of power relations by securing the misrecognition of their inherent arbitrariness (Bourdieu 1977, 164).

Pierre Bourdieu's criticism of conventional theories of knowledge is in the tradition of great deconstructive humanists such as Nietzsche, Marx, and Freud. What they had in common was their decision to take the whole of consciousness as false consciousness. Each was a great doubter in the manner of Descartes. But each took his doubt still further, into the inner fortress of Cartesian thought itself: Each doubted that consciousness is as it appears to itself; each questioned whether, in consciousness, meaning and consciousness of meaning coincide (Ricoeur 1965a, 32). Such radical doubt has corroded subjective humane values and undermined objective scientific knowledge. Such a humanism and such a science cannot be restored. But they can be transvalued and sublated by new methods and new metaphors— for example, by a deconstructive, critical exegesis of both science and values as rhetorical constructions. Such an exegesis is not merely an explanation of possible meanings as they are constructed in various disciplines, authors, or texts. It also includes, indeed focuses on, the methods by which knowledge, selves, and realities are produced.

The enemy of the symbolic realist, then, is neither the scientist nor the humanist as such. Instead, his typical adversary is the cognitive monopolist who maintains that her system is preeminent and all-inclusive and that every other version must eventually be reduced to it or rejected as false or meaningless. Symbolic realism "implies no relaxation of rigor but a recognition that standards different from, yet no less exacting, than those applied in science are appropriate for appraising what is conveyed in perceptual or pictoral or literary" or other "versions of the world" (Nelson Goodman 1978, 5).

The rubble of failed attempts to appraise theoretical works definitively attests to the futility of seeking permanent binding canons of judgement for forms of theory. "Theoretic value means value in use, and use-value is tied to occasioned want in situated contexts. [It is] therefore a virtue to have multiple, mutable, and locally validated interpretive schemata"—a multiplicity of postulates *from* which we reason (Green 1988). We thus should respect the relative validity of reasoning from different postulational systems, just as different forms of reasoning should respect the general rules of cogency and inference that make such discourse rational.

The assessment of the habitus of positivists or romantics is not a matter of purely rational deduction nor purely emotive choice, so much as it is a matter of prudential judgment. And, as Foss (1971, 246, 248–249) pointed out, "Prudence is a practical virtue, an action concept. . . . [Thus] the justification of frameworks is a function of shifting environmental demands and the species survival needs to which these give rise." Symbolic realists' conception of a critical rhetoric of reasons provides a metanarrative that facilitates such prudential judgment (Brown 1987). The point of symbolic realism is not to be truthful or untruthful in any ultimate sense, but to create with the reader a new textual space and a new rhetorical practice that, once established, would enable both rhetor and reader to transcend the ontological assumptions and cognitive and behavioral norms that have served in part as their prison. A preferred rhetorical strategy and method of logic for such a critical practice is dialectic, which is the topic of the ensuing chapter.

FOUR

JEAN-PAUL SARTRE AND CLAUDE LÉVI-STRAUSS
The Dialectic of Agency and Structure in Theories of the Social

> The things themselves, which only the limited brains of men and animals believe fixed and stationary, have no real existence at all. They are the flashing and sparks of drawn swords, the glow of victory in the conflict of opposing qualities.
>
> Nietzsche (1962)

> The concept and even the word "structure" itself are as old as Western science and Western philosophy. Nevertheless, . . . structure . . . has always been neutralized or reduced, and this by a process of giving it a center or of referring to a point of presence, a fixed origin. . . . The function of this center was not to orient the structure . . . but above all to make sure that the organizing principle of the structure would limit what we might call that *play* of the structure.
>
> Derrida (1978)

MODERN SOCIAL theory has been an arena of conflict since its inception. Central to this conflict have been the efforts of romantic or humanistic thinkers to criticize the dominant positivist paradigm and to forge new ways of understanding human conditions. These critics conceive social actors to be creators and organizers of cognitively and emotionally meaningful acts, and social events to be patterned according to commitments, intentions; and imagined consequences. With such assumptions as a starting point, humanistic social science investigates the problems of intention and meaning, the social construction and use of moral rules, the role of power in such interactions, and how such conflictual negotiations of reality create and are constrained by the cultures and political economies in which they are embedded.

Such an approach is one way of linking scientific to ethical concerns. As we have seen, however, the dominant positivist notion of scientific explanation tends to exclude the analysis of the construction of reality and meaning. Such analysis requires an interpretation of feelings, actions, rules, and reasons; but explanation in positive science speaks of causes, effects, systems, and structures, and views behavior as determined by inner or outer forces. Do these apparently fundamental differences between positivist and romantic thought-ways mean that we can have the objective, technically useful knowl-edge of structural mechanisms *or* the morally relevant understanding of human actions, but not both at once? Or it is possible for humanistic thought to take a rigorous and practical form, and for science to somehow include the lifeworlds and praxes of persons?

Classical social theorists such as Marx, Weber, and Durkheim sought to close the fissure between agency and structure, but their estates were broken up among legitimate heirs and illegitimate claimants, and their respective projects to create a unified theory of society were shattered. Newer schools, such as symbolic interaction-ism, ethnomethodology, or systems theory, have tended to reproduce the very limitations they were intended to resolve. Partly in response to these limitations, certain European thinkers have sought alterna-tive approaches to understanding human conditions. Among these are existentialism and structuralism. Existentialism focuses on the construction of reality and meaning; structuralism focuses on struc-tures of meanings as pregiven. The first assumes that social actors are moral agents who consciously intend their conduct. The second assumes that intentions are superintended by the deeper structures of the mind that lie beneath the actor's conscious awareness. For existentialists it is the actor who speaks and in so speaking creates language. For structuralists it is language that "speaks" through the actor and that, in so speaking, "creates" him.

An adequate theoretical and civic discourse requires both these dimensions. It needs to make visible those structural causes and consequences of individual and group actions which may not be apparent in the mundane awareness, or unawareness, of members. Moreover, because social policies affect human conditions and con-sciousness, sensitivity to the lifeworlds of members also is indispen-sable to any informed and responsible social intervention. One method for practicing such a discourse might be taken from the respective logics of existentialism and structuralism. In this chapter I argue that such a method is not only possible, but directly implied in both existentialist and structuralist modes of thought. I begin by discussing the dialectical social theory of Jean-Paul Sartre. Then, after treating Lévi-Strauss's theory of structure, I compare and criticize both these approaches. I argue that dialectical thought generates structures, and that structuralism invites a dialectical method of construction. Specifically, the very notion of structure implies several defining principles, each of which presupposes some dialectical process. Dialectic thus provides a method for joining understanding of the lifeworld with explanation of structural constraint.

The Existential Dialectic of Jean-Paul Sartre

What is dialectic?[1] The soft definition sees dialectic as a stylistic device of argumentation, having little or no distinct logical status. In this view, dialectic is held in low regard to the extent that it differs from conventional formal logic; and to the extent that it is worthy of respect, it is indistinguishable from clear thought in general. Kant expressed this appraisal when he spoke of dialectic as "the logic of illusion," a method useful for unmasking transcendental judgments but not for establishing synthetic truths (Kant 1885, 7; see also Popper 1940, 411).

Whereas Kant reduced dialectic by narrowing its scope, other philosophers have diluted the term to the point of meaninglessness. Neo-Kantian, Cartesian, and neo-positivist logicians have written of "the myth of dialectical reason" (Ruyer 1961), claiming that, like scientific procedure itself, dialectic is nothing more than the "purification of knowledge under the pressure of experience with which it confronts itself" (Gonseth 1948, 94). An equally flaccid definition was advanced by the sociologists Ralf Dahrendorf (1958, 1959) and Pierre van den Berghe (1963). "The minimal dialectic approach (if it can still be called that)," said van den Berghe, assumes that "(1) change is not only ubiquitous, but an important share of it is generated within the (social) system . . . , and, (2) change of intra-systemic or endogenous origin often arises from contradiction and conflict between two or more opposing factors" (1963, 695).

Yet if this definition is accepted it would be hard to find theories that are not dialectical, because most social thought from Hesiod onward has dealt with either the inner changes of social systems, the conflicts between or within systems, or both. Such definitions thus are useless for understanding the distinctive character of dialectical thought or for determining which analytic categories might best serve as tools for dialectical social analysis.[2]

In contrast to these positions, a strong view of dialectic sees it as a radical "negation of the laws of formal logic," a method aimed at "the demolition of all acquired and crystallized concepts, in order to prevent their mummification" (Gurvitch 1962, 5). The modern expression of this position started with Kant's German successors—Fichte, Schelling, and Hegel. While accepting much of Kant's thought as a starting point, they attacked his doctrine of noumenal things-in-themselves. Instead, they contended that the reality grasped by dialectical reason is the infinite whole, of which analytic understanding can apprehend only the parts. Thus dialectical reason is useful not only for negating judgments about inaccessible transcendental entities. It is also the method by which we come to know the organized totality of experience itself (Quinton 1975, part 1, 35).

Since Hegel, other writers have sought in dialectic an awakening from what Rimbaud called "the one-eyed intelligence" of positivism. Chief among these is Jean-Paul Sartre. Sartre's work often is treated as a combination of existentialism and Marxism or, more ambitiously, as an attempt to integrate Hegel's theoditic philosophy of history, Rousseau's psychology and politics, Marx's theory of alienation and economic praxes, and Hobbes's individualism, all in a kind of dialecticized Cartesian rationality. Such an interpretation of Sartre may be inevitable, in that we understand ideas in terms of other ideals that they are like or unlike. Yet it is incorrect and trivializing if it leads us to believe that Sartre integrated these elements into a static formula. Instead, Sartre made of them an emulsion. They become a single "solution" only when agitated; left to sit on the shelf, the parts settle out.

One thread that runs throughout Sartre's work is his concept of the ceaseless opposition between man's freedom of choice and the burden of his past choices. Existential freedom and objectified history would at first appear to be antagonistic siblings, born of the same late modern culture. Hegel and Marx sought to integrate existence and history by seeing history as expressive of human spirit or action, as well as analogous to human life in it cycles of evolutionary growth and decline. But other thinkers followed the historical relativist line of Nietzsche, who condemned the "excess of history" and the "tyranny of the actual" which is reflected in an "unrestrained historical sense" (Nietzsche 1957). In the case of Sartre, he began as a follower of Nietzsche (*La nausée, L'imaginaire, Being and Nothingness*), and ended as a champion of Marx (*Critique of Dialectical Reason*). To trace this development of Sartre's thought and assess its contradictions is, I believe, to reveal difficulties that inhere more generally in projects to integrate theories of human agency and theories of structural causation.

Sartre's early rejection of historical and social structural thinking is expressed in his philosophical novel *La nausée*, in which an amateur historian seeks to cure his periodic nausea by writing the biography of a Marquis de Rollebon. But the writer comes to understand that any order in the historical material that he studies is in fact imposed artificially by him and that there is no inherent meaning either in the past or in the present. "I understand nothing more about his conduct," says the narrator of the Marquis. "Slow, lazy, sulky, the facts adapt themselves to the rigor or the order I wish to give them; but it remains outside of them" (Sartre 1949).

The sickening heaviness of existence, the absurd unmeaning of what Sartre called "human reality," is prior to any possible social order or history. History, in other words, is exterior to the original materials of human existence. History may make this absurd existence meaningful, but the meanings are always created by humans; they do not inhere in the events of existence past or present. This denial of the definitive historical past is part of Sartre's more general denial of original meaning. Indeed, Sartre's later affirmation of history depended on his first providing a general affirmation of the possibility of meaning creation. What we take to be a factual historical past, said Sartre, is instead a product of the human imagination, an effort to narrate reality in order to transcend it: "The imaginary thus represents at each moment the implicit meaning of the real" (Sartre 1948, 272). Before the activation of the aesthetic imagination, history has no existence (Krieger 1968, 248).

At this stage of his thought, however, Sartre was unable to explain how one moves from aesthetic perception to critical historical synthesis. This is partly due to his having conflated three levels or processes of historical understanding: that of actors in their particular moments, that of structural forces of history, and that of the historian. This merging of levels yielded what Sartre recognized as an "inherent contradiction and ambiguity" (1948, 169–71), since the aesthetic imagination, which is the very faculty that permits us to represent human reality, is just that faculty which constitutes the unreal.

Sartre's focus on the individual imagination as the agency of historical understanding gave rise to difficulties with his concept of totalization. For Sartre, objects of the imagination, works of art, or historical representations are themselves "indivisible wholes, independent, isolated worlds" with no necessary relations to each other or to their milieux. Given these assumptions—similar in spirit to Wittgenstein's and Winch's concept of self-contained language games—how is it possible to achieve a larger totalization? This question was taken up in *L'être et le néant*. In this work Sartre represented existence as a process in which consciousness and its totalizations are immanent. In this perspective, "neither consciousness nor existence are *in* time. [Instead], time is created by consciousness as the medium through which consciousness transforms existence into a world for which it can take responsibility" (Krieger 1968, 253). Whereas the future is a freely chosen telos toward which consciousness directs itself, and the present is the withdrawal and

negation by free consciousness of given existence, the past is an
obdurate facticity that consciousness determines itself to transcend
(Sartre 1956, 107). Thus consciousness emerges from that very past
that it must negate in order to realize itself, "for the meaning of the
past is strictly dependent upon my present project" for the future
(Sartre 1956, 497–498).

That the present in a fundamental way determines the past also is
expressed in Sartre's post war play *No Exit* (1947, 171–172):

> Garcin: Estelle, am I a coward?
> Estelle: But I don't know, honey, I'm not in your shoes. You have to
>   make up your mind for yourself.
> Garcin: I can't make up my mind.

There is only one means by which the characters can "really"
decide who they are, what they did, and why they did it: They must
go on acting in such a way that their future acts confirm or refute that
"past" that has been chosen as the "real" one. Thus, the behaviorist
concept of motivation is turned on its head. It is not the stimulus that
determines the response; it is through the person's choice of action in
the present that he knows what were its causes in the past (Jameson
1961, 189–192; 1972, 210–211; see Danto 1968, chap. 9).

The admitted paradox (Sartre 1956, 489, 496) of this formulation is
tied to Sartre's identification of history conceived as the *reality* of the
past with history conceived as *knowledge* of the past. Sartre rejected any
essential distinctions between the knowledge of ordinary historical actors and that of contemporary historical scientists. Thus, on the one
hand, he concluded that the agents of history act like historians: "The
historian is himself historical; . . . he historicizes himself by illuminat-
ing 'history' in the light of his projects and those of his society" (1956,
501). But on the other hand, Sartre is unable to explain how historians
are able to achieve the formal and comprehensive totalizations that give
"history as knowledge" its special cognitive power.

How then does Sartre deal with the evident privileged access of
historians to structural causation, retrospective understanding, or
history of the *longue durée*? In *L'être et le néant* he was unable to do so,
because for Sartre the question still was one "of *my* freedom," of
"only *my* particular consiousness" (1956, 438). Human reality remains
individual reality. Groups and collective actions or forces become
unreal because essential reality can only be the cogito. Sartre conceived of the past as a creation of present consciousness, and of the
group as an artificial seriality. But without history or collectivity what
possible forces could form a continuum between individual intention
and social-historical outcomes?

Sartre repositioned himself on these issues in his post war writings. Through the war experience, de Beauvoir said, "we discovered the reality of history and its weight." And with the discovery of his own historicity, Sartre also discovered his own "dependence," which could be resolved only through solidarity with "those men who embodied it [solidarity] on earth," that is, with the proletariat, the "universal class" (Beauvoir 1963, 15–17). Sartre's task therefore became that of integrating his earlier existential conceptions of agency and will with the structural historical materialism of Marx.

Sartre took up the question of solidarity and historical action in his novel *The Age of Reason*, but his continuing loyalty to Rousseauean individualism led him to treat social order and change as a kind of *volonté générale*. The life of Sartre's protagonist, the Communist Brunet, has "meaning" and "destiny" because he shares "a whole world in common" with his comrades. "He had joined up, he had renounced his freedom. . . . And everything had been rendered to him, even his freedom. 'He is freer than I; he is in harmony with himself and with the party' " (1947, 159). Sartre linked personal agency in the lifeworld with social causality in history only by subsuming individual freedom to collective totalization. "Everything is outside: . . . solid objects, all of them. Inside, nothing. . . . Myself, nothing" (Sartre 1947, 362–363). "Solidarity" remained a social totalization of individuals without essence, a pure exteriority: "I can break the shell that separates us only if I wish for myself no other future than his, . . . share his time and his minutes" (Sartre 1951, 200). Practice is made intelligible through knowledge, and the individual historical agent is made an historian by fusion into the group.

Critics have attacked Sartre's formulation from different directions. For example, George Stack argued that Sartre's collectivist conclusion is dissonant with his existentialist premises. Stack noted a parallel between the individual's relation to history in Hegel's philosophy and the individual's relation to the group in Sartre's sociology. As with Hegel and Marx, and despite his insistence on the primacy of the person, Sartre imputed a higher rationality and sovereignty to the collectivity. There is a "necessity" by which individuals are converted into a functional element of the group through the constraining instrument of "terror." The freedom of the individual is sacrificed, for Sartre as for Hegel, in order that the "idea" of freedom be fully realized in time.

Sartre's stress on the collective thus has a number of ironies: It subverts his initial commitment to the sovereignty of individual choice; it represents a prescription of what social organizations should or must be, rather than a phenomenology of how they come to be; and most strikingly, it suggests a loyalty to revisionist Marxism at just the time when revisionists were themselves attacking the view that individuals must be sacrificed to bring about the new era (examples include Desan 1965; Kolakowski 1968: Petrovic 1967; and Schaff 1970).

This "necessitarianism" and group rationalism weakens Sartre's argument on a further ground, because he tended to substitute it for a description of how specific empirical mechanisms of dialectical transformation actually work. Sartre did cite examples of the unintended consequences of purposive action—deforestation of China led to floods and famine; an influx of Spanish gold caused inflation during the Renaissance; armies on their respective retreats bump into each other and are forced to fight. But in other areas he omitted such specific grounding. For example, in his treatment of groups Sartre asserted that a self-conscious recognition of the common purpose of the group leads the individual member to synthesize the group as a totality. There emerges an inner unifying orientation within the group that Sartre, unlike Lewin or Moreno, thought is intelligible. If such a formulation is more than a definition of a group, it leaves out important descriptive and processual distinctions: "Groups" vary greatly in the distribution and degree of self-consciousness of their members; the members' totalization may be formed on grounds other than a common purpose; solidarity may be more affective and emotional than cognitive and instrumental. Sartre's treatment of leadership put too much stress on the rationalism and sovereignty of the group and overlooked the role of charisma, the significance of the prestige of the leader on group formation, and other such transformation mechanisms.

Sartre posited a total opposition between man and nature, and between *my* will and the will of others. But in this formulation objectivity became anti-human, and humanism became subjective and anti-nature. Because Sartre saw the individual agent as the sole source of intelligibility and freedom, he was never able to articulate the practico-inert nor to conceive of objective structures as much more than seriality. This criticism also can be stated in temporal terms: There is a certain "instantaneity" in Sartre's view of group formation. Sartre's conception of group life is basically timeless; groups can experience time, change, and *durée* only as a deterioration into the seriality of their initial moments of formation (Chiodi 1970). This weakness is curious, given Sartre's comments on Lévi-Strauss's ahistoricism in the first part of the *Critique of Dialectical Reason*.

For his part, Sartre recognized the incompleteness of his earlier theories and tried to extend his extentialism to accommodate a Marxist conception of social historical structure. For example, Sartre (1969, 60) said that the projected second volume of the *Critique* would show that "there is an institutional order which is necessarily . . . the product of masses of men constituting a social unity and which at the same time is radically distinct from all of them." Yet even if we were to accept with Sartre (1960, 72) "the reality of Marxism" as "the only valid interpretation of history," we still would not have overcome such dichotomies as freedom and necessity, revolution and science, romantic conceptions of agency (now elevated to the level of class consciousness and action) and positivist conceptions of structural causality. Indeed, all these issues continue to be central to the major debates within contemporary Marxism itself (Brown 1989, 14–23; Burawoy 1979, 50–64).

The Structuralism of Claude Lévi Strauss

Despite these limitations, and partly because of them, Sartre's dialectical sociology provides a counterpoint to the structuralism of Claude Lévi Strauss.[3] One locus for such a comparative analysis is their debate concerning structuralism and existential historicism. In "History and Anthropology" (1967a, 21–22) Lévi-Strauss said:

> If, as we believe to be the case, the unconscious activity of the mind consists in imposing forms upon content, and if these forms are fundamentally the same for all minds—ancient or modern, primitive or civilized . . . —then it is necessary and sufficient to grasp the unconscious structure underlying each institution and other customs, provided, of course, that the analysis is carried far enough.

Unlike some structural theorists, such as Durkheim or Parsons, Lévi-Strauss did not treat the totality as itself the explanation of its parts, nor did he, as did Radcliffe-Brown, understand structure to be simply the regularities of observable interactions. Instead, Lévi-Strauss viewed "surface" facts and meanings as generated by a "deeper" linguistic structure. A kinship system, for example, is essentially a system of messages. It "does not consist in objective ties of descent or consanguinity between individuals . . . it is an arbitrary system of representations, not the spontaneous development of a real situation" (1976, 49). Such underlying structures are the same throughout time and unknown to the members themselves. Yet for Lévi-Strauss they provide a sufficient basis for "discovering general-laws" in "a social science [that] is able to formulate necessary relationships" (1976, 31).

The deeper structure to which Lévi-Strauss referred is not a telos of the social system itself nor merely a convenient theoretical construct. It is not a transcendent essence, nor is it emergent from lived experience or constructed in consciousness, for Lévi-Strauss rejected both phenomenology and existentialism (Lévi-Strauss 1955; Piaget 1970, 112). What then is the nature and role of the deeper structure, and in what manner is it to be decoded? While not answering these questions directly, Lévi-Strauss (1970, 247) indicated that this ultimate stuff is biochemical (1970, 62), and that the method of its apprehension is analytic rather than dialectical or hermeneutic reason:

> As for the trend of thought which was to find fulfillment in existentialism, it seemed to me to be the exact opposite of true thought, by reason of its indulgent attitude toward the illusions of subjectivity. To promote private preoccupations to the rank of philosophical problems is dangerous, and may end in a kind of shop-girl's philosophy— excusable as an element in teaching procedure, but perilous in the extreme if it leads the philosopher to turn back on his mission. That mission (he holds it only until science is strong enough to take over from philosophy) is to understand Being in relation to itself, and not in relation to oneself. Phenomenology and existentialism did not abolish metaphysics: they merely introduced new ways of finding alibis for metaphysics.

This is positivism with a vengeance: The failure to recognize that philosophy is a form of human praxis; the focus on Being without a hint of self-reflection or epistemological self-criticism; the supposition that philosophy will be vanquished by science; the depersonalization of the agent of science, the researcher; the naive refusal of metaphysics; and the assumption that phenomenologists accepted common sense as the grounds for knowledge when in fact their epoché and reduction precisely distinguished this natural standpoint (itself closer to science than to phenomenology) from reflective consciousness. Lévi-Strauss's science is naively Kantian, but without a transcendental subject (Poster 1975, 318–319; Sartre 1970, 59).

In light of this it is easy to guess Lévi-Strauss's objections to Sartre's *Critique:* Sartre's assignment of a privileged status to historical construction and his emphasis on individual consciousness, *la force des choses,* and dialectical totalization. Having postulated the mind's "imposing forms upon content," Lévi-Strauss can dispense with the question of the historical genesis of structure; having presupposed the universal and unconscious nature of this structuring activity, he can ignore the specific totalizations consciously undertaken by actors:

> In my perspective meaning is never the primary phenomenon . . . behind all meaning there is a non-meaning. Man has meaning only on the condition that he view himself as meaningful. So far I agree with

Sartre. But it must be added that *this meaning is never the right one:* superstructures are *faulty acts* which have "made it" socially. (1970, 253–254)

Lévi-Strauss also criticized Sartre for his Cartesianism in positing a solitary, traditional cogito (the early Sartre), as well as for his sociologism and historicism (the later Sartre).

> He who begins by steeping himself in the allegedly self-evident truths of introspection never emerges from them. . . . Sartre in fact becomes the prisoner of his Cogito: Descartes made it possible to attain universality, but conditionally on remaining psychological and individual; by sociologizing the Cogito, Sartre merely exchanges one prison for another. (1970, 249)

Despite such assertions, dialectic does play a role in Lévi-Strauss's domain. It is a kind of reason *people* use in constituting their cultures, thereby providing anthropology with its object:

> The role of dialectical reason is to put the human studies in possession of a reality with which it alone can furnish them, but the properly scientific work consists in decomposing and then recomposing on a different plane. With all due respect to Sartrean phenomenology, we can hope to find in it a point of departure, not one of arrival. (1970, 250)[4]

In addition, dialectic can serve an exploratory function in scientific inquiry itself. "Dialectical reason is . . . something *other than* analytic reason . . . it is *something additional* in analytic reason" (Lévi-Strauss 1970, 246). Dialectical reason is more venturesome, it builds bridges and crosses over them; it is analytic reason's own effort to transcend itself. Yet, in light of the potential contribution of dialectic to the method and problems of structure, the role assigned by Lévi-Strauss seems too modest and too vague. Indeed, just as Lévi-Strauss argued that Sartre used analytic reasoning to advance the case for dialectic, so Lévi-Strauss used dialectic reasoning to argue the cause of structuralism. Each thereby restricts the other's method to suit his own purposes even while criticizing that method for its restrictions. Such opposition and interdependence precisely suggest a necessary complementarity between dialectical and structural modes of thought.

The Reciprocal Implication of Existentialism and Structuralism

Jean-Paul Sartre had gone to the Black Forest, Claude Lévi-Strauss to the jungles of the Amazon and the streets of New York. Both Sartre and Lévi-Strauss believed that modern societies have their myths just as do primitive cultures, but with one difference. In modern societies this myth is called History. For Sartre such history naturalizes and justifies arbitrary domination and disguises the agency of historical actors; for Lévi-Strauss it masks atemporal structures and presents them as temporal historical actions. For both, but for opposite reasons, "myth is the most fundamental form of inauthenticity" (Lévi-Strauss 1969, 39). For Sartre the exit from such false-consciousness was self-conscious praxis; for Lévi-Strauss the only escape from myth was science. For each thinker, of course, the social thought of his Other was itself mythic. In Sartre's view, structuralism disguised human agency; for Lévi-Strauss, (1976, 117, also 23), "We are led to conceive of social structures as entities independent of mens' consciousness of them (although in fact they govern mens' existence)." Replied Sartre (1970, 743): "What is essential is not that man is made, but that he makes that which made him. But for structuralists like Lévi-Strauss, the future is not to be made, but to be predicted. Praxis is here eliminated in favor of process."

Sartre might have accepted Lévi-Strauss's structuralism as a supplement to his existential Marxism, for he saw in it a useful account of the practico-inert. The problem for Sartre was Lévi-Strauss's intellectual imperialism and lack of critical self-reflection. In Sartre's view, Lévi-Strauss drew his analogy between language and other social structures too easily, extended it too far, and denied the lifeworld even as a basis of his own theoretical practice. Lévi-Strauss drew upon certain aspects of the contemporary *Lebenswelt* without accounting for this in his epistemological self-understanding. The growth of bureaucratic structures, the increasingly abstract and depersonalized character of modern life, the segregation between the public techno-structure with its cybernetic discourse on the one hand, and the private sphere of feelings and emotions on the other, all were broad cultural conditions experienced by contemporary persons. Given such a lifeworld context, one might well expect the emergence of a theory that envisioned society as constituted of agentless structures: Lévi-Strauss generalized from the distinction between the subject and her language to posit a fixed disjuncture between social beings and social institutions, a distinction which reflected today's world of lived experience even while excluding the possibility of liberated action to transform it. Thus, for Sartre, structuralist science was neither justified epistemologically nor demonstrated practically. As such, it became a conservative ideology serving the existing order and, by implication, its dominant social class. For Sartre and other existential Marxists, the key question—could alienating structures be over-turned by social action—was not answered or even addressed (Poster 1975, 318; Lefebvre 1966; Goldmann 1966).

Structuralism may be revealed as ideology not only by noting its practical functions or interests, but also by criticizing phenomenologically the constitution of its object. Such a critique reveals that the "new empiricism" of Lévi-Strauss is in fact a "new idealism," and that the supposed idealism of phenomenologists issues into a new sophisticated objectivity. Lévi-Strauss went beyond the naive empiricism of earlier positivists by abandoning the natural standpoint and engaging in an explicit process of modeling his object. In this process, speech by actors in specific situations was distinguished from language as a system of abstract relations. Experience and the subject were thereby bracketed out of consideration. This new object could then be examined apart from its references to or meanings for experience. A further distinction, between synchronic and diachronic aspects of language, made it possible to focus on the structure of language while ignoring the historical process of its generation.

By constituting its domain as an autonomous object, structural anthropology also constituted itself as a science. Language, like the social institutions explained on its model, was taken to be sign systems having no necessary contents. Social institutions, like structuralism itself, became closed systems with only internal relations and no external referents. Through such rigorous distinctions Lévi-Strauss constituted an ideal object for anthropology that permitted precise logical analysis, much more so that previous positivists had done. But at what cost? By its very obdurate abstractness, the new empiricism turned out to be a new idealism, an ideal science of an ideal object (Ihde 1971, 174–175; Ricoeur 1965, 1968).

As critics in the romantic tradition have noted, however, the experience that every speaker and listener has of language provides a limit to structuralist attempts to absolutize this object. For speakers, language is that through which persons express themselves and their worlds. "To speak is the act by which the speaker overcomes the closures of the universe of signs, . . . [and] by which language moves beyond itself as sign toward its reference . . . [and] seeks to die as an object," (Ricoeur 1968, 119).

"Being is said in multiple ways,"; as Heidegger put it. Myths, symbols, icons, and words are all polysemic, they all have a range of different correct meanings. Indeed, it is possible to imagine a context in which *any* speech act can be rendered interpretable and, hence, possibly meaningful. This condition is not necessarily opposed to the structuralist project. On the contrary, it invites a conception of rules, normal forms, or structures that limit plausible interpretations and make possible what Schutz called the idealization of reciprocity. Such limitations, imposed by structures, normalize potentially chaotic happenings into expectable events and thereby enable intelligibility and communication. But structuralists eschew such a phenomenological view of language and society, and thereby reify their epistemological heuristic into an ontological principle. Myths, for example, can be fruitfully examined in terms of their inner logic without consideration of their referential aspect. But when such bracketing of the referent becomes a rigid principle, and when structuralism makes absolutist and imperialistic claims, then structuralists thereby render themselves incapable of knowing fully that of which they speak.

This is because myths, like other social linguistic structures, contain a subject matter. Myths speak of birth and death, of origins, nature, and destiny, and it is because of this that their world decoding potential can address us—that is, we are able to interpret myths because they talk about dimensions of our own experience. This applies also to the explanations offered by structural anthropology. They too depend on a preunderstanding of the meaning of myths, even though such meanings are said to be bracketed out of their analyses. For example, such binary oppositions as high and low, left and right, or raw and cooked are laden with meanings drawn from the anthropologist's own culture as well as that of her hosts. Even a structural analysis therefore involves some degree of translation. There can be no structural analysis without this indirect attribution of meaning, that constitutes the semantic field from which the anthropologist then distils homologies and oppositions. Yet such a hermeneutically enlighted awareness of preunderstanding and transfer of meaning is explicitly eschewed by Lévi-Strauss and other structuralists; it is dismissed as typical of "shopgirl philosophies" (Bleicher 1980, 226–227; Ricoeur 1973, 79).

Structuralism thus falls short of a genuine metatheory of culture and society. Like existentialism, it too invites a sublation that would at once preserve and complete it. Like positive science in general, structuralism forbids critical analysis of itself or its own conceptual instruments, which we are asked to take as eternal and unchanging. These a priori categories—metaphor and metonymy, homology binary opposition, and the like—are "conceived by structuralists to be ultimate and rather Kantian categories of the mind, fixed and universal modes of organizing and perceiving experience" (Jameson 1971, 15). A sublation of structuralism might be achieved by transforming these absolutized transcendental categories into relative historical ones. This would retain structuralism's power to solve the riddle of the sphinx—that is, to decode contradictions inherent in the social linguistic object. But it would further permit us to understand that the riddle itself is a literary genre or cultural artifact, and that our categories of understanding (and non-understanding) reflect in part the conditions and contradictions of our own cultural and historical moments. But how might such a self-reflective discourse be achieved?

Dialectic and Structure: Interdependent Methods of Logic

Dialectical thought has long been used to make logical contradictions into cognitive consistencies and historical reversals into theoretical unities. But the use of dialectic has rarely been explicit, and thus its reflexive and liberating potential has not been fully realized (Brown 1989, chap. 6; 1987, chap. 8).

Of course there are many applications of dialectic besides that between conscious intentions and structural outcome. But this antinomy closely parallels the contradictions between Sartre's and Lévi-Strauss's thought. To overcome this antinomy would be to sublate the dichotomy of romanticism and positivism in general. Lifeworld and structure, like romanticism and positivism, imply and inform each other. Paradoxes emergent from the methods of one are made tractable by methods of the other, thus presupposing some dialectical process. The very notion of structure assumes several defining principles. These include inside-outside boundaries, internal logics or rules of cohesion, and the genesis, construction, destruction, and transformation of structures and hierarchies of structures.

Boundaries. Structure can be understood as the boundary that contains some set of elements. Similar concepts are frame, ground, system, field, or form, each containing its elements or contents. All concepts are "containers" to some degree; concepts of structure take this as one of their explicit functions. And it is clear that any container can be defined as much by what it excludes as by what is inside it. The "inside" implies and cannot be understood except in terms of what is "outside." Spinoza made this point when he insisted that all definition is "negation"—*omis determinatio negatio est*—in the sense that no substance can be known "in itself" except in terms of the totality of all that it is not. And since all our definitions are stated in terms of positives, we may translate Spinoza to say that "every positive is negative" (Burke 1969, 23).[5]

We normally become aware of the structural framework of activities only when this framework has been negated. It is only in terms of structural boundaries that the object or action "makes sense," yet it is only through their opposites that these boundaries become known. A nice instance of the definition of boundaries by dialectical negation is Harold Garfinkel's (1967) conception of background expectancies that define the limits of a situation and thereby provide members with a scheme of interpretation. The background constitutes implicit boundaries by which appearances become recognizable and intelligible to the actor as the "appearance-of-familiar-events." Yet even though actors are demonstrably responsive to this background, they are unable to tell us what it is. In order for these boundaries to come into view, "one must either *be a stranger* to the 'life as usual' character of everyday scenes, or *become estranged* from them" (Garfinkel 1967, 35–37, my italics). In applying these principles, Garfinkel and his students violated these background assumptions with an air of naive incomprehension, thereby forcing their subjects to make explicit the boundaries or "normal forms" of interaction and to reveal what conduct is required to maintain them.

In his essay on "The Negative Character of Collective Behavior," George Simmel (1950, 400–401) made a similar point:

> Even from their most punctilious observance [of rules of courtesy], we must not infer any positive existence of esteem and devotion they emphasize; but their slightest violation is an unmistakable indication that these feelings do not exist. Greeting somebody in the street proves no esteem whatever, but failure to do so conclusively proves the opposite.

Social *dis*regard defines who and what is well regarded. Structures of attention define what is *not* to be attended. The limits of any situation are known through their violation. Such structural boundaries, or "frames" as Erving Goffman (1974) called them, serve as rules of relevance, or rather *ir*relevance, by which we screen out aspects of our situations that do not count. Wittgenstein illustrated this with a discussion of chess. The terms "queen," "castle," or "check" make sense only in terms of the framework of the game as a whole, that is, in terms of what the game is not. We become aware of this framework dialectically, by learning what we cannot do, such as crushing our opponent's king with a vase and declaring "I won!" Dialectic is a method for explicitly eliciting such awareness.

Cohesion. Dialectical opposition not only defines structural boundaries, it also is a method for discovering the inner cohesion of any hypothesized system. Dialectic reveals rules of congruence by showing incongruence; it affirms canons of consistency through opposition and contradiction. Structuralists themselves offer many examples of this. By working out the *negative* implications of a term they discover the structure of signification implied by that term and whether it is internally consistent (Lévi-Strauss 1967, 229–232). Using Greimas's (1970) model, for example, we could understand a given tribe's marriage rule as the sign, *S*. Opposed to this would be practices that violated the rule, such as incest or perversion, that it, − *S*. The strict negative of the rules, then, would be all conduct not included under them, such as sexual activity of children, *S̄*. The fourth term, the contrary of that which is prohibited, would not take us back to the original *S*, but would result in − *S̄*, as, for example, the practice of male adultery which, though prohibited by the marriage rules, may not be abnormal. In this sense, marriage is a negative term, dialectically transformed into a positive by its contraries. Greimas's model of meanings and transformational functions of every semantic unit shows how logical structure is constructed dialectically (Brown 1989, 117).

This schema also can be applied to a number of concept clusters in Max Weber's thought (Jameson 1975, 13–24). For example, Weber's four basic types of social action can be seen as an expression of latent dialectical structure:

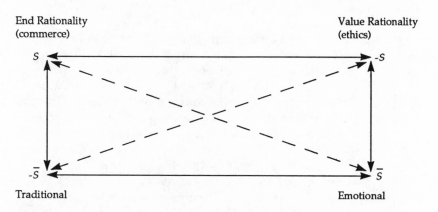

The initial sign *(S)*, "end rationality," in the sense of conduct that is rationally directed toward profit, has its contrary *(− S)* in behavior rationally directed toward ethical ends. The strict negative *(S̄)* of the initial sign is emotional behavior, while the contrary of the strict negative *(− S̄)* is traditional behavior. In these examples, the internal logic of the sign system is shown to be consistent through negation. Of course the same dialectical method can be used to show a *lack* of consistency, in which case we might reject the posited structure for having failed to meet its own rules of cogency.[6]

Genesis and Hierarchy. Besides boundaries and rules of cohesion, structure also implies at least two other questions to which dialectic helps us respond: How do composite structures come into existence in the first place? and, How do they relate to each other? These problems, as Piaget (1970, 9) put it, are at the core of structuralist thought:

> Structuralism, it seems, must choose between structureless genesis on the one hand and ungenerated wholes or forms on the other; the former would make it revert to that atomistic association to which empiricism has accustomed us; the latter constantly threaten to make it lapse into a theory of Husserlian essences, Platonic forms, or Kantian *a priori* forms of synthesis. Unless, of course, there is a way of passing between the horns of this dilemma.

One path out of these difficulties may lie in the use of dialectic as a switching device by which (1) elements are transformed into structures; (2) one structure becomes the element for some other structure on a higher level; and (3) one element becomes the structure for elements on lower levels. Virtually all disciplines have some notion of a hierarchy of elements and structures, though they often have little explicit argument as to their dialectical transformations or even what such a transformation might be. In linguistics for example, a word can be seen as a structure in relation to more elemental phonemes, or as an element in the structure that is a sentence. In logic and mathematics, Gödel and the Bourbaki circle demonstrated that every structure or system presupposes a "parent structure" from which its axioms are derived. In social theory, examples of such hierarchies of elements and structures are easy to find. The individual personality can be seen as a structure of various needs and drives, or as an element of a group; the group can be seen as a system of persons and cliques, or as an element of a larger institution or system, on up to Parsons's total society, Sorokin's civilization super-systems, or Wallerstein's world system. In effect, any variable or observation that one chooses to treat as homogeneous, internally consistent, partless, unitary, or literally atomic and without internal components or relations is thereby defined as elemental. In contrast, any variable or observation that is taken to have internal components or relations is thereby defined as emergent or as being a higher order system.[7]

Nothing that we investigate is phenomenally given as either element or structure. Instead, this depends entirely on how that range of experience is treated by a discipline as a whole or by particular individuals working within it (Wallace 1971, 49). In this sense, a key measure of the degree of development of a science is the scope of options and variations of assembly available within it for treating phenomena as either elements or structures. This multiplicity of possible perspectives is a major resource and contribution of dialectic.

Contrary to Lévi-Strauss, all structure is usefully conceived as at once construction and destruction. Elements and structures emerge or dissolve in a process of continual formation and transformation. The concept of a fluid hierarchy of elements and structures replaces the idea of a static, formal system of abstract structures. Instead of stasis, there is a continuous cognitive activity in which contents are elaborated upward and forms downward, each becoming the other in the process. Higher order structures may hover over two or more elements that are still seen as closed and complete structures. Similarly, subelements often lurk within systems that are still seen as unitary. Indeed, "discovery" may be understood as the revealing of relationships within and between structures and elements, the uncovering of connections that previously were only latent or intuited.

Even allowing for hierarchies of elements and structures, however, the question remains as to the precise means by which one is transformed into the other within any given domain of thought. By what processes exactly do variables emerge from one level to the next? How do structures become elements in larger structures? How do elements become structures for lower order elements?

Dialectic is a prime strategy for such transformations. At the core of dialectical insight is an ironic viewing of things in terms of their opposites. This involves a kind of expeditioning and distancing, a making of temporary bivouacs and sorties, in either pyramiding or minusculizing directions. For example, it is only in the juxtaposition of illegitimate power and powerless legitimacy that the concept "authority" emerges as a higher order "system" (Blau 1964, 9). Similarly, Kingsley Davis, noting the functional dependency of two such opposites as prostitution and marriage, implied that both these "systems" are "elements" to some higher order synthesis (Davis 1961, 283–284). Sorokin also showed how the perception and playing off of dialectical opposites yields syntheses on increasingly higher levels, each synthesis implying another contrary and a further totalization. In accounting for the structure of various historical periods, Sorokin pointed to contradictions, imminent characteristics, unanticipated consequences of consciously intended actions, and quantitative aggregations becoming qualitative changes, as ways by which lower order structures dialectically become elements of higher order ones (1964, 401–432; see Schneider 1964).

In a quotation above Lévi-Strauss spoke of "the mind . . . imposing form upon content." Having installed "unconscious structure" as a prior tenant in the mansions of existing institutions, however, Lévi-Strauss leaves little room to discover how consciousness is expressed in institution building and how this praxis affects and is affected by intersubjective totalizations. An alternative way of understanding forms and contents, genesis and structure, is through a "dialectic of structurings," an insistence that neither forms nor contents exist per se, but that both are dialectically constructed. Such a view draws on Jean-Paul Sartre's conception that persons are free, and that they are defined by and against the worlds which they themselves create. Instead of speaking of a strict opposition between abstract forms and concrete entities, or of intending actors and unconscious structures, a dialectical view focuses on the interaction of various levels of apprehension and construction of reality.

Dialectic examines in particular the interpenetrations and mutual implications of three modes of awareness: lived experience; the more formal methods and models used to reformulate or reify this experience; and the reflexive apprehension involved in understanding the relations between modes one and two. In such an inquiry, ambiguities, instead of being collapsed into an immediate resolution, are first developed into full contradictions. Through such a development we discover the richness of a concept or proposition and the boundaries of its proper domain. This is the most crucial moment in the dialectical process, for it is then that the mind shifts gears, as it were, and spirals back upon itself in a larger orbit. What was an unsolvable contradiction in the first circle becomes its own solution from the perspective of the second. In this expanded, dialectical view, the form and the content, the structure and the genesis, are seen in a newly totalized frame. Indeed, our formal presuppositions themselves are seen to have provided the precondition of our elemental dilemmas.

This dialectical process *within* the subject matter, so to speak, has its parallel in the thinker's relationship *to* the subject matter. Instead of the distinction between subject and object remaining static, the thinker can make her own subjectivity an object of reflection. The mental processes that were stymied by a mystery that seemed to inhere in the subject matter can themselves by examined. In such a scrutiny, our initial perplexity may become a commentary on the mystery itself. Indeed, the initial obscurity of the subject matter as we develop it—the apparent implausibility of historical motives, the meaning of certain acts—is seen to have been part and parcel of our way of looking at it, our very method for objectifying it.

In such a manner thought attempts to liberate itself by becoming aware of its own complacent arrogance, its assumption that its chosen perspective is the given, ultimately privileged one. Such a liberation is at the very heart of dialectic, but its outcome is no "proof," either of correspondence or of symmetry. The "demonstration," if there is one, is not of a hypothesis but of a method, a method for constructing social theory that would account for subjectivity even while retaining the rigor of objectivity, that would be true to the existential experience of actors even while decoding the transformation of actions into structures.

Lifeworld and structure are both excellent positions for critically viewing each other. Because we are inside of speech all the time we need a standard of criticism that is outside of speech, in language. *"We need a dream-world in order to discover the features of the real world we think we inhabit* (and which may actually be just another dream-world)" (Feyerabend 1978, 31–32). Just as lifeworld requires structure as a locus for critical detachment, so a part of structure always is its existence for the subject. This dimension of structure—the subject's (non)awareness of it—can be understood phenomenologically. Thus phenomenology of the lifeworld, as in Jean-Paul Sartre, is a resource for the full comprehension of structure. Conversely, the understanding of structural constraints, as in Claude Lévi-Strauss, is a prerequisite for freedom as much as the failure to acknowledge necessity is a form of willed unfreedom or bad faith. Individual freedom presupposes recognition of necessity, much of which takes the form of structural constraint. Necessity requires the mind to step outside its imagined potency in order to consider unfreedom and choose to accept or resist it. In this sense the critical devaluation of lifeworld brought about by structural analysis brings tragic acceptance and ironic laughter and thereby serves as a resource for awareness and liberation (Ricoeur 1980, 344–351; Poster 1975, 348; Brown 1987, chap. 6; 1989: chap. 5).

The choice between understanding of the lifeworld and explanation of structure, between individual and society, or between subjectivity and objectivity, is misconceived. Instead, it is possible to view the subject matter of the human sciences as social relations; not as mechanical motion or human intentions, but as symbolic, mainly linguistic, interaction; not as subjective or objective, but as intersubjective with varying degrees of objectification. Seen this way, both intending agents and deep structures are nodal points for relations of communicative action. Lifeworld and structure are not static opposites but dynamic crystalizations of varying durée in the same dialectical process.

Symbolic Realism: A Fusion of Horizons

If dialectic is to be our method, what might be its philosophic justification? In what tradition of discourse might we place it to provide an historical and practical warrant? Such a tradition is the study of language itself. By viewing agency and structure in terms of rhetoric, both are seen as engendered through the practice of language. In the critical rhetorical perspective—or what I have called symbolic realism—both agency and structure emerge from persuasive communication. Science itself is seen as a specialized system of communication, and communication is seen as the constitutive medium of all human experience, making such experience real in the sense of being sharable and hence capable of intersubjective (that is, "objective") verification. Unlike the purely positivist or purely meaning-interpretive theories discussed earlier, symbolic realism dialectically joins syntactic and grammatic analysis of structure with semantic and pragmatic interpretation of meaning and use.

The concept of symbolic realism draws on the Renaissance belief that the society is constituted of structures created and maintained by acts of human intelligence, imagination, and will—that social reality is an expression of *virtus* as well as *fortuna*. This practical human activity also can be understood as a structuring process, the exact nature of which contemporary scholars have only recently begun to decode. Despite their differences, for example, the works of Bernstein, Bourdieu, Cicourel, Collins, Douglas, and Foucault, all imply a method by which the debate between positivists and romantics might be overcome and by which the philosophic perspective of symbolic realism might be given empirical substance.

From such a perspective the subject matters of both structuralists and existentialists are understood to be construed through different rhetorics of reason. Neither rhetoric provides direct access to reality, since each is part of the reality that it construes. "Lived experience" no less than "structure" is constructed through linguistic practice. Structuralism and existentialism need not be reductions, however; instead they can be transcodings from one form of representation into another. The scientific realist would strip off the symbols to expose the underlying objective reality, whereas the romantic idealist would subordinate this reality to intuit the true meaning of the symbols. But transcoding is an interpretation that becomes part of the subject matter under study, just as an interpretation of a poem becomes on the next reading a part of what the poem says. Both subject matter and explanation are symbolic. The interpretation or explanation—the study—becomes a metaphor for the symbolic expressions studied. Each is deepened. Ways of doing human science, then, may be judged by whether they build a wall between us and their objects, or whether they make them newly accessible to us. In the human sciences the "objects" are the minds and works of other human beings and other norms and forms of being human. Hence an implicit telos of such disciplines is to seek greater accessibility of understanding between persons. The ideal public of the rhetor scientist in symbolic realist terms is a universal audience that constructs itself through dialectical oppositions.

Our analysis finds a space between personal agency as articulated through existentialism, and determinism as articulated through structuralism. This space is the field for emancipatory theoretical practice. Deterministic theories deny agency; subjectivistic theories vaporize it by making it impossible to find error in any group's (version of the) world. Explanatory science poses the question of the conditions of the possibility of primary experience, thereby revealing that this experience, as understood existentially, is fundamentally defined as *not* posing this question. Whereas structuralist positivism takes itself too seriously, existential lifeworlds take themselves for granted. But from a dialectical perspective, emancipation is neither unrestricted agency nor unrestricted determinism, but the *overcoming* of determinism by agency.

Rhetorical analysis deconstructs "texts" to reveal how historical forms of consciousness are constructed and, by implication, how such forms may misrepresent practical social relations of domination. This is not a matter of correcting symbolic misrepresentations of a material reality. Instead it is a question of identifying and decoding disjunctions and mistranslations between different levels and orders of symbolization. For such a project, one must reject both the objectivistic determinism of positivists and nominalists as well as the subjective humanism of romantics and idealists, in despair of their twin quests for absolute outer or inner knowledge. At the same time, a critical rhetoric of reason affirms a more sophisticated humanism and a more sophisticated science in two ways. First, it undertakes a critique of the basic forms, categories, and methods of social and historical be-ing; and second, through such a critique, it seeks to confront men and women with the choices inherent in their actual historical possibilities.

Reformulated this way, the sterile dichotomy between structuralism and existentialism becomes a fecund dialectic. A scientific critique of lay and protoscientific ideas gives an emancipatory impulse to the human studies, provided that such a critique respects the existential significance of those ideas and does not itself make absolutist claims. Many social phenomena are emergent and hence require a realist explanation. For such explanations to be critical and transformative, however, they must not become reified, must not lose contact with the lived experience from which they emerged. Stripped by critical rhetorical analysis of its absolutist and objectivist illusions, social thought rediscovers its in-and-for-itself, its practical and emancipatory will to know.

By investigating our linguistic constraints and capacities, a critical rhetoric of reason sees persons both as carriers of preformed social linguistic structures and as agents who perform culture and speech. A revision of our symbolic representations is thus a re-visioning of the world. To be free means to have some mastery of this process. Human agency requires potency in transforming structures of meaning and practice.

FIVE

METAPHOR AND KNOWLEDGE OF HISTORY I
Organicism and Mechanism in the Study of Social Change

Alles Vergängliche/Ist nur ein Gleichnis
Goethe, *Faust* (Part 2)

Once you leave you're out in the open; it rains and it snows. It snows history.
Bernard Malamud, *The Fixer*

The problem of describing to others how members of a remote tribe think then begins to appear largely as one of translation, of making the coherence primitive thought has . . . as clear as possible in our own.
Godfrey Lienhardt, *The Institutions of Primitive Society*

THE PURPOSE of this chapter, like that of the next and of the book as a whole, is to help bring the epistemology and the aesthetics of social and historical discourse into closer alignment. As such, it is part of a larger project for our times: to restore the integrity of knowledge and agency in public reason.

The separation of science and art as forms of collective self-knowledge and public speech is recent. In the preindustrial era, historical writing was considered a genre of literature, and literature was considered a craft. Literature, like the other arts, was very close to artisanry, and history, as a literary genre, therefore seemed very close to life. It involved, for example, the writing of diaries, sermons, eulogies, orations, and essays. With the rise of the factory system, however, art and literature were distinguished from the degraded world of industry and the market, and came to be viewed as unique forms of creation and experience. Literature was no longer seen as an everyday activity in which all educated people could partake. Instead, it came to mean a set of treasured texts produced by godlike madmen. This new romantic conception "fetishized art and concealed or mystifyied the processes of its production. Literature thus ceased to be thought of as an art by which ideas could be conveyed effectively and elegantly. . . . More and more it came to be regarded as a magical or religious mission, which only those endowed with the gift of prophesy or second sight could fulfil" (Grossman 1978, 5–6).

At the same time, with the rise in prestige of science, positivist theories of knowledge replaced explicitly rhetorical ones. Within historiography, attention shifted from the rhetorical methods of historical writing to the factual bases for historical knowledge. Literature and historical science were separated, and the epistemological justification for narratives as cognitive was forgotten. The *res publica*—public reason through the republic of letters—had thrived throughout the Enlightenment and the early Romantic period, particularly in France, England, and Scotland. But during the nineteenth century, poets ceased to speak with politicians, scientists, and statesmen. Historians withdrew into the universities, and history came to be written by professors instead of poets. "The old common ground of history and literature—the idea of mimesis, and the central importance of rhetoric—has thus been gradually vacated" by both historians as well as literary artists (Grossman 1978, 7).

These long-term changes have been accompanied by long-standing controversies over the purposes, methods, and scope of historiography, making the study of social change a labyrinth of changing theories. Those who would find a way out must rise, like Helios, to a higher level of discourse and illuminate the very logic of social science itself.

In this chapter, I map two well-trod paths in this labyrinth: functional evolutionism and experimental empiricism. The evolutionists view societies as social organisms whose internal developments follow the pattern dictated by an immanent nature. Evolutionists take their cues from Aristotle and conceive of change as slow, orderly, continuous, and teleological. Endogenous and historical changes are thought to harmonize to produce a progressive movement and entelechy. In contrast, the empiricists assert that any theory of change must derive from a close empirical investigation of the thing changing. Thus empiricists oppose any a priori assumptions about the nature, direction, form, rate, and outcome of change, and reject what they deem to be metaphorical models. Yet they too invoke a metaphor—the world as a machine—for their redescription from the organistic model.

The next chapter goes beyond this debate between evolutionists and empiricists by critically analyzing two further approaches to the study of social change: French structuralism and existential phenomenology. The first, structuralism, generally is not thought of as a form of historical sociology. Using the writings of Lévi-Strauss, Louis Althusser, and the *Annales* school as instances, however, I argue that such an historical sociology—or perhaps an anti-sociology—is implied in the structuralist approach. Similarly, phenomenology generally is thought to focus on those essences of consciousness that are prior to historical awareness or action. But I describe an existential, hermeneutic, social phenomenology that draws more from the writings of Merleau-Ponty than from the early pure phenomenology of Husserl. And I argue that such an approach offers a method for decoding the historicity of awareness and conduct, a method that has direct implications for all the other approaches to historical construction, as well as for any project for instituting historical change.

My argument assumes the form of a semiotic square of opposing positions. Within the dialectic of these oppositions the noumena of historical science may appear. As each of the four basic approaches is criticized from the perspective of the others, resonances are set off among them so that they organize themselves into a structure of oppositions, contraries, and negations. It is not the case merely that the various approaches to the study of social change are separated by their differences, however, or even that they are related in spite of their differences. It is more accurate to say that they are interrelated and interdependent by virtue of their mutual exclusions and antagonisms. My purpose thus is not to rigidly isolate these approaches, nor to champion one above the others, nor even to plea for a facile harmony or cooperation. Instead, using Greimas's model, I draw their differences as sharply as possible in order to make explicit the implicit interrelatedness, through negation and complementarity, of each approach with all the others.

I take the dominant approach, functional evolutionism, as the sign, S. I then criticize this thesis, evolutionism, from the perspective of its contrary, experimental empiricism, or $-S$. In the next chapter, this contrary $(-S)$ is itself negated by a structuralist critique of its fundamental assumptions. In this manner the structuralist approach to historical sociology emerges as the negation of the contrary $(-S)$ and the strict negative, or $\bar{S}$, of the initially posited sign (S), evolutionism. Finally, I argue that a phenomenological approach to historical explanation is the negation of this negation, that is, $-\bar{S}$, in that it reverses the assumptions of structuralism. The phenomenological study of change stands outside of all other modes of historiography yet at the same time is presupposed in all of them, suggesting that all modes of historical thought are both structures of consciousness as well as forms of historical practice. These relationships may be represented as follows:

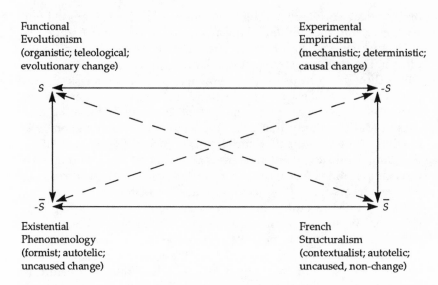

Functional
Evolutionism
(organistic; teleological;
evolutionary change)

Experimental
Empiricism
(mechanistic; deterministic;
causal change)

Existential
Phenomenology
(formist; autotelic;
uncaused change)

French
Structuralism
(contextualist; autotelic;
uncaused, non-change)

In the final section of the next chapter I transcode these four modes of historical science into the four "world hypotheses" or root metaphors as discussed by Stephen Pepper, and relate these to four tropes of linguistic figuration—synecdoche, metonymy, metaphor, and irony—as elaborated by Giambattista Vico, Kenneth Burke, and Hayden White. I conclude that the deployment of one or another of these tropes is unavoidable in any linguistic representation of reality and that, therefore, the scientific and the artistic dimensions of historical sociology are inseparably conjoined.

The Cognitive Status of Metaphors for Historical Science

The question of the cognitive status of metaphors tends to appear whenever philosophers discuss the fundamental questions of similarity, identity, and difference. This is not only because metaphors are employed in every realm of knowledge; it is also because metaphors are our principal instruments for integrating diverse phenomena and viewpoints without destroying their differences.

Despite its apparent centrality, however, until modern times metaphor was not acknowledged to have an explicitly cognitive function. Aristotle, for example, was ambivalent about metaphor. He did say, "The greatest thing by far is to be master of metaphor." But he also assumed that language plays little part in creating what it describes. Given Aristotle's division of the uses of speech into three categories—

logic, poetic, and rhetoric—metaphor may be used to illustrate a point or sway a crowd or as a poetic ornament of style. Yet, as he put it, "All such arts are fanciful and meant to charm the hearer. Nobody uses fine language when teaching geometry" (*Rhetoric*, 3.1404a). This view of metaphor prevailed for many centuries, and under the joint influence of plain-speaking Protestants and early positive scientists, the function of metaphor—along with "fine language" in general—was further demoted.

Beginning with Vico, however, this traditional view has been opposed by philosophers such as Nietzsche, Coleridge, Croce, and Goodman. Vico challenged both Aristotle and especially Descartes by arguing that the transparent certitude of mathematical reasoning derives solely from the fact that we ourselves create the "world of forms and numbers" with which mathematics deals, its elements being fictions that we freely devise. Instead of seeing metaphor as an embroidery of the facts, such thinkers viewed it as a way of experiencing facts and, by making them objects of experience, giving life or reality to them. In their view, poetic imagination stretches the mind and reality, the word and the thing, through metaphor. By capturing the precise physiognomy of the experienced world, metaphor was thought historically or logically to precede the concretized meanings of literal or scientific discourse. Still, by stressing the emotional and precognitive nature of poetic revelation, the romantics reinforced the traditional dichotomy between metaphor and scientific thought and devalued the functions of metaphor in the constitution of rational argumentation. By energetically distancing themselves from scientists, they placed themselves in the company of schizophrenics, aphasiacs, and children, whose utterances, by the romantics' own criteria, could not be distinguished from poetic metaphor.

Another view of metaphor is the symbolic realist or tension theory. Borrowing the romantics' insight that creative thought is metaphoric, this view extends the idea of metaphor as a logic of discovery to include science as well as art. Moreover, it distinguishes creative activity in both these fields from the normal science or art that goes on in each. In this view, metaphor is just as vital to natural science as it is to poetry. In science, however, the referents are of very special sorts: The analogy is between a purely formal (ideally, mathematical) theory or model and some empirically visualizable phenomenon (ideally, observable through controlled and calibrated methods). But even this difference fades when we speak of the "root metaphors" of science. For here metaphors serve to define the boundaries of a given domain of discourse and to set limits for subtheories that can with consistency be extrapolated from it (Berggren 1963, 461; Toulmin 1961, 79).[1]

Original metaphors lack the precision that comes with elaboration. Newton's image of the eye as a camera, for example, acquired precision only after he had developed the theory of optics that was its specification. All referential language is polysemic, but in conveying new ideas such imprecision is indispensable, since an image of the field of study has to be posited before it can be specified. The discourse constituted by metaphors exudes a halo of virtualities that imply dimensions yet to be spelled out and aspects yet to be known. The only remedy for this condition is an impossibility: that we should know everything about a domain before we have conceived it.

Historical sociology, like science and art, also must represent its world with metaphors. Social and historical scientists, however, generally have not understood scientific theorizing to be metaphoric and, hence, they have felt compelled to choose between a literalistic, reductive scientific positivism on the one hand, and a vaporized conception of creative intuition on the other. This forced choice is based on erroneous assumptions about the natures of scientific and artistic knowledge. The choice for students of history is not between scientific rigor as against poetic insight. The choice is rather between more or less fruitful metaphors, and between using metaphors or being their victims.

All this is especially true of root metaphors—those sets of assumptions, usually implicit, about what sorts of things make up the world, how they act, how they hang together and, usually by implication, how they may be known. As such, root metaphors constitute the ultimate presuppositions and frames of reference for discourse on the world or on any domain within it. Root metaphors differ from models or illustrative metaphors in two ways. First, they characteristically exist below the level of conscious awareness. Ordinary speech is made of frozen metaphors; root metaphors are akin to frozen models—they are a kind of submerged or implicit model underlying the writer's thought (Black 1962, 239). Second, root metaphors are comprehensive. Thus, unlike models or ordinary speech, root metaphors are the implicit metamodels in terms of which narrower range models or discourses are couched. We might say that root metaphors describe worlds, whereas models describe the contents of those worlds.

Two such metaphors in the study of history are the organism and the machine, as expressed respectively by two principal schools of historical science—functional evolutionism and experimental empiricism.

History as Organism: Functional Evolutionism and the Empiricist Critique

In the dominant, functionalist, version of evolutionism, society is compared to an individual biological entity. In social Darwinist and

Marxian theories the comparison is not to the single organism but to the biological species; here the imagery is one of competition among individuals or classes and survival or dominance of the stronger (Peel 1974, 193). Varieties of evolutionism occur depending on specifications as to the moral status of change (for example, as progress, development, or decline); its processual nature (as convergence or as differentiation); its rate (in spurts or as a gradual unfolding); and its mechanisms (divine intervention, class struggle, or natural selection). We also can distinguish old-fashioned evolutionists, who were "utopian" in giving an account of the past based on a vision of the future, and new evolutionists, who are "ideologues" in reifying the present as the telos of the past (Mannheim 1936).

To define the essential features of the biological metaphor, it is useful to examine its original Aristotelian formulation, where it is presented didactically and explicitly. The evolutionary and the homeostatic aspects of contemporary functionalist thought, for example, seem to be a congeries only because their root organic metaphor is not specified. Once it is made explicit, as in the writings of Aristotle, these two different aspects of functionalism can be seen as alternative elaborations of the same biological image.

Aristotle had seen two poles in previous Greek speculation: change, becoming, or cause was stressed by Ionian nature philosophers such as Thales and Anaximander; permanence, being, or form, was central for Plato.[2] Aristotle unified these notions in his concept of form as cause. The material cause of the atomists is incapable of explaining the *why* of becoming, he said, for it lacks that which the concept of becoming itself makes intelligible—the unity of the thing that it welds into a whole. Those who see reality only in form, however, cannot explain how this reality came to be, and so treat the form as eternal and everything else as illusion, and hence tell us nothing of the world. Thus for Aristotle genuine wholeness must be the product of becoming, but at the same time it cannot be the mere mechanical aggregation of parts. Instead, a true whole (that is, a universal species or class, or any society, period, or unit of scientific analysis), emerges only where all parts are dominated by a single purpose and strive to realize it (*Physics*, 2.8).

Aristotle also claimed that if "natural things are exactly those things which do move continuously," then "unnatural" or "accidental" things must be those which do not. The natural and the unnatural were thereby distinguished by the criterion of regularity of occurrence and, indeed, Aristotle insisted that this distinction be made *before* a scientific investigation of a thing could be undertaken:

> It is obvious why there is no science of [the unnatural or] accidental,
> for all science is of that which is always or for the most part, but the
> accidental is in neither of these two classes. (*Metaphysics*, 11.8)

This method was then applied to politics and society. Men and women unite "because of a natural instinct to leave behind one of their own kind, and of the desire for self-sufficiency." From this self-generated union come families, clans, gens, and phratries, which unite to form villages and city-states. The city-state is thus the end of a natural, regular teleological evolution. It is a species, a good, the fulfillment of man's nature as a political animal (*Politics*, 2.2). Not all peoples have reached this state of self-realization, it is true. But Aristotle's theory is concerned with the "natural" process of development, not with "accidents" or "monstrosities." Not all acorns become oaks. In each particular case this depends on local conditions of soil, climate, and so on. It is for just this reason that to understand oaks or anything else as a general class or species, science must focus on their ideal development, that is, what they become "if nothing interferes." Thus there are some things that simply are not suited for scientific investigation (specific historical events for example), and even with proper scientific subjects (such as the polis), any occurrence that cannot be associated with the unfolding of that thing's telic potential must be treated as an "accident" and excluded from scientific study.

Thus, for Aristotle, natural things that change according to the law of their nature or telos are the proper subjects of science, whereas unnatural or accidental events fall outside this purview. Moreover, as change is regular, continuous, purposive, and self-generated, it is possible to see in primitive societies, which are at an earlier stage of growth, the former stages of modern societies. These basic assumptions have informed theories of social change from Aristotle's time down to the present day, as the following statements illustrate: "The education of the human race," said St. Augustine (1910, 10.14), "has advanced like that of an individual, through certain epochs or, as it were, ages, so that it might gradually rise from earthly to heavenly things and from the visible to the invisible." "As the germ bears in itself the whole nature of the tree, and the taste and form of its fruits, so do the first traces of Spirit virtually contain the whole of that history" (Hegel 1956, 57). "New, higher relations of production never appear before the material conditions of their existence have matured in the womb of the old society" (Marx 1946). "*Cultures are organisms*, and world history is their collective biography. Every Culture passes through the age phases of the individual man. Each has its childhood, youth, manhood, and old age" (Spengler 1928). "Culture may be classified . . . , stage by stage in a probable order of evolution. . . . The institutions which can best hold their own in the world gradually supercede the less fit ones, and . . . this incessant conflict determines the general resultant course of culture" (Taylor 1878/1924). On these assumptions it follows that "Every time we undertake to explain something human, taken at a given moment in history—be it a religious belief, a moral precept, a legal principle, an esthetic style, or an economic system—it is necessary to go back to its most primitive and simple form, to try to account for the characterization by which it was marked at that time, and then to show how it developed and became complicated little by little, and how it became that which it is at the moment in question" (Durkheim 1965). "An evolutionary universal, then, is a complex of structures and associated processes the development of which increases the long-run adaptive capacity of living systems in a given class. This criterion is derived from the famous principle of natural selection" (Parsons 1966). Though spanning many centuries and ideological points of view, these seminal statements all express the notion that society is, or is like, an organism.

This organic image of society is so deeply rooted that scholars often fail to recognize it as central to their own social thought. Nonetheless, some writers have argued that the procedures of Aristotelian evolutionists like Comte and Spencer have been "thoroughly discredited," as Howard Becker put it, and hence may "be dismissed without further ado" (1940, 525). Even by 1920, said Murdock (1949, xiii), "evolutionism in the social sciences was completely defunct." But other commentators, such as Teggart, Bock, Nisbet, or Lyman, have shown that much sociological theorizing continues to commit the same Aristotelian fallacy that supposedly was laid to rest many decades ago.[3]

Talcott Parsons's work provides an example of the continuity of the Aristotelian explanation of social change on the model of organic growth, especially his *Societies: Evolutionary and Comparative Perspectives* (1966). In the manner of Greek and Christian scholars, and of the eighteenth-century moderns and nineteenth-century champions of progress, so Parsons suggested that "human society" has generally passed through the stages of "primitive, intermediate, and modern." This is not merely a logical taxonomy, any more than it was for Aristotle, Spencer, or Comte. On the contrary, Parsons identified the logical series with "socio-cultural evolution" that, "like organic evolution, has proceeded by variation and differentiation from simple to progressively more complex forms." This is to be a universal history of "Total Society," the key explanatory concept in which is the "evolutionary universal . . . a criterion derived from the famous principle of natural selection." The particular histories of specific peoples are, by implication, either to be ignored or slotted into the logico-temporal scale of development from Australian primitive to American modern (Parsons 1964, 1666; see Nisbet 1969, 263).

In Parsons's theory of historical change, then, certain characteristic functions are seen as inherent in the "nature" of society, that is, as part of its essential definition as a class. Hence these functions tend to be elevated to a status ontologically superior to that of the specific actions within specific societies that they are intended to explain. The a priori assumption as to the nature and evolution of society is used as the principle for selecting data to support this assumption, and should exceptions be found to the "natural" development or stability, these can be labeled "accidents," "chance historical events," or "mutations," rather than being examined as possible disproofs of the posited order. Given such an approach, the task becomes that of finding those characteristics from which a posited state of equilibrium or change can be deduced. The "findings," as Kenneth Bock put it (1963, 236), are "then presented as an analytic statement of what *must* happen rather than a merely empirical generalization of what did happen."

Boas and Maitland in the nineteenth century, Teggart and Hodgin in the early twentieth, and Nisbet, Bock, and Gellner today, all have attacked such thinkers—from Plato to Parsons—who have made use of the organic metaphor. Their experimental empiricist critique is as follows: The dualism between "natural processes" and "accidents" has led to the search for causes or processes of change outside of specific historical events. By calling the subject matter natural before investigating it, laws of development are invoked to determine which aspects of the phenomenon should properly be considered part of its development and which, being accidents, should not. This has led to the practice of dismissing inconvenient data as irrelevant and of using the assumption of biological growth as a classification system for those data that happen to fit. Rather than seeking regularities by comparing discrete things or events, Aristotlian laws of development are established a priori for certain given phenomena. They are not demonstrated with reference to data; instead, they become the principle for selecting the very data they presume to explain. This is a tautology in the formal sense, in that the thing to be explained (society) and the thing that is supposed to explain it (society's coming to be) are both known by the same indicator (the "nature" of society). Hence, though the "Aristotelian fallacy" resonates with the teleological method of common sense, it is unacceptable as modern empirical science. By contaminating their independent and dependent variables, the evolutionists have rendered their theses untestable.

In contrast to the faulty procedures of the evolutionists, experimental empiricists have insisted that all explanatory concepts be operationalized to refer to specific historical events, that all events to be explained be included in the analysis, and that all concepts and events be described in logical and temporal sequence. When events occur outside the predicted sequences, rather than dismissing them as deviant cases or accidents, the investigator must accept them as falsifying evidence and either abandon or modify her original hypothesis (Bock 1963, 237; Gellner 1965).

This mode of explanation assumes that change occurs when a critical event takes place outside the thing to be explained. Such an event may come from another society (for example, trade with China changed the Roman Empire). Within a single, hermetic society, however (such as Japan in the eighteenth century), the event will be found in one institutional area that causes change in another. Thus, empiricists are committed to experimentalist methods of controlled comparative observation and verification, and reject the functionalist assumptions of telic rationality in social order and of functions (as distinct from events) that explain the evolution of institutions or social systems.[4]

History as Mechanism: Experimental Empiricism and Its Limits

The decline in use of the organic metaphor began in the sixteenth and seventeenth centuries with the work of Galileo, Newton, Bacon, and Descartes. Life went out of nature. Physical imagery began to replace the organic. Nature, and soon history, persons, and society, were seen as a machine. One of the first explicit transfers of mechanical thinking to the social realm is found in Hobbes's *De Cive, or The Citizen* (1979, 10). For Aristotle man was a social animal, for Hobbes he was an antisocial machine:

> For as in a watch, or some such small machine, the matter, figure, and motion of the wheels cannot well be known except it be taken in sunder, and viewed in parts; so, to make more curious search into the rights of states, and the duties of subjects, it is necessary . . . they be considered.

Other writers elaborated this metaphor. "I esteem the universe all the more since I have known that it is like a watch," said Fontenelle (quoted by Cassirer 1969, 50). "Let us conclude boldly," asserted La

Mettrie in *L'homme machine* (quoted by Needham 1955, 236), "that man is a machine, and that there is only one substance, differently modified, in the whole world." "Here as elsewhere," added the literary critic Hippolyte Taine (1982, 12), "we have but a mechanical problem: Though the means of notation are not the same in the moral and physical sciences, yet as in both the matter is the same, equally made up of forces, magnitudes, and directions, we may say that in both the final result is produced after the same method."

The metaphor of mechanism eventually penetrated into the study of history, which in the nineteenth century had still been closer to literature than to science. Peter Gay (1974, 210) affirmed this shift toward mechanism: "This pressure toward objectivity is realistic because the objects of the historian's inquiry are precisely that, objects, out there in a real and single past." In the same spirit Perry Anderson insisted that historians should seek to establish

> the mechanism of single events or the laws of motion of whole structures. Both are equally amenable, in principle, to adequate knowledge of their causality . . . for rational and controllable theory in the domain of history. (1974, 8)

Historical sociologists have been even more forceful in seeking to assimilate historical understanding to causal analysis on the model of mechanics. "The most important phase of historical work," said Max Weber (1949, 176), "namely, establishment of the causal regress, attains validity only when in the event of challenge it is able to pass the test of the use of the category of objective possibility, which entails the isolation and generalization of the causal individual components. . . . " The "ultimate objective" of such an approach, declared Theodora Skocpol, "is, of course, the actual illumination of causal regularities across sets of historical cases" (1979, 39; see Nichols 1985). "The 'logical' argument against Evolutionism . . . is valid," said Ernest Gellner (1965, 18), because the evolutionary series of developmental stages "as such explain . . . nothing." By using it "we cannot attain truth about the mechanism of a given social transition." In contrast to evolutionism, for history on the model of the machine,

> as anywhere else in empirical science, the explanation of a phenom-
> enon consists in subsuming it under general empirical laws; and the
> criterion of its soundness is not whether it appeals to our imagination,
> whether it is presented in suggestive analogies, or is otherwise made
> to appear plausible—all this may occur in pseudoexplanations as

well—but exclusively whether it rests on empirically well-confirmed assumptions concerning initial conditions and general laws. (Hempel 1942, 45; see Mandelbaum, 1960)

This conception of history—as a nomothetic theoretical enterprise seeking causal laws that explain objective facts—is legitimated by contemporary positivist philosophy. The mechanistic metaphor at the root of this approach is defended by logicians' analysis of the Aristotelian tautology, by Hempel's discussion of covering laws, and by Ryle's demonstration that to be a cause a thing must be an event and not a process or a law (see Hempel 1942, 1959; Ryle 1954; and Stinchcombe 1978). Other philosophic approaches, however, have encouraged criticism of the mechanists' formulation. These include structuralism, hermeneutic phenomenology, critical theory, and pragmatic philosophy of science. Such alternative approaches focus on the questions, What is an event? What is our unit of study and how can we know it?

All the empiricists believe that a properly conducted science of history requires the controlled comparative analysis of observable events. Yet a principal problem of this position, a problem that few of its practitioners have acknowledged, is their assumption that events and their interrelationships are unambiguously available for inspection. Once skepticism arises about the warrant for ordering various happenings under the concept "event," the entire method of logic of the empiricists is called into question (Patcher 1974).

A central aspect of the problem of conceptualizing the event is that of establishing boundaries. In what sense does an event refer to a phenomenon bounded in space and in time? Positivist historians typically have treated events as if they were equally and mutually available to all who examine the historical record. But how is this historical record to be interpreted, or even known to be an historical record in the first place? How can happenings be properly conceptualized as events? When does an event begin and where does it end?[5]

In addition to these difficulties in delineating events out of historical happenings, critics have attacked the experimental empiricists' assumption that explanations of events are constituted of "If X, then Y" statements, "causes" preceeding "effects." That is, one set of events is explained as having been caused by another, prior, set insofar as both sets of events are instances of a more universal covering law. Hence, questions arise concerning the nature of a causal relationship. What we see then is the potential for a two-pronged attack on empiricist historicism. One prong pierces the assumption of an accessible fact world that can be unproblematically conceptualized as events. The other punctures the assumption that these events can be accounted for by machine-like causal relations.

Crying "Back to the things themselves," hermeneutic phenomenologists launched this attack by holding that our notion of facticity is itself a construction that must be put aside if we are to get at the essential be-ing of phenomena. Such a perspective, of course, represents a radical departure from the dominant mechanistic standpoint, which is so central to the modern habitus that it is difficult to imagine how we could criticize or even doubt it. Yet such a critique has been developing since Kant, is adumbrated by Hegel and Dilthey, and is given twentieth-century expression by Husserl, Heidegger, Merleau-Ponty, and Gadamer.

This attack is as follows: The naturalistic fact-world is not in itself a finding of science; instead it is an assertion about the nature of Being in general. As such it is a metaphysical proposition and hence its cognitive authority depends on its philosophic justification. It is true that positive science gives procedures for deducing logical relations between concepts, such as revolution, colonization, etc., which are considered the events. Yet, as the logical positivists themselves discovered, these procedures offer no help in knowing the relationship between the conceptual categories and the contents to which they are purported to refer (the happenings). Moreover, because this approach is based on the metaphor of the machine, it entirely omits intentionality, which for many scholars is central to historical action and historicist explanation.

The usual method by which empiricists deal with such difficulties is to describe the so-called logic-meaningful nature both of the events themselves and of their causal relationships. If we unpack this phrase—logico-meaningful—we discover that its logical aspect rests on the assumption that events and their relationships are logical in the degree that they possess the properties of Aristotle's logic of ends and final causes, which may or may not reside in the consciousness of the individuals or groups who are undertaking the activities so described. The logic involved here is telic, in which the various elements of action are organized around some purpose or end through which one knows them to be what they are. That is, the telos shapes the happenings into an event, much as for Aristotle the architect's blueprint defines the house, or the form contained in the acorn unfolds as the oak.

Such explaining in terms of ends or telos is frequent in everyday life, at least in occidental societies. For example, if we ask, "Why is Mary so dressed up?," a plausible answer would be, "She has a date (and wants to look her best)." The purpose or goal of the actor is taken as determining or accounting for the action observed.

As we have seen (chap. 3), there are epistemological difficulties with such formulations, at least insofar as they claim to have scientific validity. More importantly, in terms of the empiricists' own assumptions, a distinction must be made between applying such telic logic to individual persons and applying it to whole groups or societies. It is plausible to speak of goals or purposes in accounting for individual action; but are we justified in explaining social-historical changes in terms of the goals, purposes or ends of institutions, societies, or historical epochs (Mandelbaum 1960)? Moreover, in terms of causal reasoning, in what sense can some *future* state or goal be said to have brought about a *previous* action or event?[6]

Another difficulty with "logico-meaningful" assumptions concerns their reference to meaning. "Meaningful," the second half of the term, rests on motivational plausibility. Here, the empiricist assumes that she and her readers share a common vocabulary of motives, and that the reader will accept as proper and fitting the mental states and relationships attributed to others, presumably because the reader would see them as appropriate to himself. Philosophers have reflected on the nature of understanding, meaning construction, and interpretation in historical and anthropological research—cases where it is least possible to assume a commonality between the vocabulary of motives of the subjects and the readers of the study. And these scholars have shown that intelligibility involves translation. For example, after a highly thorough and rigorous defense of empiricist historiography, in which he rejected hermeneutic and phenomenological approaches, Brian McCullagh's own logic of mechanism forced him to reverse his position and conclude that "all historical descriptions are interpretations" (1984, 233). But such a conclusion runs contrary to the entire case that McCullagh had so scrupulously developed. And having already dismissed Heidegger, Gadamer, and other cognitive relativists, he was unable to account for the paradox to which his argument had led him. By ignoring or rejecting hermeneutic methods, empiricists have been unable to supply or account for the missing motivational element of their own explanations.

In sum, empiricists have failed to account for the apparent contradiction between a first mode of historical understanding that stresses meaning interpretation, and a second mode based on causal relations that both disdains yet appears to presuppose the first. We thus are faced with two apparent contradictions within the logico-meaningful method. The first contradiction is between teleological interpretation of meanings and deterministic explanation of facts. The second is between the two levels of telic logic—that of an intending consciousness, and that of social groups. Historical scientists in the experimental empiricist mode have not adequately dealt with these contradictions. Indeed, to the extent that empiricists invoke or presuppose the logico-meaningful form of accounting, they themselves are guilty of the very mentalisms and tautologies of which they accuse evolutionists.[7] This difficulty appears to be unavoidable, if only because of the logical and practical impossibility of either a science of the total event or an apodictic basis for defining which aspects of events are relevant.[8] As Simmel (1977, 82) said,

> A science of the total event is not only impossible for reasons of unmanageable quantity. It is also impossible because it would lack a *point of view* or *problematic*. Such a problematic is necessary in order to produce a construct that would satisfy our criteria for knowledge. A science of the total event would lack the category that is necessary for the identification and coherence of the elements of the event.

This suggests that the telos for organizing happenings into events must be an intellectual telos, that is, the cognitive purpose of historical scholars. Such cognitive purposes are implicit in the root metaphors through which historians craft their accounts. Yet mechanists, by rejecting metaphoric thinking in principle, remain unreflective of their own methods of logic.

Root Metaphors and Historical Figuration

It should be clear that my purpose in undressing the metaphors of the organism and the machine is not to deplore metaphoric thinking, or even to criticize these particular metaphors. Once it is understood that they *are* metaphors, however, their relative adequacy in light of other possible metaphors may be more clearly seen. Mechanism is a good place from which to see the tautological nature of biologistic thinking. Conversely, the biological metaphor is more able to deal with immanent factors, intentionality, and transformations of systems than is mechanism. Similarly, features peculiar to both these metaphors can be limned from structuralist or phenomenological perspectives. For example, phenomenologists show us that both organicists and mechanists devalue human agency in history.

Such a critical self-consciousness is illustrated by George Kubler's reflections on appropriate root metaphors for the history of art:

> The biological model was not the most appropriate one for a history of things. Perhaps a system of metaphors drawn from physical science would have clothed the situation of art more adequately . . . , especially if we are dealing in art with the transmission of some kind

of energy; with impulses, generating centers, and relay-points; with increments and losses in transit; with resistances and transformers in the circuit. In short, the language of electrodynamics might have suited us better than the language of botany; and Michael Faraday might have been a better mentor than Linnaeus for the study of material culture. (1962, 9)

All approaches to historical science are equally metaphorical but not all are equally empowering. Thus, in considering approaches to historical science as modes of public discourse, we should note especially how they differently privilege the role of historical actors (Burke 1984). By analyzing alternative paradigms poetically and rhetorically we also can see that both art and science are metaphoric, and therefore that scientific (or political or artistic) revolutions are processes by which original, poetic metaphors become literal and prosaic. Conversely, science, art, or historiography describe a literal reality only to the extent that their metaphoric constructions of experience have become frozen. Realistic representations appear as such only when a given approach to historical science has become a commonplace, a dead metaphor that is taken as a literal description. Realistic representation is convincing not because it is realistic; instead, it is realistic because we already have been convinced:

> The value of "dead" metaphors in argument is above all prominent because of the great force of persuasion they possess when, with the aid of one technique or another, they are put back into action. This force results from the fact that they draw their effects from an analogic material which is easily admitted because it is not only known, but integrated, by means of language, into the cultural tradition. (Perelman and Olbrechts-Tyteca 1969, 543)

The history of historiography, like the history of science, politics or art, abounds with examples of absurdities later taken as truths, that is, of spritely new metaphors that have become frozen. *"Créer un poncif,"* to create a commonplace, this was Baudelaire's ideal, to invent something so unprecedented it would at first be taken as absurd, only to have a discourse form around it, a discourse that transformed the initial absurdity into banality. Similarly, "the world *as* a machine" for Descartes became "the world *is* a machine" for Newton (1966). By this means a metaphoric half-truth of scientific or artistic invention may become institutionalized as whole doctrine, not only accepted, but *indispensable* to the further experiments done under its aegis.

Philosophers have argued that such ordering schema are prerequisites for any rational thought or, indeed, for ordering perceptions into experience (Kant 1949; Hoffman and Honech 1981). In this sense, root metaphors are frameworks for interpreting meaning within which sensa become facts, facts become concepts, and concepts become discourse. In *World Hypotheses* Stephen Pepper (1942, 91) suggested how the formation of root metaphors might take place.

> The method in principle seems to be this: A man desiring to understand the world looks about for a clue to its comprehension. He pitches upon some area of common-sense fact and tries if he cannot understand other areas in terms of this one. The original area becomes then his basic analogy or root metaphor. He describes as best he can the characteristics of this area, or, if you will, discriminates its structure. A list of its structural characteristics becomes his basic concepts of explanation and description.

For example, the *organicist* approach reconstructs and integrates selected elements of its field into components of a synthetic process. Actions or events are explained to the extent that they can be ordered around some superordinate telos that defines the nature and purpose of each particular element. A hierarchy of reality or meaning is thereby created. The evolutionary approach in historical science is an instance of such organicist thinking in that it posits—evolutionists would say "discovers"—a "stage" of "development" that has been or will be arrived at in or by history. This schema is then used to determine what will be considered a part of "History" and what will be its significance. It is in terms of the evolutionary whole, in other words, that the historical parts are constituted and comprehended.

By contrast, the metaphysics of the *mechanism* is clearly expressed in early modern philosophy of science: It is reductive, naturalistic, and nominalistic. Its style is analysis rather than synthesis, reduction to primary elements rather than elevation to a transcendent telos. It is as though the organistic view had been turned on its head; in place of the parts being instances of the whole, as the parts of the body take their essence from their function in a larger system, instead the whole is seen as an instance of the parts, much as a machine exists as such because of the aggregative causal actions of the elements within it.

Root metaphors provide frameworks for determining which kinds of data and not others appear as evidence. As organicists, for example, historical scientists must focus on or constitute those facts that can be orchestrated into some given *process* of development. By contrast, mechanists orient themselves toward the kinds of happenings or events that can be made to stand for general causal *laws*. In either case, however, an analysis of root metaphors rejects either a dogmatic commitment to any one approach to historical science, or a cynical rejection of them all. Instead, our negative dialectic can yield a positive cosmopolitanism or what Kenneth Burke called an athletic skepticism. Such a stance requires that the author appreciate the limits of her chosen mode of discourse, respect the etiquette that it implies, and not imperialistically extend it beyond its proper application.

If historical scientists were to recognize the metaphoric elements in their narratives and theories, this would not degrade historiography to the status of ideology, propaganda, or fiction. Instead, it could serve to correct the tendency to become captive of one's ideological preconceptions which are not recognized as such but honored as *the* correct perception of reality (White 1978). Such ideological thinking is created by attributing literality to theories that are elaborated, perforce, from metaphors.

Literalist discourse that has forgotten its origins in communal rhetorical practices can be revealed as ideological in retrospect, as when a newer theory supplants an older one. The hidden ideology of discourse also can be unmasked dialectically by juxtaposing two literalist paradigms each of which posits a uniquely true nature of history or society. In abandoning absolutist claims made in the name of any particular root metaphor, however, we need not plunge into an absolute relativism. Instead, we can affirm a pluralism that respects the relative rights and privileges of each approach to historical science, and thereby celebrates our capacity to define who we are and what we might become.

Six

METAPHOR AND KNOWLEDGE OF HISTORY II
Structuralism, Phenomenology, and the Tropes of Linguistic Figuration

The fundamental methodological problem of any human science lies in the division [*découpage*] of the object of study . . . . Once this division has been made and accepted, the results will be practically predictable.

Lucien Goldmann (1970)

Drum, da gehäuft sind rings
Die Gipfel der Zeit,
Und die Liebsten nahe wohnen, ermattend auf
Getrenntesten Bergen,
So gib unschuldig Wasser,
O Fittiche gib uns, treusten Sinns
Hinüberzugehn und wiederzukehren.

Hölderlin, *Patmos*[1]

EVERY HUMAN group has some notion of its origins, nature, and destiny, usually expressed through rite, myth, and theological doctrine. For modern societies, these questions tend to be cast in secular, often scientific, terms. In particular, the study of our origins as peoples is articulated in what is called historiography or historical science, as well as related discourses such as archaeology, paleology, or historical sociology.

Drawing on the symbolic realist perspective, I argued in the last chapter that historical knowledge is metaphoric. Historical construction is mediated by root metaphors through which we make experience (or the "historical record") comprehensible or, more strongly, through which we *have* experience of history. In developing this position I first established the cognitive status of metaphor. To say that the natural or human sciences are metaphoric is not to devalue their cognitive power, but to reveal that this power emerges from language. Given the cognitive status of metaphor, I then showed how most historical science construes its domain either as an organism or as a machine. Having treated evolutionism and empiricism, I now examine structuralism and phenomenology to argue that each is a distinct mode of linguistic figuration, a prosaic deployment of one of four major poetic tropes.

Structuralism: A Contextualist Alternative

The structuralist approach to historical science may be considered in relation to the original project of Bock and Nisbet. Both these scholars had been interested in empirically grounding the sociological study of change. One of their presumptions—so obvious it was never made explicit—is that social change has gone on and is still going on. This supposition, rarely if ever challenged in sociology, has never been justified by its propounders and, hence, it is subject to philosophical criticism. Such criticism, in turn, could provide the basis for new approaches to historical science. In discussing social change, Bock and Nisbet object to the evolutionists' assumption that the forces of change are always at work. In contrast, they assert that whether and to what extent social change is going on is itself an open empirical question. However, they do not consider the possibility that social change has *never* gone on, that there is no such thing as social change.

This possibility appears strange to modern Occidentals, but it has been normal for most peoples and times. Virtually all cultures make the distinction between Being and Becoming, and the assumption that "there is nothing new under the sun" merely reflects their having posited the ontological superiority of Being. For example, in the Vedic tradition, Being is stressed as the one reality, and all change is seen as *maya* or illusion. Similarly, for Lévi-Strauss action in the world is an endless restageing of a few fundamental myths. Indeed, Lévi-Strauss's position itself can be seen as a modern expression of Plato's original vision. In this view there is no history. Instead, history is the appearance of change, and reality for science consists in those forms through which these appearances become visible. Temporality, in other words, is produced by historians and other mythmakers. And for structuralists, "that production would be scientific only if it demarcated the diachrony of structures, not the intentional acts of individuals or groups" (Poster 1975, 62). The structure of histories replaces history as narrated actions or events, a structure in which discontinuity and differential temporality prevail.

Structuralism, then, differs radically from the other modes of historical science. In the evolutionist approach, for example, the task is to organize data to fit a logically necessary evolutionary scheme oriented toward a transcendent telos; for empiricists, by contrast, the task is to identify empirically different types of events, and to show what causal relations may exist among them, without presupposing any developmental process or necessary outcome; finally, for social phenomenologists, the focus is on the intentions and projects of individual actors and how these unfold in a field of scarcities and constraints. Despite their differences, all these approaches presume the centrality of processes, events, or actions unfolding in time. These assumptions, however, are suspended by structuralists. In reconstituting Marx as a structuralist sociologist of change, for example, Althusser rejected the assumption of evolutionists concerning origins, as well as that of empiricists concerning causality, and he denied the analytic relevance of the individual historical actor presupposed by phenomenologists. "Instead of the ideological myth of a philosophy of origins and its organic concepts," said Althusser, "Marxism establishes in principle the recognition of the givenness of the complex structure of any concrete 'object,' a structure which governs . . . the object and . . . knowledge of it. There is no longer any original essence . . . but instead, *the ever-pre-givenness of a structured complex unity*" (Althusser 1970, 198–199). By such an intellectual strategy, structuralists seek to avoid "the twin confusions of 'mechanistic' materialism and the idealism of consciousness" (Althusser 1970, 202).

The reconstitution or translation of other modes of historical science into the structuralist one also is seen in Lévi-Strauss's reformulation and integration of history and ethnography. In going back to the sources, said Lévi-Strauss, Durkheim discovered that he had misinterpreted the opposition between history and ethnography. The opposition was not between two different *disciplines*, as he had previously imagined, but between two different *methods* within each of the disciplines. History and ethnography had been either antiquarian empiricism focusing on particular facts and events, or "conjectural history" of the evolutionary anthropologists. Instead of analyzing the full complexity of systems of significations, earlier scholars had collected and classified the facts genealogically (see Hubert and Mauss 1964, 7–8). The previous error was above all one of method. By contrast, what was needed in both history *and* ethnography was a structuralist approach. And, thanks to this method, ethnography as well as historical sociology "can henceforth escape its confining alternatives; either to satisfy an antiquarian's curiousity . . . ; or to illustrate a posteriori, by means of complacently chosen examples, speculative hypotheses on the origin and evolution of mankind" (Lévi-Strauss, 1976, 48).[2]

In this new science, how is social change to be treated? For the structuralist, there are two histories—that of symbols and signs that are taken as real by historical actors, and that of the grammar and syntax, the "structural combinations in a limited number," through which these symbols are encoded. The first is surface appearance that is treated by conventional historians; the second is a deeper reality to be treated by social scientists. The two together are like a kaleidoscope in which the combination of identical elements always yields new results. The "history of historians," as well as the meaning given by members to their own experience, is present in this kaleidoscope as a congeries of contents. The job of the social scientist is to identify the basic patterns or structural combinations into which these contents may fall (Lévi-Strauss 1976, 16; see 1967, 253–254).

This imagery not only rejects evolutionary and causal determinisms, but also the volition of individual actors. The history of historians "has a meaning and should have, because this is the only way to give a wider meaning to civilization itself." But as a structuralist social scientist, Lévi-Strauss also can claim that whereas history has a meaning or meanings from "inside the society of the observer," this "ceases to be true when we try to reflect a broader point of view and look at it from the outside" (quoted in Steiner 1966; see Lévi-Strauss 1967, 257).

Still, what of the treatment of social change? How do the shifts occur from one arrangement of the kaleidoscope to another? If the "history of historians" is ignored in structuralist historiography, what is left? Indeed, the structuralist approach to history would at first appear to be a contradiction of terms, since we usually conceive of history as an unfolding narrative of meanings or a causal progression of events in homogeneous linear time. By contrast, in structuralism, meanings and events are unimportant and time is neither homogeneous nor linear. Althusser, for example, pointed out that the category "labor" is to be understood not as a simple fact or occurrence, but as the complex process of the structured whole of society. A simple fact, category, or event, therefore, "is not original; on the contrary, it is the structured whole which gives its meaning to the simple category" (Althusser 1970, 196).[3]

Structuralism thus begins with a commonplace idealist polemic against empiricism, but then proceeds to introduce a reconstituted "empiricism" of its own. The earlier idealist critique insisted that signs were not merely shadows of things, echoes of the original voice of experience, but that signs exist only as part of a system. Instead of stressing the meaning of signs as representations of things or events, in this view, one must focus on the structure of alternatives in which they are encoded. Contemporary structuralism goes beyond this idealist critique by seeking to show concretely and operationally how these structures of signs actually work. In so doing the structuralists reconstitute traditional empiricism, as well as the meanings of such concepts as representation, actuality, and concreteness, locating them not in the thing and its name, as formerly, but in a structure of signification (Gellner 1974, 120).

Seen in this way, social formations are discontinuous rather than historical in any progressist, eschatological, cyclical, or causal sense. Instead, for the structuralist, subsequent stages of history are always anterior to the present. Humanity's future is already behind it, not in the sense of cycles of rise and decline, but in the sense that, since each society produces its own temporality, history in the usual sense is simply an internal product of, and subordinated to, universal structures as they manifest themselves in particular societies.

As Lévi-Strauss said of structural history, it

> would make itself by itself. Society, placed outside and above history, would be able to exhibit once again that regular and, as it were, crystalline structure which the best-preserved of primitive societies teach us is not antagonistic to the human condition. (1976, 3–32)

Evolution or causation is replaced by structure, praxis is supplanted by process (see Sartre 1970a, 743). Change for the structuralist is reduced to turns of the kaleidoscope, transformations in basically synchronic structures, shifts that may be brought about by disjunctions between "internal" factors such as the system of rules in any given society and the system of signs that represent them, or by "external" factors such as environmental changes. In either case, however, man's projects and intentions appear to create only the contents of societies, but not the way these contents are structured. Instead, the relationship is exactly the reverse; the structures engender the contents. As Lévi-Strauss put it, "I claim to show, not how men think in myths, but how myths operate in men's minds without their being aware of the fact" (1969, 12).

The foregoing might give the impression that structuralist historical sociology is a program of anthropologists and philosophers rather than a practice of empirically oriented historical scientists. This is not the case. The entire *Annales* school, for example, may be taken as representative of the structuralist approach to historical science (Stoianovich 1976).[4] The founder of this school, Marc Bloch, attempted in *La société féodale* to redefine the concept feudalism as a type of society in much the way that Durkheim redefined our conception of the sacred as a category of a social-cognitive structure. By proceeding topically and comparing cases, rather than chronologically by narrating events, Bloch reconstituted what he called "a total social ambiance" of complex structures of collective consciousness and action.

Given Bloch's view of time as itself a meaning content *within* history rather than a form *for* history, the fixed relationships between different "historical series" was shattered. Previous to the *Annales* writers, historians had assumed a uniform time as the medium through which historical phenomena have their existence. But this assumption, said structuralists, is itself what imposes a continuity and homogeneity on diverse phenomena. Thus Lucien Febvre, another *Annales* founder, called for a historiography that would not be located within—and thereby posit—a supposedly even and objective time-flow (Grossman 1978, 25). Similarly, Fernand Braudel destructured time into *histoire événementielle, histoire conjoncturale,* and *historie de longue durée.* Each of these histories has its own time. Only the first—the most superficial history, "is on the scale . . . of individual men"; it is akin to the "history of historians" described by Lévi-Strauss. The second history has "slow but perceptible rythms." The third history, of the long span, "is a history that is almost changeless" (Braudel 1980, 2, 20, 21). In the same spirit, Emmanuel Le Roy Ladurie recommended that we concentrate on what he called "immobile history" in which demography, technology, and society form a relatively stable albeit complex structure, as he believed they did in Europe between the fifteenth and the early eighteenth centuries (Le Roy Ladurie 1974).

Homogeneous space, like homogeneous time, also is nullified in the structuralist approach. Fernand Braudel, for example, in his monumental *La Méditerranée et le monde méditerranéen: L'epoque de Philippe II,* makes the structural constitution of a given space the object of his analysis, rather than positing the prior existence of such space as a physical entegument for historical action. This history has its own "geographic time," it is a "history whose passage is imperceptible" (Braudel 1980, 3).

These features may be summarized as follows: Whereas the evolutionists assumed a homogeneity of space and time, thinking in terms of one humanity, one world, one history, the neo-positivists segregated these into different peoples, places, and histories. They argued that it was arbitrary to posit a single telos for all of history, or to presume any telos at all. Yet they did not believe that our very idea of history itself, whether unitary or multiple, was itself arbitrary; they argued that there were different histories, but it did not occur to them that there might be no history at all, or that such histories were mere surface appearance, and that the unity of time—an assumption of any history or histories—was itself an arbitrary presupposition.

Thus, in contrast to Weberian social historians of politics as well as Marxist students of economics, *Annales* historians such as Marc Bloch, Lucien Febvre, Fernand Braudel, Pierre Goubert, and Emmanuel Le Roy Ladurie "have challenged the conception of a linear time which guarantees continuity of development and have asserted instead the multiplicity of 'times,' each finite, differently structured, proceeding at different velocities, and marked by ruptures" (Iggers 1975, 175–176). Refusing to depict the history of the modern West as the culmination of world history, they have insisted that each epoch be studied in terms appropriate to itself and to universal principles of the functioning and transformation of structures. Unconcerned with origins, and refusing to see societies as part of a continuous developmental process, they construe histories to be multiplicities of times and structures, in which homogeneous events and time become illusions of members in particular societies.

The Phenomenological Alternative: History as the Creation of Meaning and Form

The fourth approach to historiography rests on still another set of assumptions and thereby provides the basis of a critique and a method for recentering historical knowledge gained from any of the other perspectives. The formal propositional knowledge of historical scientists, say phenomenologists, achieves its status *as* such knowledge only by glossing the embedded character of the actors' lived experience. For example, just as Garfinkel (1967) showed that the rationality of everyday life is largely a retrospective reconstruction of chaotic process, so it would seem that the rationality of historical science is not so much the description of a preexisting structure, as it is an active construction of meaning and order, a studious instituting of history more than a study of history's institutions.

Put slightly differently, as theoretical descriptions of a factual past, the other approaches to historical science idealize the pretheoretical historicity of persons. In so doing, these approaches remain opaque to their own praxis and meaning. From the phenomenological viewpoint, when the study of the past becomes scientific in any of the other modes, it ceases to be a study of history (Habermas 1968a). This is because the intellectual interest of such modes of historical science is to seek universal, or at least general, formulations. In pursuit of nomothetic generalizations, however, these modes transform all history into the present by projecting it to the level of processes, laws, or structures that can apply at any time or place. The specific historicity of subjects is made either timeless or wholly contemporary, either explicitly, as in structuralism, or implicitly, as in evolutionism and empiricism. In contrast, a phenomenological approach sees history as the coming to be of meaning. It thus seeks to bring to awareness the essential preconceptual ingredients that permit the life-worlds of both historical actors as well as historians to appear in consciousness. In the phenomenological approach one does not prescribe to the historian what he ought to do or what historical reality must be like; instead one describes the dialectical relation between the scholars' historical attitude and the historical dimension of the actors' life-world.

To see this is to begin to make historical science critical in two ways. First, it aids the analyst to reflect on her own practice, helping her become aware of the roots of her implicit preconceptualizations in the soil of historicity. Second, it yields a more adequate understanding of human actors as they confront *their* situations (Shiner 1969, 274). A next step would be to penetrate the logic-in-use of historical subjects, and to deepen the dialectic between it and the formal logic of theoretical consciousness (Kaplan 1964; Bourdieu 1977). Such a dialectic would engage both the subjects being studied and the analyst herself, as each tries to construe an only partly shared historical world (Gaines 1975, 5). In this manner, a phenomenology of historical knowing can yield a coincidence of the historicity of consciousness and the consciousness of history, a dialectic between the discovery of one's own historicity through the recovery of lived historical experience (Ricoeur 1965b, 33). Such an approach would make human agency central in our understanding of historical construction.

These points were taken up by Merleau-Ponty in the first chapter of *Les aventures de la dialectique*, where he noted that the historical scientist is not basically different from historical agents and that this similarity permits a shift from one of these "levels of praxis" to the other. Max Weber adumbrated this idea with his insight that historical matter is "a human choice become situation." For Weber this conjunction of situational constraints and human freedom was the animus of history. This is the phenomenological kernel of Weber's historical thought. A "rationalization" in Weber's sense is created only when historical actors choose to advance the themes of some given historical system, rather than developing other themes that would generate other particular systems. Just as historical actors build meaning structures of which their lived history is constituted, so active historians reconstitute such meaning structures, thereby making them part of the historical system upon which contemporary actors may draw. History is made, by actors and historical scientists, when order is created from contingency. Phenomenological historiography shows from the standpoint of the present how this was accomplished in the past.

When we think of methodology as logic of method and not merely as research technique, it becomes evident that each of the principal methodologies of historical science also implies a philosophy of history, some determinate construction of the historical field. This is true of the existential phenomenological approach as well, except that in this mode the historical field is *determined to be indeterminate.* In the other modes it is assumed that there are processes, laws, or structures in or of history that the historical scientist discovers. As a philosophy of history, existential phenomenology relativizes all the other philosophies by rendering them human constructions that bear no ultimate necessary relationship to their domains of application. Or, more precisely, existentialists hold that the domains of application of theories of history are not historical fields as such, but the contemporary field of praxis of the historian.

Phenomenological historiography shares Nietzsche's wish to restore human will to the center of the stage of life.[5] Nietzsche saw that the emplotment of history in one or another way reflected the interests and projects of official and folk historians. But for him there was no one true way—indeed, he saw the belief in any one, absolute, true version of the past as a vestige of the Christian belief in one, absolute, true God, or in Christianity's secular counterpart, positive science, with its belief in one, true body of natural laws. Against both these constrictive notions of historical truth Nietzsche asserted the relativity of every vision of the real (White 1973, 332). For Nietzsche every history, whether lived or written, was a contingent construction or reconstruction, an act of human will.

Thus, in the existential phenomenological mode, history has no objective meaning, because history does not confront man as an object but as a field of existential choices. Man is cast into a morally meaningless universe in which he is compelled to define himself. Driven by care, anguish, and fear of death, man is confronted by a heritage that contains a multiplicity of histories. The individual creates his history not on the basis of objective processes, laws, or structures of the past, but by decisions oriented toward the future (Iggers 1965, 8). In this view, history has no intrinsic meaning—no immanent telos, no laws, no structure. It is, as Alexandr Herzen said, "all improvisation, all will, all enterprise. There are no frontiers, there are no timetables, no itineraries." In the same spirit Jean Paul Sartre asked,

> Does history have a meaning? Has it an objective? For me, these are questions which have no meaning. Because History, apart from the

man who makes it, is only an abstract and static concept, of which it can neither be said that it has an objective, nor that it has not. And the problem is not to know the objective but to *give* it one. (1952, 353).

Seen in this way, the writing of history is a moral activity of retrospection. By retrospectively viewing the past the historian creates space for prospectively viewing the present. For example, a great beauty who died at twenty-six did not live as a great beauty who would die at twenty-six, but she must appear to the historian at every point in her life as one who *will* die at twenty-six (MacIntyre 1981). Hence, retrospection, which makes no sense for lived experience, is just the perspective that makes sense of, that constitutes, relived or remembered experience. In a dialectical manner, however, such constitution of the past becomes a society's awareness of its own continuity, its moral self-definition in terms of an origin and, hence, a destiny. Seen this way, even the "disinterested" academic writing of history assumes political and ethical import (Pocock 1968, 237). Historical interpretation has the farness of retrospection, but it also includes the nearness of empathy; for it is precisely the distance between the historical actor's conscious intentions and the historian's knowledge of outcomes that provides the space for the phenomenological historian's practice.[6]

Phenomenological historical science operates between the theoretical forms of historical accounting and the actor's contingent historicity that is the precondition of moral and political judgement. Historical understanding in the existential phenomenological mode begins with the assumption that historical actors are moral agents, capable in principle of intending their own conduct, even if their conduct is conducted within larger processes and structures, and even if their intentions are superintended by quasi-natural laws. But if historical actors are taken as moral agents, it follows that their futures must always be contingent on human will, and that "the past" is that past that peoples have chosen to claim as their own. Recognition of the contingency of the future and of the ambiguity of the past does not denigrate the efforts of historical scientists. But it does call attention to the relative character of evolutionary tendencies, causal relations, and deeper structures in history, and it provides a barrier against their theoretical reification.

An example of the fruitfulness of such a perspective is provided by reconstituting Tilly's (1978) analysis of the conflicts in England at the turn of the eighteenth century.

The participants saw their interests more or less clearly. . . . In comfortable retrospect we may question the means they used to forward their interests; scoff at tearing down poorhouses, anger at the use of troops against unarmed crowds. Yet in retrospect we also see that their actions followed a basic, visible logic . . . . Two modes of social organization locked in battle to the death. The new mode combines the expansion of capitalist property relations with the rise of the national state.

Tilly showed how the broader historical context of conflicting sets of rules and meanings bears on our interpretation of the textual action. The context was the struggle between the traditional moral economy and the new possessive individualism and nationalism of capitalism. In this context, the textual action—"tearing down a poorhouse"—comes to mean "protesting the definition of poverty in the system of capitalistic property relations." The authors of this text—the historical actors themselves—may see their interests (their authorial intentions and immediate audience), more or less clearly. Yet in applying a hermeneutic phenomenology to both text and context, we see how such interests or intentions emerge from a richer set of relationships than could be derived solely from a phenomenology of either the individual authors or the "historical forces at work." Men and women of eighteenth-century England not only used language to justify their political action, they also acted politically to justify their linguistic usage. They were engaged in the creation and imposition of meaning through discourse, a discourse in which traditionalists sought to pursuade capitalists through the rhetoric of action that theirs was the superior system of signification. Whereas language is often viewed as political, through a phenomenological analysis it becomes possible also to view politics as linguistic.[7]

This existential phenomenological view of history may seem bizarre at the outset. That the past, like the present, is subject to creation by contemporaries is a seemingly perverse idea. Normally we think of the past as passed. History is something one reads about in books or visits in museums. It is made up of architectural ruins, old swords, yellowed documents, Egyptian mummies. Yet history, at least in the West, is constantly being rewritten, and this rewriting is not so much in response to the progressive accumulation of new data as it is a reflection of each generation's need to recreate its own identity and advance its own projects.

"History" as a cultural artifact is always and can only be "contemporary." In order to be history and not simply a material document or a collection of dates, past events have to be imaginatively recreated in the consciousness of historians and people who read their works. Such an imaginative reconstruction becomes contemporary because it involves selection and valuation that perforce are done from the "contemporary" viewpoint of those who rethink and write about the events of the past.

History thus is never neutral, it is always subject to ideological control. For example, historians can study and recreate a "heritage" for a people and thus make it available to them as an object of their own awareness and an aspect of their self-perception. As Edward Shils put it,

> For the most part, individuals accept in varying degrees what they have become, not always happily. If they succeed in changing themselves . . . they acquire for themselves the results of pasts other than those previously present in them. They usually enter into an already charted territory with its own already established rules, demands, and exigencies. They acquire a past which was not theirs previously. (1981, 48).

If we follow Nietzsche instead of Shils in developing this idea, we discover two main types of history: official history of the masters that claims to be the only correct one, singular and eternally true; and an unofficial, emancipatory history of the oppressed that encourages as many visions of the past as there are projects for winning a sense of personal worth for human beings.[8] Official, legitimated history is that notion of the past that is endorsed by elites and enforced by sanctions. As a kind of ruling class geneology, it is taught in academies, tribal councils, and regal courts. By contrast, a second, subterranean history exists in the consciousness of people, close to the collective memory, but not expressed through official media or in public places (Halbwachs 1980). This second type consists in whatever informal notions of the past individuals or groups bring to bear on their everyday struggles in the present. Unofficial or popular history, though it has not obtained official recognition and the stamp of public approval, nevertheless operates as a form of folk wisdom among the population, finding expression in nostalgia, fables, anecdotes, traditions, apocryphal stories, fairy tales, suppressed geneologies, ethnic legends, reveries, and the like.

Official and unofficial history are different in two principal ways: cogency and coercion. Official history characteristically is articulated with precise inner cogency. It tends to be transmitted on the printed page, conveyed in official media, or carved in stone. In contrast, unofficial or folk history characteristically is highly malleable precisely because its expression has not been rationalized and justified in terms of official canons of reasoning, whatever these may be. These properties of official history facilitate its use as ideology, that is, as a logically organized system of belief that rationalizes contradictions, mobilizes collective action, and suppresses dissent.

The second major difference between folk and official history is that the latter is buttressed by political and economic power. In contrast, folk history is found at the interstices of social life, in small places and sequestered arenas. The very rationalization that is a source of authority for official history interdicts its entry into these idiosyncratic domains of daily existence.

In countries where the political use of history by elites is proficient, as in Mexico or the Soviet Union, the state may succeed in monopolizing the memory of oppressed communities and in blocking possibilities of creating counter-hegemonic ideological discourses with any capacity for mass appeal. Then disaffected groups may withdraw from official discourses into communal, familial, or individual history, or into radically alternative forms of encoding the past. "The various transformations of the myth of Inca Ri in the Andes provide a good example of 'recoding' when they were incorporated into the collective memory of some contemporary movements amongst Andean peasants. Although transformations of this myth at the semantic level offer interesting possibilities for study, the story of Inca Ri also demonstrates how the collective appeal of a myth is influenced (i.e., increased or reduced) by links . . . with organization and rebellion" (Rivera 1982, 22–23).

Popular movements and organizations may find their own intellectuals to help them make a history that is politically useful. By rationalizing old tales, discarded theories, or popular myths around a contemporary struggle, oppressed groups create or are provided with a sense of themselves as part of an historical process, a view of their resistance as the continuation of an earlier tradition. The history formulated and diffused in this fashion will share some features with official history, but often in an inverted fashion. Ruling ideas may be reclassed as revolutionary ideals. As Albert Memmi said, "The colonized fights in the name of the very values of the colonizer, uses his techniques of thought and his methods of combat (1967, 129)."[9] But the position and interests of groups lower in the social order also will be reflected in their history. In addition to its cognitive component,

> to the extent to which it deals with personal experiences which are sometimes painful, this [collective historical] memory also has an emotive element. The emotive element is, in turn, infused with moral relevance, with notions such as "justice," "equity," and "freedom" that cannot be reduced to the economic demands that inspire popular struggles. Consequently, the accounts, the testimonials and the stories about these struggles often contain an ethical nuance that is

communicated through ideological legitimizations, teachings and morals. The act of testifying then becomes, not an "objective" account of what is recalled, but an act of moral judgement generated from the values of the present. (Rivera 1982, 18).

Historical scientists thus can be agents of cultural imperialism who wish to colonize the past along with everything else, or they can serve as advisors to the present inhabitants of that lost land who wish to claim it for themselves.

Among moderns, it should be noticed, this unofficial or emancipatory historical discourse is supposed to reside typically among primitives, children, uneducated immigrants, and old wives. Indeed, advocates of official history may seek to delegitimate unofficial history precisely by arguing that the latter is magical, superstitious, naive, or not properly scientific. Since emotional sustenance tends to be received through committed as opposed to manipulated relations, however, and since folk history is primarily a language of a committed, affective common life, it may be that despite the authority which official history may lend to the forces that be, folk history on the personal level will retain its compelling and sometimes subversive power.

In the modern West, where discourse as such no longer has magical, sacramental, or hierophantic associations, "science" and "theory" have attained a unique significance. In Weberian terms, rational-legal authority has emerged to unparalleled prominence. In this context, the rationality of scholarly histories holds forceful ironies. The two great revolutions in human thought—science and historicism—have for centuries been opposing forces (Barraclough 1956). With the scientization of history, however, science finally appears to be achieving victory. But this is not quite so. For the very formalism and scientization of histories that is supposed to reinforce and legitimate their hegemony is precisely the vehicle by means of which they come to be relativized and diagnosed as ideology. The relativism of norms that is engendered by historical consciousness makes the absolutist claims of any mode of historiography untenable. Indeed, the more "scientific" or "official" is the mode of historiography, the more determinate is the past that it establishes. But by establishing a determinate past, it thereby relativizes everything in the present, including our methods for knowing such a determinate past. Thus, through an ironic peripety, the very cogency and rationality of modern official history can be used to unmask such history as an official legitimation or, conversely, to legitimate an unofficial counterhistory. In these terms, for example, one can view the whole corpus of Marx's work as an ironic reformulation of bourgeois rationality to create, dialectically, an antibourgeois theory of social change.

To the degree that rationality in the West is a basic means of legitimating political authority, all formal language tacitly belongs to the political domain. As such, it may be exposed for its potential ideological relevance. Scientific language may mention very little about specific political issues, but it may nevertheless be particularly ideological precisely because its rationalistic appeal directs attention away from the absence of explicit political content even while conveying it implicitly. The ideological significance of formalized histories, then, is not merely that they abstract the concrete significance of the historical material under study, but also that their very abstractness is of concrete *political* significance to contemporary actors. Rationality *is* one of the paramount symbols of modernity and authority in the world today. A phenomenology of historical experience thus becomes a critique of contemporary ideology: It shows how the language of historiography, which may seem not to be politically inspired, is actually politically charged.[10]

Phenomenological analysis opens up space for such revelations. In the same way that psychoanalysis outlines a symbol *as* a symbol by stretching it into another realm of discourse, so phenomenological analysis may reveal forms of historical discourse to have multiple references. In so doing, such an analysis of histories might become as concrete as the psychoanalytic reading of a text, assuming that there is a grammar of power just as there is a language of the libido. To identify the precise form of the historical discourse would be a first step in wrenching it from one realm (historical science) and stretching it toward another (political rhetoric). A critical hermeneutic analysis of metaphors and tropes is crucial in this, since that which "goes without saying," which "everyone knows," which "has always been and must always be this way," is established as such through encodation in metaphors that have become frozen in natural language, become the words without which people cannot see the world. Such a decoding would involve an elaboration of the symbolism and syntax of the historical discourse as an implicit language of power, so that more precise translations—that is, less arbitrary diagnoses of history as ideology—could be made. Much has been said of how ideology *conceals* its political intentions but, to be successful, it also has to *reveal* something of its purpose, just as, to be successful, a sexual proposition must get some of its message across even while concealing most of it. By ironically viewing appearance and substance interchangeably, each from the viewpoint of the other, phenomenological historical science engages, officially or subversively, in such concealments and unmaskings.[11] It thus would appear that the difference between official and folk history is but a surface distinction. Once we recognize that what is one day official history might the next day be unofficial history, and vice versa, then the main distinction between them becomes practical and political.

Historical Science and the Tropes of Linguistic Figuration

In his *Critique of Pure Reason* (1949b), Kant sought to identify the a priori grounds for a science of nature, to name the presuppositions for the possibility of this type of knowledge. The same question may be asked with regard to knowledge of history (Simmel 1977, vii). What are the presuppositions of this intellectual construct? On what grounds must it be based? I have described four modes of such knowledge, each of which is a different response to this question. Yet all four responses also are versions of one single response, which is as follows: All knowledge is symbolic construction; it is knowledge in some frame of vision. Each of these modes of historical science is also an articulation of experience through language, encoding it into different symbolic forms.

Corresponding to the four root metaphors, there are four tropal models of encodation available in language. These are synecdoche, metonymy, metaphor, and irony. Through these root metaphors and tropes are formed evolutionist, empiricist, structuralist, and phenomenological approaches to knowledge of history. Seen as linguistic constructs, each mode of historical consciousness is a deployment of one of the basic root metaphors and tropes, for these are the media of verbal figuration. Root metaphors and the tropes not only are means for representing a reality that is already present; they also are means for making that reality appear, for making it experiencable and conceivable, for making it "real." This generative aspect of language applies to all root metaphors and tropes, in that all of them are mediations for the presentation of what is or has been. But each of the root metaphors and its respective trope provides a different form of emplotment, each is a different system of notation, as it were, telling reality in a different way. Each thereby not only delimits differently the horizon of what can possibly appear as real, but also the kinds of relationships that can possibly obtain among the things in this reality. Root metaphors and tropes thus constitute the world and its processes in the very act of assuming a posture before them. Each also implies a different mode of argumentation. This projective dimension of language was forgotten when science disengaged from rhetoric in the seventeenth century, thereby rendering science blind to its own poetic nature. A metaphoric and tropal analysis of historical sociology is thus part of the effort to recover a reflexivity in the social sciences, to render them truly nonideological in the sense that their texts would consciously take into account the possibility of their otherwise representing the world.[12]

Modern linguistics at least since Jakobson, and perhaps since Vico two hundred years before, subsumes prose discourse and poetic texts under a general theory of figuration. Through stylistic analysis we come to see familiar prosaic dimensions of poetic texts and poetic dimensions of prosaic expressions. This conflation of poetry and prose also allows us, more generally, to link the languages of art and the languages of science. Artistic as well as scientific inquiries require some protocol of discourse in terms of which their experiments become meaningful. Because they are themselves symbolic enactments, however, no such protocol can assert with consistency an absolute hegemony over others. This catholicity rejects the claim that there is a single correct version of what happened in history or how or why. Instead, we become aware that there are a number of possible correct views, though each may be differently encoded. It is not a question of one approach best corresponding to the basic facts of history, since each approach to historical science defines differently what are to be taken as basic facts. We do not ask whether Dürer or Degas represents the human nude more correctly. Instead we see them—along with the science of anatomy—as different systems of notation (Gombrich 1966, 81–98). Should not the same be true of different modes of historical figuration?

If we borrow Stephen Pepper's (1942) observations on ways in which the strange can be made familiar, we find that his four root metaphors or "world hypotheses" are akin both to the four master tropes and to the four main ways of historical knowing.[13] Or, put conversely, the four modes of historical science are uses of four different *root metaphors* as frameworks for four different *tropal models* of historical reality, as follows:

Root Metaphor	Linguistic Trope	Historical Science
Organicism	Synecdoche	Evolutionism
Mechanism	Metonymy	Empiricism
Contextualism	Metaphor	Structuralism
Formism	Irony	Phenomenology

Note that metaphor appears twice in our schema, once as root metaphor in relation to all four world hypotheses, again as a kind of model, as one of the linguistic tropes. Root metaphors define the nature of a world; linguistic tropes are, respectively, the methods for articulating that world's contents. Invoking metaphor on two different levels also is appropriate to the nature of metaphor itself, since metaphor is not only a particular trope, but also encompasses the other three tropes as well, in that each is a special variety of metaphor. Metaphor takes one thing to stand for another; synecdoche takes the whole to stand for the parts, metonymy takes the parts to stand for the whole, and irony takes opposites to stand for each other. This can be represented by again using Greimas's schema.

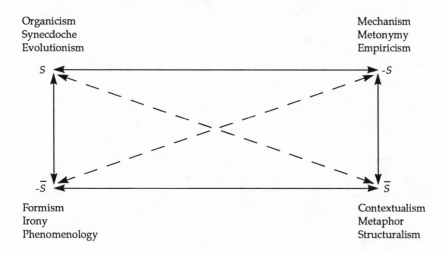

Organicism
Synecdoche
Evolutionism

Mechanism
Metonymy
Empiricism

S $-S$

$-S$ S

Formism
Irony
Phenomenology

Contextualism
Metaphor
Structuralism

The *organicist* approach reconstructs and integrates selected elements of its field into components of a synthetic process. It "explains" actions or events by ordering them around some common telos. Synecdoche—the taking of the whole for its parts—is the tropal mode for this type of encoding. Synecdoche operates, for example, in organistic metaphysical doctrines that proclaim the microcosm to be a representation of the macrocosm, as in the medieval realist Great Chain of Being. The logic here involves the establishment of a hierarchy of reality or significance organized around a superordinate telos—in this case a divine meaning. The evolutionary approach in historical science also is organistic in that it posits a synthetic development of history in terms of which specific historical parts are constituted and comprehended. This view is synecdochal in that in it every particular thing appears as an emmanation of a total process or order.

If synecdoche was the preferred mode of tropal encodement in medieval metaphysics, metonymy—the taking of a part for the whole—is the trope of modern positive science with its root metaphor of *mechanism*. In metonymy any conception of order is seen as aggregating from particular things or, indeed, is reduced to particular things. Behaviorist reductionism is perhaps an extreme example of metonymic encodement, in that it sees all higher order categories, including order itself, as represented by primary elements or parts.

Mechanistic explanations are inclined to represent historical actors as media for extra-historical forces. In Kenneth Burke's dramatistic terms, the "acts" of the "agents" are conceived as representations of nomological "agencies" that are generated by the "scene" under study.

> The Mechanistic theory of explanation turns upon the search for the causal laws that determine the outcomes of processes discovered in the historical field. The objects that are thought to inhabit the historical field are construed as existing in the modality of part-part relationships, the specific configurations of which are determined by the laws that are presumed to govern their interaction. (White 1973, 17).

Although the locus of attention is in the events, their explanation is not complete until the law that governs them has been identified, much as the complete understanding of a spring watch or a mill wheel requires that they both be seen as embodying a law of mechanics. For empiricists, however, this law is merely a convenient generalization standing for all the specific instances it covers.

The governing assumption of the *contextualist* root metaphor is that an historical field is explained when all of its primary elements are related to each other. Because it organizes its materials into concurrent durations of simultaneous significance, on the basis of which historical structures can be distinguished, contextualism favors synchronic rather than linear representations of historical time. The root metaphor of context thus yields the structuralist approach to historical science, in which each of the various parts are understood in terms of each other metaphorically. Metaphor is at work, for example, in an explanation that makes the Mary cults, the design of cathedrals, and the ethos of chivalry each a representation of the others. Structuralists thus might think in terms of such metaphoric images as "Cathedrals are frozen theology," or "Chivalry was the Mariology of knights," and then elaborate these illustrative metaphors into structural models of medieval society that invent and redistribute historical meanings.

The root metaphor of *form* seeks to define the essence or inner meaning of unique historical actions, events, or moments, either as individuals or classes, either concretely or abstractly, within a given field of inquiry. While lacking in precise analysis or synthetic explanations, the formist approach compensates with dramatic vivacity and verisimilitude in its accounts of particular agents or forces. Formism does not posit a reality or structure apart from contents, but rather sees "form" in and through contents just as, conversely, contents are constituted as such in and through form (Brown 1989 [1977], 40–43). As in Hegel's notion of the being of mind as its act of self-awareness, so form is the being of contents in an act of self-articulation. Form and essence are thus an identity, the unity of knowing and being. The rendering of contents into a form through which they are accessible as an object of knowledge is not an abstract operation. Instead, it is the essential principle that operates in all the processes by which experience becomes intelligible—by which we *have* experience. Form is thus a basic principle of the life of the mind, in this view, and is in no way separate from its contents or its expressions. The relationship between the phenomenology of essences and the forms of social-historical life is both dialectical and integral, in the sense that each is immanent in the other (Baillie 1967 [1910], 42).

Form is never available to us as such in experience and, hence, we can never properly make use of it in the abstract for purposes of explanation. Similarly, essences of experience become visible through formal articulation. In the formist view, then, facts and laws, even if exhaustively known, do not provide history; indeed, they can never provide more than a background for it. This is because history is the story of the coming to be of meaning, rather than a body of laws about facts. Meanings are not facts (except to the extent that facts also are meanings), and laws are not stories or narratives. History does not find general laws about facts; instead, through forms it defines human essences within ideographic particulars (Simmel 1977, 150, 157).

The trope appropriate to formism is irony, which involves not merely stating the opposite of what one means (for that is merely a lie), but stating simultaneously two logically incompatible meanings and leaving it to the auditor to determine which is the intended one. Historical science from an existential phenomenological perspective thus is ironic, since to do science means to presuppose a social-historical determinism, whereas to do existential phenomenology means to presuppose agency and intention. The agent and the structure—two opposites—are made to stand for each other. The "tension" of irony, what gives it its dramatic richness, lies exactly in its revealing the contradictions in the relationship between the intentions of human actors and the outcomes of historical events, and between the prospective awareness of historical agents *in* history and the retrospective awareness of writers *of* history. As I have implied above, this mode is itself emancipatory since it requires for its completion the active participation of the audience: For irony to operate its auditors must resolve the intentional ambiguities of the text and impose their own determinate meaning. Thus irony not only sees the historical actors as having been agents; it also casts the contemporary reader into the role of agent, for it is she who must determine the facticity and meaning of the past. It is this ironic tension between two or more modes of awareness that signals the critical self-consciousness of both historical actors as well as historians. It is the Kantian moment in a Hegelian dialectic, when in the conceptualization of historical determinism we establish our freedom, and in the recognition of historical constraint we apprehend the freedom of historical actors (Brown 1987, chap. 8; 1989 [1977], chap. 5).

Scientistic social thinkers would reject this translation of their discourse into tropological terms, for they suppose that plain English—that is, nonpoetic descriptions of the facts—protects them from value bias. What they overlook, of course, is that even nonpoetic language is conducted through metaphors and tropes without which discourse itself would not be possible. Literal or nonpoetic language uses metaphors, but they are frozen or dead metaphors rather than vivid ones—for example, the leg of a triangle, the mouth of a river, a weighty argument, a deep thought, a round number. The scientistic viewpoint thus assumes that things can be described prelinguistically, before the world was given names. But this is impossible, for it assumes an extra-linguistic, extra-cultural point of view. There is no such thing. There *is* a logical equivalent, however, to seeing and experiencing things "before they were named." This is to see things from the perspective of *another* name—that is, to see things poetically. This method of thought also can be expressed in semiotic terms: Every discourse that claims to be realistic presumes that its semantic system has only two terms—the signifier and the referent. It thereby omits the term that is essential to language and to every act of the imagination—the sign.

Thus my purpose in exposing the root metaphors of historical science is not to suggest that historical knowledge is impossible, nor to point to an alternate discourse that would be realistic in some ultimate sense. Instead, following Kenneth Burke, Stephen Pepper, and Hayden White, my concern with root metaphors and the four master tropes is their role in the constitution and the description of social historical truth (Burke 1969, 503). This interest impels us to focus on the use of tropes as basic modes of figuration, systems for properly describing or explaining reality. Our interest also invites us to distinguish root metaphors and tropal models from merely illustrative figures of speech, since it is mainly though the first two that reality is taken to be correctly described. Root metaphors impose a "nature" on reality, as did, for example, the medieval root metaphor of the world as a text or the Enlightenment image of the world as a machine. Similarly, models are tropes whose implications have been elaborated into a logically cogent system, as in Newton's theory of optics—based on a camera metaphor of vision and developed through metonymy into a system of logically interrelated principles. By contrast, the use of tropes merely to illustrate some item in the text is closer to scientistic notions of language, since in this usage figuration has little ontological or epistemological function (Brown 1989 [1977], 107–172).

The tropes are linguistic orientations, expressed through root metaphors, that provide a notational system in which certain kinds of data, and not others, appear as evidence. Organicists, for example, take as data those facts that can be orchestrated into some given *process* of development. Mechanists focus on the kinds of events that can be made to stand for general causal *laws*. Contextualists count as evidence those occurrences which display homologies that can be fitted into a *structure* of the epoch, society, or institution under study. Finally, formists include the *intentions* of historical actors as evidence for both historical *explanans* as well as *explanandum*.

Our analysis shows that each of these modes of historical figuration implies and depends on the others. For example, the phenomenologist, in insisting that the past is always a reconstruction from a contemporary perspective, must admit the impossibility of a complete or singular historical account. As our knowledge of the past is constrained by our ignorance of the future and fragmented by the diversity of present perspectives, there is no reason in principle not to posit a diversity of histories, each with its own temporality. But this is just what the structuralists have done. In the structuralist mode, human time, which always requires the reference point of a present, is bracketed or forgotten. But if the phenomenologists' focus on human acts blocks our awareness of time that is not of our own making, the structuralists' focus on changeless structures blocks our awareness of our own historical being. Evolutionism provides an antidote for this double forgetfulness by positing an anology between lifetime and the time of civilizations: Both persons and epochs experience growth and decline, creation and death, destiny and fate (Danto 1968, 18; Ricoeur 1983, 224).

The phenomenological approach not only ironizes the intentions of historical actors, it also ironizes the intentions of historians in each of these four modes. On the one hand, formists make us see a field of historical praxis upon which meanings are generated that contradict each other, and in which the intentions of particular historical actors are negated by the aggregated intentions and scarcities that we call forces and events. On the other hand, organicists, mechanists, and contextualists invite us to seek theoretical knowledge of the past whose sign is not contradiction and negation, but an agreement of minds. Thus, whereas the existential view of historical praxis engenders skepticism of such theoretical knowledge, the evolutionist, empiricist, or structuralist views of historical process, laws, or patterns engender theoretical dogmatism. From the first point of view there is no meaning or truth *of* history, though there are truths and meanings *in* and *for* it. From the other points of view there is no meaning or truth in or for history, but there can be truths of history if we are willing to suspend our conception of history as lived praxis. Thus any attempt to conjoin these views poses problems the resolution of which contradicts, respectively, either the very essence of lived experience, or the very essence of theoretical knowledge.

In contrast to either skepticism or dogmatism, however, suppose that the objects of both experience and knowledge were framed a priori by our modes of discourse. Suppose, that is, that tropes functioned both epistemologically and ontologically, projecting our objects of knowledge as well as mediating our knowledge about them. Then it would be pointless to assert the direct correspondence between subject and object, as in dogmatism, or the unbridgeable discrepancy between subject and object, as in skepticism. Once we focus on the use of language rather than on consciousness, then the traditional dualism between the mental and the physical, between knowledge and its object, falls away, and we begin to see that the starting point for human ontology and epistemology is not an abstract ideally logical private inner consciousness, but the shared, rule-governed, social reality of language (see Apel 1967; Simmel 1977, 200–201; Ricoeur 1965b, 42; Keat 1981, 205).

The different modes of historical figuration are in effect different expressions and elaborations of basic linguistic tropes; they are modes of poetic insight that have been formalized into social science explanations of historical data. Yet none of these modes has apodictic authority over the others; and if one mode of representation seems more realistic than the others this is not because of its superior epistemological or ontological status, but because we are more used to speaking in its code. The lack of absolute superiority of one mode of figuration over the others is not guaranteed by some common foundation of all of them outside of language, but rather because all these discourses are enclosed in the same ineliminable integument. Each is an island of intelligibility within the common sea of words.

Thus the cognitively responsible relationship to our modes of inquiry is neither absolute dogmatism nor absolute skepticism. This is because both of these attitudes seem to free us from the obligations to provide an intellectual warrant for our thought modes, to respect the rules of our own language game, and to accept moral responsibility for the practical interests that, as rhetorical constructs, our thought-ways may serve. By contrast, a cosmopolitan and self-reflective attitude requires that those who author historical science recognize that they thereby are authorizing some version of our origins, our nature, our destiny.

The relativization of perspectives that our analysis has yielded reminds us that we have a choice of modes of historical understanding. In light of such an awareness, it becomes intellectually irresponsible to insist that any one approach is dictated by self-evident facts or logic, for we now know that modes of historical science have their definitions of facts and their own methods of logic. Each approach contains its internal rules and obligations. Rather than inviting an amoral solipsism, the relativization of approaches may encourage us to be responsible for such intellectual commitments, to bear moral witness to our theoretical practice.

Such a witnessing is not only a contemplative and merely theoretical attitude, but also an act of decision. Self-knowledge involves an awareness of one's responsibility to the future, and this venturing anticipation requires some conception of the past. As both Bultmann (1957, 162) and Betti (1980, 72) pointed out, historicity is not a natural attribute of persons, but something that is siezed by them as part of their own realization as human beings. To be more than the determined products of our relative historical environments, we must affirm the challenge of attributing meaning, including the attribution of meaning to the future and to the past. Consciousness of the modes and methods of historical figuration is an invitation to true historicality, to a life that not only claims a past but also, through this, embraces responsibility for the present and for the future.

Among the ancient Greeks, fate and the gods set the context for texts on moral action. Today it is our conceptions of history and society that provide the frameworks for human will and conduct. On what stage and in what tongues might current moral dramas be enacted? Representations of history and society can mystify our moral contexts by reifying them into purely formalistic language; they can nullify our actions by reducing them to mere behavior; they can obscure our collective circumstances by confining themselves to primal tribes or micro settings. But historical science also can reveal the scarcities inherent in any social order, it can summon before us alternative possible worlds, and it can thereby confront us with our collective moral and political choices. This in itself is no cause for elation. The very idea that we are responsible for the larger political and historical morality of our discursive practice is a source of existential anguish. Still, to see historical science as linguistic figuration is to accept an openness to human existence and an indeterminancy of the past, and at the same moment to affirm the possibility of our creating a better future. It cannot show us how to determine human history, or even that history has any given and necessary moral content. But it can free "history" from antihumanistic determinisms.

SEVEN

BUREAUCRACY AS PRAXIS
Toward a Political Symbology of Formal Organizations

Leopards break into the temple and drink the sacrificial chalices dry; this occurs repeatedly, again and again; finally it can be reckoned on beforehand and becomes part of the ceremony.

Franz Kafka (1971)

TODAY WE face increasing demands for elite technical and theoretical knowledge to manage complex institutions of our advanced science-oriented society. At the same time we feel an increasing need for nonalienating forms of participation, self-governance, and work. The policy sciences, and especially sociology, are similarly divided. On the one hand, they employ methods and theories that presuppose a causal epistemology and a determined social world. On the other hand, the very practice of policy planning presupposes that the social world can be transformed, at least by social engineers. This second assumption, however, implies that human conduct is not determined, but that people can be agents. The contradiction between these two assumptions—of causal determinism versus intentional change—has not been resolved, with the result that in practice individuals tend toward one pole or the other—as private citizens toward alienation, as public planners or managers toward elitist reification.

In this context active citizenship tends to atrophy, while the role of the official, given his positivist methods, becomes that of implementing cost-effective programs within a moral and institutional status quo. Similarly, policy research or managerial science tends to become an instrument of the very bureaucratic domination that creates the problems it is trying to solve. As a rhetoric, a way of expressively structuring a world, the policy sciences lend legitimacy and persuasive power to the dehumanized vision that their objectivist methods create. More sensitive citizens, managers, and planners tend to be aware of this, but generally they lack the conceptual framework that would enable them to reflect on the moral implications of their actions and the political uses of their research, and to reincorporate both into a deeper, more dialectical approach to theory and action.

One antidote to this situation would be a view of formal organizations that encompassed both politics and moral consciousness. Such a view would provide for predictability and control, not based on objectifying causal formulas, but on human experience and ethical accountability. The methodology of such an organizing practice has yet to be spelled out. Indeed, my ethnomethodological and Marxian comments in this chapter suggest a transformation of the concepts of "organization" and "planning" themselves. The conventional meanings of these terms derive from the utilitarian efforts of men such as Saint-Simon and Frederick Taylor. But today, in a world where organizing and planning have become the objects of theoretical and practical critique, the terms require new metaphors and methods.

Reprise

"Social structure" and "structures of consciousness," like system and lifeworld, tend to be separate domains in social theory. Yet there is at least one area where they might be joined: The theory of formal organization. This body of thought recommends itself for several reasons. It grows out of classical theory yet is largely American; it is oriented toward problem solving for capitalist corporations yet it is rich in theoretical findings. Moreover, when social scientists seek empirical embodiments of their concepts of structure, it is to formal organizations that they most often turn. And because it is a privileged site, theoretical innovations about formal organizations are likely to influence social theory and research in general.

At first there appears to be a radical disjunction between Marxian, Weberian, and Durkheimian approaches to formal organizations. For Marx the very rationality of firms stripped away feudal myths and laid bare the larger irrationality of exploitative relations. Yet the bureaucratization of industrial life, though alienating in itself, also brought workers together physically, psychically, and eventually politically. Thus Marx viewed productive relations under capitalism as a present evil that would make possible and necessary a long term good—the proletarian revolution.

In contrast, Weber focused on rationality inherent in organizations.[1] He saw action in modern bureaucracies ideally as oriented toward the solution of problems, that is, bureaucrats set goals and organize work so as to achieve them. While drawing on Marx's ideas concerning instrumental rationality, Weber viewed bureaucracy as a short-term good but a long-term evil. Though bureaucracy could solve specific social problems, Weber feared that society in general would become bureaucratized, leaving little space for affective human relations. To this long-term evil, however, Weber had no solutions. He had only an historically intermittent resolution: the eruption of charismatic forces that would respond to breakdown of rational bureaucracy and join people for a time in new communions.

Durkheim's thought has affinities with that of both Weber and Marx. For Durkheim instrumental reason and anomie were features of the complex division of labor characteristic of almost all aspects of industrial societies. In Durkheim's view the very ordering of personal relationships in terms of means-end rationality could establish conditions permitting irrationality, egoism, and anomie. These "pathologies" could be treated within the official framework of the organization itself through the formation of occupational associations; or, as was later discovered, they might be resolved through hidden, unofficial relationships that develop informally among the personnel. Yet this informal organization constitutes in fact a basic reformulation of the entity as initially understood. Departing both from Weber and from Marx, Durkheim's solution to anomie in society and in industry was neither charismatic renewal nor revolution. Instead, he recommended that organizations themselves be humanized through an enhancement of affective relations at the worksite.

In American organization theory, ideas of Weber and Durkheim (but not of Marx) were reduced to the service of positive science and efficient management. For example, Weber's notion of bureaucratic rationality, initially advanced as an ideal type, was adopted as a paradigm by American sociologists and "applied" in practice by Frederick Taylor. Likewise, in American theory there is a positivistic emphasis on behavior and a reluctance to examine the lifeworlds of persons for interests or intentions. Thus American studies of organization have concentrated on the behavioral aspects of the rational system, and have tended to lose sight of the structures of consciousness and society that are presupposed in the performance of rational activities.

Yet the study of consciousness was not altogether rejected. Durkheimian thought, in effect, has been invoked to account for the failure of rationality to manifest itself as fully as the Weberian paradigm would have us expect (Parsons 1951; Merton 1957, 131–207). This focus on the deviancies and dysfunctions that prevail as persons resist or default on the rational imperatives of the organization constitutes an implicit recognition of the phenomenological basis of activity. Studies by Mayo, Roethlisberger, Dickson and their descendants presupposed notions of structures of consciousness to explain why modern organizations did not live up to (or sometimes outlived) their rationalistic promise. But in dealing with such anomolies, the Americans inverted Durkheim's recommendations. The strategy was not the political revolution of Marx, nor the critical stoicism or charismatic renewal of Weber, nor even the communitarian aggroupment of workers of Durkheim; instead it was the education of technocratic managers to be more sensitive to the psychological needs of employees. This research did not yield a sociological explanation of psychological states as Durkheim had attempted; instead it reduced political and organizational issues to personal troubles (Carey 1969).

More recently, however, there has been a neo-Weberian revival in Anglo-American organization theory. This body of work is probably sociology's richest mine of predictive generalizations. Instead of reifying Weber's ideal type, writers such as Stinchcombe (1959), Blau (1965), Etzioni (1961), Woodward (1965), Hage (1974) and others have followed Weber's comparative historical method. By tracing relationships between various organizational factors, these scholars have developed logically cogent and empirically grounded models of organizational behavior. For example, through comparative analysis of large numbers of factories using assembly line technologies, continuous process technologies, and single unit production technologies, Woodward argued that there is a discrete range of styles and structures of authority possible with each of these means of production. Likewise, Etzioni has shown that persuasion, force, and rational rewards are three patterns of authority; that emphasis of one diminishes the others; and that, according to the degree of any of these patterns, one can predict other features of the organization. Similarly Hage has illuminated correlations between degrees of hierarchy and rates of innovation in firms.[2]

Three questions arise on the basis of this body of work. First, does what we say about formal organizations have anything to do with the people who inhabit them and of whose actions they are constituted? Second, do these formal organizations exist as hermetic behavioral systems, or can they be understood only in terms of their political, economic, and ideational contexts? And third, how might we fuse macro-structural and micro-interactional approaches to the study of formal organizations?

To treat the first question we might turn to the micro-sociologies of consciousness that have developed out of the Durkheimian tradition, with important influences from European phenomenology through Alfred Schutz and from American pragmatism through George

Herbert Mead. Using such an approach we would focus on discursive practices in order to decode the structures of consciousness that prevail as part of rational decision making itself—both as an on-going activity as well as a prospective and retrospective rhetoric of legitimacy. Similarly, we would examine the political and linguistic processes and micro-structures out of which are constituted "authority," "credentials," "rules," and the like. In short, we would not confine the study of structures of consciousness to deviant or disfunctional modes.

In addressing the second question we may receive help from recent Marxian scholarship. That is, we would investigate organizations in terms of systems of accountability, persuasion, and coercion, both in the society as a whole as well as in the offical operations of the organization. Moreover, our attention would be drawn to the political economic context and the ruling ideas in the environment of specific organizations.

An answer to the third question requires the integration of neo-Durkheimian micro-sociology of organizational enactments and neo-Marxian macrosociology of the larger political economic context and processes of organizations. If this amalgam could be fused with neo-Weberian studies of organizational structure, hierarchy, and decision making, a more embracing understanding of organizations and organizing, and of social structure and process generally, would become available. Such an integration may be possible through the concept of the organization as a paradigm for communicative action.

Garfinkel's Demystification of the Weberian Mystique

One step in the direction of a sociology of consciousness for organizations, albeit partly unintentional, has been taken by ethnomethodologists: Most ethnomethodological studies are of organizations. Suicide clinics, kindergartens, social welfare agencies, and juvenile justice systems all are organizations having official goals, formal procedures, professional staffs, and so on.[3] In their studies of such systems, Cicourel, Garfinkel, and others have revealed what might be called the nonrational basis of rational conduct. Just as Marxian macrosocial analysis has shown bureaucratic rationality to be substantively irrational, likewise, when subjected to microanalysis by ethnomethodologists, the supposedly rational procedures of formal organizations turn out to be absurd and yet, in their very absurdity, these procedures provide the rhetoric and rationale for their own legitimacy. By looking beyond the question-begging assumptions of functionalists (and by looking beneath the analytic categories of

Weberians), ethnomethodologists have shown that the activities themselves—whether their consequences be called manifest or latent, functional or dysfunctional—are composed of what ordinary folk would call nonrational elements. Indeed, it is precisely of such nonrational elements that the business of organizing consists. By unmasking rationality as itself a social construction, Garfinkel demystified the Weberian mystique.

Garfinkel's contribution may be highlighted by contrasting it to theories current before his work. Previously, the idea of rationality had taken two expressions. One was that the actors themselves were rational; that is, they projected goals and, in a means-end calculation, decided what would be the most efficient way to achieve them. It then was noted that this formulation could make any action appear "rational"—that is, any outcome could be seen as having properties unachievable except by the particular actions preceding it. This reduced the idea of rationality to a tautological description of the behavior initially observed. A second, predominant view placed rationality in the organization rather than in the individual. In this view purposive action was seen to have intended or manifest consequences as well as unanticipated, latent ones. Then, those outcomes that seemed nonrational or unrelated to the stated organizational goals were labeled "unanticipated," while those that seemingly flowed from the stated goals were labeled "manifest" or "intended" (Argyris 1973).

The pre-Garfinkelian conundrum, therefore, might be stated as follows: Either the actors could be seen as always behaving rationally, in which case the concept of rationality would be rendered empty; or some actions would be seen as rational and others—those yielding unintended consequences—as irrational. However, this latter approach raised problems of its own. First, it appeared to reify human motives to nonhuman entities—the social system or its components. Second, it seemed to be arbitrary; that is, the goals or purposes of the organization appeared to be open to the choice of the sociologist herself. Just as there are different individual lives from which different rational purposes could be reconstructed, so there are different organizational purposes or even different organizations— that is, the "same" organization interpreted from different points of view (André G. Frank 1957).

Thus, even within a single organization, the problem remained as to which (or whose) version of the organization's goals the sociologist was to take as her point of reference. And if the analyst chose to accept the official goals espoused by the organization's leaders and thence label as "dysfunctional" various "deviant" behaviors, her analysis could hardly resist becoming a scientized apologetic for management (Mariner 1971). Moreover, as with organistic thinking in general, the theory itself remained tautological in that behavior was seen to have caused itself; that is, the same evidence was used both to demonstrate the nature or goals of the system, and to explain how these were brought about. In formal terms, the dependent and independent variables were both known by the same indicators. Given the pretensions of many sociologists to objectivity and value freedom, these difficulties were embarrassing.[4]

The foregoing gives us a perspective on the contribution of Cicourel, Garfinkel, and their followers, for they have provided a third view of rationality. In theoretical as well as in detailed observational studies, these scholars have demonstrated how rationality is employed by social actors retrospectively as a rhetoric to account for actions that, from a rationalistic point of view, were chaotic and stumbling when performed. Moreover, Garfinkel and others have shown this to be the case in the actor's individual lives, in their group processes, and in their roles as members or spokesmen of institutions.

If the demystification of rationality in all its forms surprises or horrifies us, Garfinkel offers no respite. He merely shows what "rational activity" is and suggests that this is all there is. For example, in "Some Rules of Correct Decision that Jurors Respect" (1967, 104–115), Garfinkel describes in detail the talk, bargaining, and muddling that go on in jury discussions and how rules, rather than guiding this process, are emergent from it. The jurors at first do not quite know what they are doing, but as their sentiments take shape through the contesting of various viewpoints, they begin to invoke rules of evidence and rationality to justify positions at which they have arrived or which they are in the processs of forming. The rational justification of their decisions crystalizes at about the time that the decisions do, or in many cases even afterwards, when a summary is being prepared for presentation to the court. Thus Garfinkel shows us how rationality does not instruct us as to what action to take, nor is it a property inherent in conduct or in the social system as such. Instead, rationality emerges in interaction, and then is used retrospectively to legitimize what already has taken place or is being enacted.

One could extend Garfinkel's findings to apply to the *prospective* use of rationality in organizations. The organizational plan, for example, can be seen not as a set of instructions for what actually will take place, but as an ideological device that functions to build constituency, to define the limits of responsible opinion, and in general to impose the planners' or managers' definition of reality upon discourse and conduct within and around the organization. Just as statements made by jurors must be susceptible to rationalization in terms of the emergent rules of evidence, so talk about what is going on, to have legitimacy as public discourse within the organization, must be couched in terms of the directorate's statements of the organization's nature, purpose and goals.

This rhetorical function of rationality appears to be inevitable. For example, even if the organizational plan is taken seriously as a set of instructions for future action, it is readily reinterpretable as the covering vocabulary for the difficulties that will unfold as attempts are made to follow it. That is, in actual practice of implementing the plan of action various problems are produced, and the responses to these problems are then reconceptualized as the "solution" or the achievement of the organization's "goals." According to Garfinkel, this upside-down process is in fact what rationality is all about. A good example of this is the work of coroners, who must classify bodies as dead by "accident," "criminal intent," "suicide," or "natural causes." According to the coroners' instructions, the number of categories available for defining the dead body is limited. However, corpses do not come already labeled. The coroners' instructions are thus in effect instructions on how to generate a set of difficulties, the solution of which will constitute the production of the instructions' goals. The coroner, in doing his duty, finds convenient ways to solve the problem of fitting recalcitrant cadavers into the categories of an organizational agenda. Again, such postmortum efforts to restate chaotic process in terms of some formal structure are what "rational action" is made of (Douglas 1967, 186–188).

Thus rationality, rather than being the guiding rule of organizational life, turns out to be an achievement—a symbolic product that is constructed through actions that in themselves are nonrational. Probably we could even say that the dichotomy between rationality and nonrationality is itself ultimately ungrounded, emerging mainly from the legitimacy in our culture of "rational," and the illegitimacy of "nonrational," conduct. Precisely because this particular hierarchy of legitimacy prevails in the modern West we tend to legitimize our activities by accounting for them in terms of rationalistic vocabularies of motives. At the level of micro processes, however, the dichotomy between rational and nonrational conduct breaks down completely, suggesting that both these forms of activity have the same basic components.

Such a radical critique also suggests a means of radically reformulating organizational theory. Rather than seeing organizations as preexisting instrumental entities producing various products, we may now also see them as on-going processes of organizing. Moreover, just as Garfinkel bracketed the facticity of "rationality" in order to see how it was constructed, so we can imagine other studies that would bracket "authority," "hierarchy," "structure," "leadership," and other received factors of organizational analysis, in order to see how such "facts" actually emerge in interactions.

It is not hard to see how empirical phenomenological studies would be conducted of the above factors or of other aspects of organized social life. Indeed, merely to posit such a program suggests a reframing of much microsociological research on the procedures by which various selves and behaviors become defined as rational and normal. Investigations have been made in formal organizational settings, for example, with reference to the maintenance of professional definitions of "doctor" and "patient" during gynecological examinations (Emerson 1970) and in psychiatric diagnostic sessions (Daniels 1970; Goffman 1961b; Scheff 1966; Szasz 1961, 1970). Similar studies have shown how hermaphrodites manipulate their sexual identity in families, offices, and clinics (Garfinkel 1967), and how Basques, Native Americans, Blacks, or overseas Indians negotiate their identities respectively within ethnic or larger national cultures (Lyman and Douglass 1973; Brown 1989 [1977]). Likewise, we may now reinterpret in organizational terms the "work" involved in classifying applicants for welfare, or in sustaining morally normal definitions of actions performed within an illegal abortion mill or a nudist colony (Weinberg 1965). For heuristic reasons such studies tend to focus on extreme situations where the definition of reality is more precarious. Yet this very feature makes them all the more useful in showing how the most taken-for-granted factors of organized life are the products of considerable intersubjective work.

By reinterpreting such microsociologies of consciousness as studies of formal organizations, it becomes clear that the latter are essentially processes or organizing enacted by persons. Given this view, the factors by which the organization is analyzed, such as power, authority, or technology, can be translated into actions that people engage in in order to generate and maintain various features of the situation. Through close analysis of linguistic and other communications, investigators have told us how persons get redefined by organizational professionals as objects to be worked on, clients to be serviced, or deviants to be controlled. In so doing, however, such studies represent a kind of micropolitical sociology. The study of reality creation is a study of power, in that definitions of reality, normalcy, rationality, and so on serve as paradigms that define what conduct is permissible within them. Moreover, if we ask what would be the equivalent of ethnomethodological theory at the macro political level, we are thrust directly toward neo-Marxist theory.

Marx, Metaphysics, and the Mundane World

Ironically, our reinterpretation of Garfinkel's studies reveals their affinity with the neo-Marxist critique of instrumental reason. Horkheimer (1947), with Adorno (1973), to name but two such theorists, argued that means-end rationality has provided both an instrument as well as a rationale for technocratic domination. For example, just as rationality can provide a rhetoric for legitimizing past conduct (à la Garfinkel's microsociology), so it can be employed as a *prospective* rhetoric for closing off unwanted alternatives and advancing one's own group's agenda. Moreover, by focusing discourse on the efficiency of alternative means, instrumental reason displaces attention from the appropriateness of pregiven ends and the class interests that they serve. Thus, by showing that "bourgeois rationality" constitutes, in effect, a class ideology, neo-Marxist theorists suggest a way that micro-studies of the social construction of meanings might be linked to political economy, collective structures of consciousness, and class-based concepts of rationality, reasonable opinion, normalcy, and social order.[5]

In addition to shifting upward from microsociologies, then, we may also shift downward from Marxian political economy to the *Lebenspraxis* of formal organizations. Perhaps, as Marx "materialized" Hegel, so we can invoke Husserl to "phenomenologize" Marx.[6] One way this might be done is to interpret the Marxian "base" as a phenomenological *Lebenswelt*. The *Lebenswelt* encompasses our preconceptual experience, the categories through which such experience is mediated, and the conceptualized reality resulting from apprehensions mediated by those categories. Thus, as Piccone (1971, 24–25) said, "far from being a passive process, perception itself is a form of labor" involving "the conceptualization of those features of reality deemed relevant, that is, determined as essential in relation to some telos." Though most experience is mundane experience, the *Lebenswelt* also is the domain in which concepts are invented and historical projects formulated. Moreover, the mechanical matching of precategorical experience to the categories of mundane experience depends on the original constitutive labor that generated the conceptual repertory. Now, if we follow Husserl, this reality-producing labor is performed by a "transcendental subjectivity" that generated these concepts but that is constantly repressed in mundane experience, that is, in alienated everyday life under certain social and historical conditions.[7]

In addition to interpreting the "base" as *Lebenswelt*, a Marxian use of Husserl also requires us to interpret as transcendental subjectivity the organizational worker himself. Systematic efforts to suppress transcendental consciousness characterize bureaucracies throughout the industrialized world. Members of such organizations are limited to mundane experience as it is predefined largely by the official categories of that system. This collapsing of the transcendent into the mundane results in distorted communication (Habermas 1970, 114). In such systems the determinants of action are not freely accessible to the consciousness of the actors, who must act instead under intentions formed behind their backs.

Yet the very location of the worker at the nexus of the official norms and goals and the actual exigencies involved in creating the appearance of their accomplishment, forces the worker to function as a transcendental subject. Like "primitive man" who must patch together accounts of what goes on around him (Levi-Strauss 1970), so the modern worker must make "myths" ad hoc that reconcile the actual processes of his work with the official rhetorics of the organization. Anyone who has performed alienated labor knows that the most difficult part is not learning the instrumentally rational techniques, but establishing a *lebensweltiche* relation to them through which one may preserve some autonomy in the very process of presenting oneself as a cheerfully obedient, robot-like thing. ("Learning the ropes" or "making out" in organizations involves precisely this.) "Revolution"—or the de-alienation of organizational practice— would permit this covert transcendence to become open and normative, no longer deviant or subversive, but in the service of organizational products that are, or include, humane organizational process as well.

Toward a Political Phenomenology of Organizations

One means of integrating neo-Durkheimian and neo-Marxian theories with each other and with neo-Weberian organizational studies may lie in the concept of the organization as a paradigm. By paradigm, I refer to those sets of assumptions, usually implicit, about what sorts of things make up the world, how they act, how they hang together, and how they may be known. A paradigm in this sense might be considered a "mini-habitus" or a "collective root metaphor" in use. Paradigms function as a means of imposing control as well as a resource that dissidents may use in organizing their awareness and action. That is, we can view paradigms as practical as well as cognitive, and as a resource as well as a constraint.

The above conceptualization may be arrived at via two complementary paths. First, we may expand Marx's notion of "ruling ideas" to encompass what Kuhn intended by the term paradigm. In so doing, the rich tradition of Marxian analysis of the political economy of consciousness is made available as a resource for studying how paradigms govern conduct. Second, we may extend the concept of paradigm to stress its pragmatic institutional aspects, not merely its cognitive ones. Thus we could speak of paradigms for discourse and conduct, and even for organizational behavior, in addition to paradigms for research and theorizing within a given disciplinary domain.

Having proposed the above reformulations, we are able to advance a new hypothesis: Organizational change is analogous to scientific change as described, say, by Brown (1989 [1977]), Imersheim and Kaplan (1974), Kuhn (1962), or Masterman (1970). If this analogy can be convincingly made, a way would be cleared for the empirical study of how new paradigms within specific organizations are generated and what conditions must be present for a paradigm shift. For example, we would seek to discover in discursive practices the correlates of what Kuhn has described in logical terms as anomalies, overextensions, or excessive ad hoc adjustments in the currently dominant approach.

Much of scientific activity, like most of what goes on in organizations, involves tacit practical as well as explicit formal knowledge. That is, the relevant knowledge is often a matter of application, such as *how to employ* the official procedures and *when to invoke* the formal description of those procedures, rather than abstract knowledge of the formal procedures themselves. Paradigms, in other words, may be understood not only as formal rules of thought, but also as rhetorics and practices in use.[8]

This stress on the practical side of paradigms—their function in organizing scientific activity—suggests that paradigms may serve a similar function in the more explicitly formal organizing of nonscientific work. Scientific paradigms implicitly offer various questions to be answered, methods to be followed, tasks to be accomplished, and the like, all in a particular manner. In a similar fashion, organizational paradigms provide roles to be enacted in particular ways, in particular settings, and in particular relation to other roles. These roles need not be specified by rules for enactment. As Brown (1989 [1977]), Kuhn (1962), Polanyi (1958), and Wittgenstein (1979, 140–142) have argued, explicit rules are neither necessary nor sufficient to direct scientific activities; and, as Garfinkel has shown, organizational activities are no different in this regard.

This tacit intersubjective property of paradigms constitutes in effect the "agreement" among members that enables the orderly production of role enactment. That is, the structuring of organizational interaction requires members to rely upon shared but largely tacit background knowledge that is embodied in an organizational paradigm. Roles as well as the definition of "problems," "responsible opinion," "leadership," and so on, are afforded by the dominant model. Such rules and roles are not a static description of the organization, however, so much as the official rhetoric in terms of which unofficial negotiations take place (Manning 1980, 4; Strauss 1978).

The maintenance of paradigms requires political organization, and with this the imposition of sanctions against violators of the paradigm's implicit rules. The achievements of science are testimony to the skill scientists have exercised in solving the problem of rule enforcement, even when these rules are only tacit, for scientific progress is critically dependent on the ability of the community of practitioners to direct researchers toward their paradigm's puzzles.

With the above provisos in mind, I propose that formal organizations be considered paradigms in operation, different in degree and content, but not in essence, from scientific paradigms in use. In this I draw on Wolin's application of Kuhn's ideas to political societies:

> My proposal is that we conceive of political society [read: formal organization] itself as a paradigm of an operative kind. From this viewpoint society would be envisaged as a coherent whole in the sense of its customary political practices, institutions, laws, structure of authority and citizenship, and operative beliefs being organized and interrelated. A politically organized society contains definite institutional arrangements, certain widely shared understandings regarding the location and use of political power, certain expectations about how authority ought to treat the members . . . and about the claims it . . . can rightfully make upon its members . . . . Further, in its agencies of enforcement and its systems of rules, a political society possesses the basic instrumentalities present in Kuhn's scientific community and employs them in an analogous way. (1968, 149)

What Wolin says about political societies is truer still of formal organizations. "Normal science, for example, often suppresses fundamental novelties because they are necessarily subversive to its basic commitments" (Kuhn 1962, 5). Similarly, formal organizations enforce certain types of conduct and forbid others, defining which "experiments"—in the form of group or individual initiatives—will be nurtured, tolerated, or suppressed. Through its complex set of information systems, structures of reporting and accountability, and

political groupings based on departments or status, formal organizations, like scientific communities, have mechanisms for determining
what will constitute reasonable and productive "theory and
research"—that is, policy and operations.

Like scientists accounting for an anomaly, so organizational members have paradigms available to them, paradigms that provide
pre-scripted accounts for rectifying untoward behavior. Bureaucratic
rules, for example, often prescribe the account that is to be given by
a functionary to justify or excuse actions taken toward clients. For
instance, the telephone operator responds to customers' complaints
by quoting from memory the rules of telephone conduct required of
the situation (Lyman and Scott 1970, 56). The invocation of "the
rules" of an organization, with their connotation of violation and
prison, is a means of imposing conformity and curtailing dissent. As
Edelman described them, these rules "are unseen and untouchable
and hence, like all dogma, not to be violated, altered, or questioned.
Their invocation is a signal that discussion of the merits of the issue
is out of place and profane, that what is involved is the transmission
and conservation of a sacred tradition. Reference to 'the rules'
therefore evokes a symbolic political setting that is extremely confining" (Edelman 1964).

Paradigms provide accounts for the performance of a bureau, and
these may be given dress rehearsals "in-house" before they are
presented to the audience for which they were designed. Accounts
also may be tried out in New Haven, so to speak, before being shown
on Broadway. At each presentation, audience response may be
literally taken into account, that is, incorporated into the account in its
next incarnation (Blumstein et al. 1924, 551; Lyman and Scott 1970,
57). Though there is enormous diversity in the accounts given by
different organizations in different settings, it still should be possible,
in C. Wright Mills's terms, to "identify characteristic vocabularies of
motive in relation to typically recurrent situations" (Stone and
Farberman (1974 [1970], 470). Various industries present different
ideological themes to different audiences (Seider 1974, 809). For
example, the weapons industry appeals to national defense, whereas
retail merchandisers appeal to social responsibility to consumers. A
process of interpretation also is involved in choosing the relevant
audience, constructing the account, and noting and responding to
audience feedback. If the account is to be taken as successful it must
help the organization reach its goals, restore its identity, and recreate
order in its relationships (Hewitt and Stokes 1975, 7). The strength of
an organizational paradigm may be measured by the range and
veracity of its repertoire of accounts—the various vocabularies of

motives available within the paradigm by which members can credibly justify or excuse themselves when attacked. In the same sense, organizations, like scientific disciplines, are divided into different product lines or industrial sectors. And, like scientists adjusting their theories in response to criticism, organizations are ready to revise their accounts in light of audience feedback.

Like scientific disciplines, organizations also have histories, undergo internal and external changes, and experience strains. The dominant paradigm may be confronted and even overthrown by an insurgent one, or it may be modified to absorb its challengers. Workers may unionize, the market may shift, ideological movements may emerge. In much the way that leaders in a scientific community seek to adjust their paradigm to account for novelties and anomolies, so leaders of formal organizations adjust their collective rhetoric to accomodate unexpected changes. To the extent that they succeed in this, their efforts constitute a kind of puzzle solving. As long as the organization can handle its "puzzles" and make minor adjustments in the paradigm to accord with the new "facts," that organization is proceeding in a manner reminiscent of normal science (Wolin 1968, 150). To the extent that it is superceded by other forms of organizing, however, there will have occurred a paradigm revolution.[9]

Of course not all disciplinary or organizational orders are morally equivalent. An advantage of a rhetorical perspective is that, by making communication, practice, and agency central in our analytic vocabulary, we become able to assess the ethical content of organized systems. The paradigmatic rhetoric of a formal organization makes the content of precategorical experience accessible to conscious awareness as some given object. The paradigm defines the nature and meaning of that which the organization is. An example may illustrate the power of such rhetorics to define a social and moral world. Today the spokesmen for cybernetic systems theory argue that formal organizations are (or are like) a giant computer, with its input and output, its feedback loops, and its programs. This machine—the organization—is in turn guided by a servomechanism—the techno-administrative elite. To see this imagery as a thing made, as a symbolic artifact rather than as the fact, is to reject it as a literal description of how the organization "really is," and to unmask it as a legitimating ideology. By doing a close textual analysis, we can make it clear that in the paradigm of cybernetics the vocabularies of personal agency, ethical accountability, and political community have atrophied. In their place, the organization, initially conceived as serving human values, becomes a closed system directed by elites and generating its own self-maintaining ends (Stanley 1978). With cyber-

netics as a paradigmatic self-image for an organization, "rational,"
"reasonable," and "responsible" come to be defined in a particular
way, according to particular stockshelves of arguments, rules of
reason, and protocols for action. These serve as boundaries for public
debate and policy options. Put differently, though the "marketplace
of ideas" in organizations may be relatively free for those who operate
within the regnant paradigm, this paradigm may serve oligarchs and
constitute a powerful barrier to entry.[10]

All of us to some degree design or tailor our worlds, but we never
do this from raw cloth; indeed, for the most part we get our worlds
ready to wear. This is perhaps most often the case when the world in
question is that of formal organizations, citizenship, and policy
formation. For such *public* worlds, the constitutive building materials
are largely supplied by national trade associations, industry lobbies,
policy research centers, government agencies, leading universities,
corporate advertising firms, major wire services and newspapers,
national television networks, and the like. Should one invoke facts
and arguments or rules of reason not sanctioned by these sources,
one is unlikely to get a public hearing. And what is true for the polity
in general is truer still for formal hierarchic organizations. In these
arenas, attempts to express nonlegitimate opinions publicly can result
in the loss of one's job.

Thus, in addition to studying the negotiation of reality, we might
also analyze the *imposition* of (a paradigmatic) reality by more powerful groups. Such analysis would focus on the mechanisms, and the
amassing of control of the resources, for symbolization and legitimation of organized life—ownership patterns, opinion leadership, clique
interlocks, and so on. It would go on to see whether such control
overlaps extensively from bureau to bureau, from organization to
organization, and from industry to government to state. Such an
inquiry also would explore whether such overlaps emerge from
class-based mobility ladders, collective ideology, and cooptation, and
whether these mechanisms in turn reflect corporate aristocratic
hegemony over national organizational life (Domhoff and Dye 1987;
Perlo 1957; Woodmansee 1975).

In hierarchical organizations (or in a bureaucratized society) it is
not only the means of economic production that become concentrated, but also the means of autonomous reflection. As large
organizations emerge, elites exercise their powers more broadly,
controlling complex interconnections over an ever widening field. But
at the same time there are fewer and fewer positions from which the
major structural connections among different activities can be perceived, and far fewer men and women who hold such positions

(Mannheim 1940, 59). There comes to be not only a concentration of control over the *contents* of reality (the means of production), but also over the *definition* of reality (the foundational assumptions concerning what constitutes "property," "rights," "obligation," "legitimacy," and so on).

From such a perspective our subject matter becomes not only organizations as instruments, but also organizing as process. Moreover, to the extent that a bounded system exists, it is seen as composed of rules that define the domain and protocols of conflict. "Organizations" thus become a continuous process of enactment in which notions of goals, purposes, or functions are used by actors as rhetorics to enhance their relative position or identity or to make their definition of the situation more compelling. For example, such an approach reformulates the view of organizational heirarchy in which differences in status are thought to serve a vital function for the organization (Davis 1961; Davis and Moore 1945). In this functionalist view, more income, privileges, deference, and other rewards that constitute higher status serve as incentives to recruit persons to higher and more demanding positions, and to insure that they perform the duties attached to those roles in an efficient manner. By contrast, it is possible to understand hierarchy as a set of dynamic relationships, as processes of negotiation and domination among people who bring different perspectives and resources to the interaction. Some persons or groups may have greater interactional skill per se; others (to borrow from the instrumentalist model) may bring possessions, attributes, or competencies that are especially valued or feared. The creation and contesting of hierarchy is not a zero-sum game nor are all the relevant utils commensurable or transferable. One can even imagine great differences among participants' definitions of the relevant rules of the interaction, or even blatant violations of rules that have been agreed upon. Organizing can still proceed so long as the actors continue to feel that interacting is preferable to not interacting at all (Helmer 1964, 301–302).

At the extreme however, the contesting of interests may require participants to invest an enormous part of their resources in redefining the form that the interaction will take (open warfare) or it may encourage an unbridled exercise of advantage (naked power). Thus there may emerge a mutual interest in stabilizing typifications of role and status differences as a strategy both of acknowledging and of using such conflicts. As status differences come to be regarded as "normal," the pressure by "higher status" persons prompts "lower status" ones to acknowledge the "superiority" of the more powerful, thereby establishing a status consensus. The validation and continual reenactment of these power relations may create a class system in which the use of power is limited by the values used to legitimize it, and in which the compliance of social subordinates becomes routinized.

Status hierarchies are never entirely static, however, for high-status persons will tend to expand the scope of their legitimate exercise of power, while lower status persons will seek to restrict it. Consequently class systems normally involve the creation and maintenance by lower status persons of strategies of withdrawal, confrontation, or subversion, and by higher status persons of social distance and exclusion, prestigiously novel activities and possessions, public disclaimers or power intentions and activities, stress on the difficulties associated with high status, restriction of public media to expressing high-status ideology only, and rhetorics asserting that class differences are necessary to the pursuance of common or transcendent goals.

At some moments—such as strikes or revolutions—the insignias of rank may be perceived as "ploys," "myths," or "ideologies" by those "oppressed" by them. But in mundane experience these symbolizations are accepted not only as normal, but as concrete reality itself. Thus, "blue collar" and "white collar" are perceived not as exterior insignia, but as the very identity of workers and their functions. Contrary to the instrumentalist view, which sees such insignia as an incentive for efforts, in our model they are viewed as the dramatic ritualization of the process of conflict or, more precisely, and when practiced by management rather than workers, as an effort to "freeze" the language game into that range of moves at which the high-status persons have won. The key to the executive washroom is not merely a reward for a job well done; more importantly, it is a means of controlling the action.

A similar rhetorical deconstruction could be undertaken of other features of organized life, such as rationality, goals, or decision making. Weber himself made only a qualified claim for the rationality of formal organizations, saying that they possess formal as opposed to substantive rationality (Gross 1964, 142). Weber noted that bureaucratic institutions are the only ones that can appeal to criteria of formal or instrumental rationality to justify themselves. In other words, bureaucratic authority is legitimated by its instrumental effectiveness and, in this sense, it is nothing other than successful power. This central insight of Weber has been elaborated by the same sociologists who criticize Weber's ideal type when it is taken as an empirical description of how organizations actually work. By showing that organizations are by no means as rational or purposive as the Weberian ideal type implies, these researchers inadvertantly vindicate Weber's account of how managerial power is made legitimate (MacIntyre 1981, 25, Jehenson 1980, 227). By requiring members to subordinate their in-order-to motives to the official organizational goals and purposes, elites attempt to substitute their own "objective" public vocabulary of motives for the "subjective" private ones of lower level members. In other words, organizations are constituted through a "rhetoric" that attempts to hide its partisanship.

This does not mean that elites are always, or even mainly, in control. Indeed, reasoning from the above observations, we could say that making decisions is not the most important exercise of organizational power. Instead, this power is most strategically deployed in the design and imposition of paradigmatic frameworks within which the very meaning of such actions as making decisions is defined. But this is not to say that power to manipulate the paradigm is held exclusively by those at the top. In business firms, for example, conscious decisions usually represent a choice between options within an official paradigm that management itself has established. Yet at the same time that this decision making is going on, a subtle, diffuse, hierarchically low-level complex of negotiations is being enacted. What emerges from these more subterranean activities is a redefinition of the official paradigm in the very process of its application. In putting the official rules of relevance into practice, there emerges a set of unofficial, inarticulate "rules of *ir*relevance" by which information entering into the official organizing frame is screened and manipulated. This can be stated simply by the dictum that input limits output, adding that those responsible for the output or production of decisions rarely have full control of the paradigm in use that restricts the formulation of their options.

Here lies an irony in the rationalistic model of organizations. Executives *can* control the rules of relevance—the official paradigm; but the rules of *ir*relevance—the paradigm as it is tacitly used—are not so amenable to managerial control. This distinction between rules of relevance and rules of irrelevance is important. As Brown (1987), Garfinkel (1967), Kuhn (1972), and MacCormac (1976) have shown, we normally become explicitly aware of paradigms only when they are contradicted. Likewise, the boundaries or rules of situated interactions tend to become apparent only when they are contested. Stated conversely, organizational paradigms constitute not only a structure of selective attention, but also one of inattention by which we screen out aspects of our settings that are not relevant to our immediate focus and interests.[11] Yet—and here is the irony— executive control is by nature neither subtle nor implicit; instead it is official and direct. Hence, the more this type of control is exercised, the narrower will become the gates through which information must pass, and it is exactly such information that must form the basis of managerial decisions.

Decision-makers have tried to impose the principles of rationality and objectivity on the inflow of information. But to the extent that the notion of decision making is considered apart from the diffuse, low-level negotiation of paradigms, such efforts have little success. This is because the criteria by which the rules of selection are established contain in themselves a range of possible responses to selected data. Thus the greater the number and levels of rules used to control inputs into the decision process (clean up the data, screen out noise), the fewer the premises included and the narrower the range of options available (Weick 1969). These logical limits inherent in the nature of formal rules, and the practical limits inherent in their application, mean that there always must be some constraint, however small, on managerial power. And within this range of autonomy the exercise of selective inattention by low-level participants normally will be directed toward immediate interests that have nothing to do with the presumed goals of decision-makers.[12]

None of this is to say that there is no structured hierarchy or formal decision making in organizations, but only that these features emerge from the negotiated interactions between players and factions which, over time, sediment into cumulative accommodations and commitments which then constitute "hierarchy," "policy," and "organization" itself.

In sum, organizational realities are not external to human consciousness. Instead, they are constituted through paradigms in a process of communicative interaction. Revision of our paradigms of perception and expression is thus a re-visioning of our worlds. This is as true for the artist or the scientist as it is for the citizen or manager or bureaucratic politician. All such actors can be seen to share a basic affinity—they create and use paradigms through which experience acquires significance. By stressing the world-creating aspects of discursive practices, such a perspective also provides a bridge between theoretical and organizational praxes, as well as between what experts do and what workers do in their workaday lives. We all create worlds. The more we are able to create worlds that are morally cogent and politically viable, the more we are able, as workers and as citizens, to manage or to resist.

EIGHT

SOCIAL PLANNING AS SYMBOLIC PRACTICE
Toward a Liberating Discourse for Societal Self-Direction

> What I am trying to do is grasp the implicit systems which determine our most familiar behavior without our knowing it. . . . I am therefore trying to place myself at a distance from them and to show how one could escape.
>
> Foucault (1971)

THE HUMAN and political meaning of modernization lies not so much in the advances of the sciences as in their systematic application to society. Only with the development of scientific methods to guide psychic and social processes has the victorious course of modern science become a dominant political and ethical factor. Science has emerged as a kind of religion, an ultimate frame of reference for determining what is real and true. As such it serves as a vocabulary for public discourse on policy issues in virtually all areas of social praxis. Scientific management, scientific warfare, scientific welfare—the application of science in all these fields seems to prefigure a totally rationalized, efficiently administered social order (Gadamer 1967).

Yet in such a world of technical calculation, what is the place for personal agency and dignity, and for a morally legitimate civic order? Indeed, is there not a fundamental conflict between technicism and humanism, between utility and humane values? Such a conflict is expressed in many forms—positivism versus romanticism, reason versus intuition, analysis versus evaluation, increasing demands for elite technical knowledge versus increasing demands for participation and self-governance.

Positivism and romanticism are two sides of modern consciousness. On the one side are the followers of Comte and Saint-Simon, on the other those of Schiller and Rimbaud. Once confined to French salons and German universities, today this conflict has become both violent and global. In its ultimate form, it is a conflict between survival and dignity (Arendt 1965, 224; Hegel 1952, 149–150; Stanley 1978). Given such global apocalyptic potentials as Malthusian food scarcities. Nth country nuclear dilemmas, and "ecocide" brought about by environmental pollution, many thinkers have advocated (or warned against) technology as a means of salvation (e.g., Kahn and Weiner 1967). Yet, in its ultimate application, applied positivism means the instrumental use not only of material tools, but also of reason and of persons themselves. In our present circumstances, the manipulativeness of scientific means for maintaining order and effecting change tends to negate our humanistic ends. That is, virtually all of the proposed technical and institutional solutions to major national and global problems require greatly increased statist regulation and control of citizens, from airport security checks to governmental population planning. At the same time, in accepting the humanistic criticisms of these instrumental techniques, we appear to consign ourselves to fatalistic passivity in the face of acute human misery and real threats to survival.

In this context it becomes vital not only to imagine alternative social orders but also to invent alternative means for achieving them. Unless we are up to this task, "survival" in both postindustrial and Third World nations may require that persons be reduced to a factor of planning or production, things possessing no intrinsic worth, dignity, or moral agency. Auschwitz is an example of such a society, but so is Walden II. Such an abolition of freedom and dignity in the name of survival through instrumental reason would be the end not only of Western humanism, but of *any* civilizational conception of the human as a privileged status in the polity and the cosmos.

The problem for planning is parallel to the problem for philosophy, the human sciences, and politics in modern democratic societies: how to reconcile systems efficiency with human agency. Theoretically, this requires the interconnection of two apparently opposite paradigms—positive science and life-world. Practically, it requires that persons be prime agents in maintaining the boundaries and continued existence of their collective systems by mastering internal complexity and environmental inconstancy. Stated in more traditional terms, the practical requirement for reconciling systems efficiency and human agency is that *citizens effectively govern their polity.*

The rift between the scientific, positivist side of social science and the interpretive, romantic one runs parallel to this chasm between the positivist technicists and their romantic critics in the broader culture. The first group speaks of facts and necessities, the second speaks of rules and meanings. The first tells us how to solve our scientific and practical puzzles, the second tells us that the application of these methods of puzzle solving is dehumanizing our culture and polluting our planet. The first points to genuine social ills, the second criticizes the cures as more pernicious than the ailments. The first group speaks of efficiency, the second speaks of freedom. Neither group responds adequately to the other, yet both often argue in the name of human caring. If somehow the positivist and romantic positions could be joined we might be able to find survival with dignity. In so doing we also would create a truely humane culture and an authentic understanding of ourselves.

If we take these theoretical ideas to heart, how might they affect our methods of planning and management? The idea of an emancipatory approach to social planning seems a contradiction of terms. "Planning" suggests instrumental, objectifying reason; "emancipation" connotes personal agency and self-direction. Unless we can conjoin the two, however, we are likely to face choices between survival and dignity, between the efficient management of complex systems and the humanization of our existence without them. The problem is not only the purposes of social policy but also the means of social planning. It is in part a problem of method. In our times even advocates of human emancipation have employed the most dehumanizing techniques. Yet what methods would be appropriate to genuine emancipation? Which techniques would represent a liberating *process*, as well as yielding a presumptively liberated product?

Though the exact nature of a post-postivist, post-romantic approach to societal guidance has yet to be defined, one can imagine some of its likely features. This task is advanced by using West Churchman's notion of "inquiring system" (1971). Churchman argued that all policy analysis, social planning, or applied research must be done through one or another inquiring system, a paradigm or model that consists of the presuppositions and methodological canons by which the problem is defined and attacked. Churchman described a range of inquiring systems (IS), using as differentiating labels the name of the principal philosopher whose premises inform them. The array includes the Leibnitzian, Lockean, Kantian, and Hegelian IS's, all of which are combined and optimized in the Singerian IS. Churchman's typology can be extended by defining still another inquiring system, an "emancipatory IS," based on a view of reality and knowledge as historically specific products of interaction, a view that sees citizens, and not merely techno-administrators, as the human authors of the world.

Consistent with Churchman's nomenclature, we might dub the emancipatory IS after Merleau-Ponty. How might such a Merleau-Pontean orientation be expressed in actual planning practice? The following are suggestions for this, generated by comparisons with principal aspects of conventional approaches.

Social Planning as Reality Construction

In contrast to the Singerian analyst who posits an objective reality that can be used to gauge possible actions, the Merleau-Pontean also asks how particular social realities are created as ideas and events out of the great din of images and happenings. Truth for the Merleau-Pontean is agreement that enables action by confirming or altering what is "normal" or "to be expected." Social reality is viewed as shaped by intentions and actions instead of as a purely objective thing-world against which the rationality of actions can be measured.

Merleau-Ponty and other social phenomenologists suggest that past, present, and future realities can be viewed as currently prevailing sets of shared assumptions about specific situations. This implies that there are multiple social realities, each the product of our (and other persons') experience and reason and not external to it. Our everyday realities emerge from the meanings we inherit, impose, and invent. Since we do not exist alone, we are continuously asserting and having validated or challenged our definitions of what is going on. From our repertoire of such definitions we constitute our reality. This means that instead of continuously discovering a wholly external verity—the reality-out-there—we are, wittingly or not, continuously adding, verifying, or revising our stock shelf of versions of what is apparent and what is real, what is abnormal and what is to be expected.

What does this mean for planned social interventions? First, the results of planning—the plan and its implementation—are understood to be products of interaction. These results can be said to constitute a reality construct for the group. Second, since this reality construct is only one among other possible constructs, what remains unknown or unexplained may not be attributable simply to inadequate data or instruments. Further efforts to fill in details on our cognitive maps may get us even more lost, since the unknown items may be in principle inaccessible in the terms of our given reality construct. In such cases, instead of seeking further degrees of exactitude, we might reflect on the assumptions of our reality construct to understand how we define "data" or "options" in the particular, now inappropriate, ways that we do.

The Merleau-Pontean planner also expects that future reality constructs will be as different from those of the present as will future technologies or social structures. She will assume, in other words, that the future is a situation in which the dominant reality, and not just the technology, are invented as well as inherited, and in which culture is transformed as well as transmitted. This is because conceptions of reality change along with changes in hardware and social organization. This is almost always overlooked by orthodox forecasters and planners.[1] Predictions may well occur as forecast, but their occurrence will likely have a different meaning for people who actually experience them than it would for the forecasters. One can note people's understanding of this in this typical response to new predictions, "I guess they [the people of the future] will be ready for it by then."

The Merleau-Pontean expects reality to continue to be negotiated in the future. This means that the kinds of realities within which occurrences will be given specific meanings will vary from those prevailing at present. To a large extent reality constructs guide the efforts spent on developing or implementing a plan. The idea of an urban crisis, for example, shaped the political and moral experience of liberal activists, even if it had little impact on the experience of most inner city dwellers. Extra-systemic actions and events also can dramatically alter collective reality constructs, often influencing member's conception of "system" itself. For example, the Soviets' launching of Sputnik helped Americans redefine their conception of the quality of their own education system; the assassinations of the Kennedys and King helped shape the perception of the danger and immorality of unlicensed weapons, as well as the character of America as a "violent society"; the oil crisis altered Americans' view of their role in the global economic system.

Another implication of the above is that meaning cannot be attached to experiences that are singled out according to pregiven rules of interpretation (rules that systems analysts and managers presume they can define for their underlings). Instead, the focus of the actors' attention and the meaning which they give to what they attend are two ways of describing the same process. Perception, project, and meaning simultaneously cooperate in what Dilthey called a hermeneutic circle of interpretation (Dilthey 1957; Brown 1978). This leads to two further points: First, the notion of a firm, agency, or social movement responding to a problem in the environment is misleading. On the contrary, the stimulus—in this case a problem—can be known or defined only in terms of the responses it elicits. In this fundamental sense the process of societal guidance creates its own subject matter. The environment is not merely out there; it also is *enacted*. Second, the notion of "defining information inputs" that later will undergo "objective analysis and interpretation" is equally misleading. Each of these two activities is presumed to be separate from and serial to the other; in fact, each is a way of doing the other. Moreover, the unitary process in which "data gathering" and "interpretation" both are involved is at once subjective *and* objective—that is, it is an intersubjective process of creating objectified meanings.

For the Merleau-Pontean, then, planning provides frameworks for structuring appearances, for creating that which becomes accessible and validated as reality. The potency of such planning practices transvalues their own legitimacy and purposes. The planner can no longer justly claim to be in the grandstand watching behaviors pass in review. Instead, as part of the parade, she can either clear or clutter up the way. Field planners are perfectly aware of this: They spend little time over the design board and much of their days outside their agency meeting with representatives of various publics. As these interactions help shape the environment, planners shift from scientific prediction to self-fulfilling (or self-defeating) prophesy. And, since the implementation of plans often depends on the support or responses of those who are affected, they in turn affect the efficacy of the plan.[2]

Elitist Planning versus Mutual Learning

In Western societies knowledge is conceived largely as a stock that agents of social change draw upon as needed. When a situation calls for strategic interventions, ad hoc models are put together from this stock by interest groups seeking to define options that will enhance their positions. This is true despite large government expenditures for research, because such research is chiefly directed at measuring existing programs or identifying substitutes, and not at producing alternatives based on new definitions of the problem. Some additional options are generated through research sponsored by public service organizations that ostensibly impart minimal "value loading." But in practice most research produces options that reinforce the predelictions of its establishment sponsors.

The positivist planning processes requires an elaborate compilation of detailed information about the present situation to justify the programs or facilities that are recommended. The implicit objective of this approach is to avoid criticisms based on experience from the past. In our changing technical and social environment, however, adhering to a rigid plan almost always assures that the results will not be responsive to future conditions.

If various groups are to better shape their own destinies, new sets of optional futures and new methods for generating them are needed. Hence the capacity for rapid learning on the part of social change agents will not be enough. Unless she can take clients along on her learning trip, the expert will find her models are unlikely greatly to enhance that constituency's capacity for self-direction. The planner must become expert at helping groups redefine their own situations. She must act as stage hand rather than script writer, helping to structure the learning experience so that she and her clients can jointly reconceptualize problems and discover new possibilities for concerted action (see Burchell and Listokin 1982; Friedmann 1973; and Miller, Schooler, and Miller 1977).

Positivist social design proceeds as if all factors are susceptible to advanced prediction by experts whose roles in the process are restricted to stereotyped tasks under the control of a centralized executive. Most of our familiar physical and social structures derive from this deterministic model. Such products as industrial plants, apartment buildings, legal contracts, and systems of administration usually are built according to predetermined forms and procedures. The assumption is that the desired outcome requires little reconceptualization by the planners and only marginal participation by the users. Such an approach is appropriate where the environment is predictable, the context static, agreement well established, and where the planning authority controls the key resources. Often, however, such conditions do not exist and elite control is neither feasible nor desireable. Of course, it is possible to decree that organizations or communities will conform to predetermined patterns. But external conformity, even if obtained, will not by itself assure the desired results. Deterministic certainty is achieved at the expense of local initiative, openness to opportunity, and appreciation of wholeness. By seeking to reduce error to the degree that is possible in the design of roads and bridges, such methods may brutalize everyone involved.

In contrast, the value of Merleau-Pontean design can be measured by the extent to which it provides more encompassing reasons for being on the scene. In such an approach, ordinary aspects of life can become part of some larger quest. For example, through one's job one can plan one's life as a career. Goods and services can not only attend to functional needs, they may also serve as a basis for communication, a source of learning, and a model of resource use. Good designs not only solve problems, they also allow individuals and groups to discover and value more of themselves, to recognize their abilities and take charge of their lives.

The Merleau-Pontean approach to social change thus aims at enhancing people's acumen and talent for using uncertainty creatively and for turning obstacles into opportunities. Since a definite future is assumed to be unknowable, taking risks is viewed as unavoidable. Rather than waiting for complete knowledge to be available to serve as a basis for action, the Merleau-Pontean begins by initiating a self-developmental process. Doing is viewed as an exercise of practical intelligence rather than an execution divorced from reasoning. The conceptual process of planning is integrated with practical experiments of action. This emphasis on learning thus builds on a classical conception of democracy in assuming, as John Stuart Mill put it, that participatory government is both strong and good because it produces "active self-helping" citizens (Mill 1958; see Delli Priscoli 1982; Friedmann 1973; Hampden-Turner 1971; and Thucydides 1951).

In the imagined world, programs for social or economic development are carried out with vigor and on an optimum schedule. In the experienced world, slippages and shortfalls abound. It is impossible to identify with precision the extent to which one or another element of the program may lag. Perhaps the completion of the steel mill will be delayed, perhaps staff training will fall behind. Rationalistic systems and purely deductive models fail to provide guidance when shortfalls occur. Attempts to suppress unforeseen events through deterministic planning tend to increase the perception of chaos rather than insure order.

By contrast, a key point in the Merleau-Pontean approach is that "things" such as factories, health centers, roads, office buildings, or public spaces, will help create and express the meaning of any given place. Thus ordinary features of the firm or community are to be used to encourage a pattern of life that elicits the participation of members in making their actions significant and productive. In this way, also, a reservoir of talent is created for coping with unforeseen events. Moreover, when inevitable shortfalls occur, instead of passively blaming elites, people take responsibility for remedial action.

Reformulating Means and Ends

A purely technicist or positivist approach focuses on means and ignores ends. A purely utopian or romantic approach focuses on ends and ignores means. By contrast, the Merleau-Pontean sees this very distinction as arbitrary and at best heuristic. Thus "goals, like sub-goals, can usually be regarded as *means* toward achieving other goals existing at a higher level of generality" (Boguslaw 1965, 76). To pursue such a deconstructivist logic evokes value considerations that the means-ends rationality of positive science and planning is incapable of addressing. Its only recourse, therefore, is to confine its application to heuristic or piecemeal programming where the statements of goals can be presented without challenge or ambiguity. Such an approach in effect reduces ends to means since both may be calculated by the same arithmetic—the felicitous calculus of utilitarian economics. Indeed, positive planning, systems analysis, and management presuppose comparability of means and of ends. Comparability of means is made possible by the concept of efficiency. Comparability of ends is made possible by the concept of benefits. Both are subsumed under a concept of utility in which both means and ends can be calculated. As I have discussed elsewhere (1987, 64–79), this entire formulation is ideological insofar as it presumes the universality of a historically specific market economy. Such an economy transforms the world into one of commodities that can be priced, compared, and exchanged through the cash nexus, thereby enabling the comparability of both means and ends independently of any consideration of "extra-rational" or "noncognitive" concerns such as honor, loyalty, ethics, or tradition.

The collective moral and cultural life, however, are presupposed by a utilitarian market system but not calculable within it (Bell and Kristol 1971, 56). Suppose, for example,

> that the use of electro-convulsive or chemo-therapy could be shown to relieve depression: we might still legitimately reject such techniques on other grounds, such as the absence of self-reflective engagement by the person treated, the power relations involved in the therapist-patient relationship, and so on. It is entirely mistaken to claim, as some advocates of these techniques seem to, that the objections on these grounds merely counterpose "value-judgements" to "effective practice." For effectiveness cannot be specified independently of values, and the character of a therapeutic technique, as well as the goal to which it is said to contribute, must be subject to normative evaluation. (Keat 1981)

The view that goals or ends are guiding principles for planning also has been challenged in the literature on organization theory itself. Thompson and McEwen (1958) argued that organizational purposes are continually redefined and renegotiated and therefore can not serve as an a priori criterion of control. Other studies showed that the actual outcomes of organizational or planning efforts regularly do not correspond to their purported purposes or ends (Zald 1970, 1965; Etzioni 1965, 126–127). This led to a distinction between "official" and "operative" goals of plans or organizations. The former were seen as mere front work for the organization, whereas the latter were viewed as the actual or real purposes at work. The operative goals were sought either in the outcomes of the implementations of the plans or in the motives of the planners. Yet both these efforts to preserve a rational and purposive view of planning proved to be circular and redundant. In the first case, identification of goals with outcomes added no new information. Indeed, if the actual goal is "derived or extrapolated from the organizational patterns" (Etzioni 1965, 136), then it comes into existence *after* the patterns which it purports to explain (Warriner 1980, 13) and therefore cannot be a cause or explanation of them. In the second case, the search for purposes or ends in the motives of the actors themselves turned out to have the same character as the official goals that had earlier been rejected: They also were reflections of what audiences were thought to accept and approve rather than explanations of action (Burke 1984; Mills 1959; Gerth and Mills 1953, 114–124). Statements of ends are not statements of prior causes of behavior but post hoc means for "dissonance reduction" (Weick 1969).

The segregation of means and ends typical of conventional approaches to planning also suffers from the logical and moral difficulties of utilitarianism more generally. Our values, goals, or ends usually are not the hard calculable data that are required by the utilitarian model. Instead, ends are characterized by logical complexity, errancy of desires, multiple levels of stakes in game play, uncertainty inherent in social reality, disjunctions between immediate consequences and justification of ends, and the like. But the utilitarian model holds that given our aims, and given the facts that determine which aims are attainable at what costs, the morally correct answer follows. But of course our aims are rarely simply given. Not only are they shaped by culture and tradition, but increasingly we have direct control over them.[3] As examples, psychoanalysis on the individual level and mass advertising on the collective level both instrumentally manipulate desires, motives, and ends. More broadly, socialization forms certain kinds of people who have certain kinds of desires and satisfactions. It is the socialization (the means) that determines which kinds of people (the ends) come into being. This is exactly the opposite of what is assumed in the utilitarian viewpoint of conventional planning and management (Gellner 1974, 99).

The Merleau-Pontean planner recognizes that the reduction of ends into means and the elevation of means into ends is a rhetorical and political process. She thus seeks to return control of this process to ordinary citizens by cultivating awareness and responsibility for such transformations. As this ideal is realized, the dividing line between citizen and expert becomes amorphous, as does the positivist dichotomy of means and ends. In purely instrumental rationality, the choice of ends and means divides in practice into two stages involving an appropriate division of labor between corporate paymasters or political patrons on the one hand, and technical analysts or planners on the other. The former are seen as setting the ends, while the latter are thought of as preparing cost-effective means to achieve them. Such an approach is highly unsuited to policy analysis as mutual learning. First, workers and citizens are removed entirely from the planning process. Second, an unwillingness to consider a change in goals and objectives renders most learning experiences superficial, in that the distinction between the ends and means of action, though conceptually arbitrary, functions to control awareness and limit understanding (Huxley 1937). An emancipatory approach would recognize that means, no less than ends, have normative implications. Mutual learning involves a reorientation of action and a reshaping of goals. Given such a process, the planner, executive, or community leader ceases to be seen as a bias free analyst of optimal courses of action. Instead, she becomes a key actor in an interorganizational process that is essentially political and rhetorical, in that planning becomes discourse intended to persuade.

Ultimate Perfection versus Excellence by Stages

The positivist approach expresses an inability to conceive of ordinary actors as capable of shaping their own history; it reflects the assumption that the future—an ultimate perfection once it has been built—is already possessed in the minds of the planners. Most programs for social change take this view. They depict conditions at the end of a horizon. Although lip service is given to the implementation process, the technical effort and the allocation of resources generally are based on the target date of the plan. Executives, politicians, and planners tend to promote the ultimate product while giving little attention to the intervening stages of development or to the patterns of life and values they imply.

In the positivist approach one emphasizes the correction of deficiencies. One begins by assessing the initial situation and then comparing what exists with an ideal hospital, sales effort, or community. The ideal is generated by cataloging all of the desirable features that have been found in experience or imagined by philosophers. This becomes the basis of a list of things to be taken care of. The target in town planning, for example, is conceived of as a finished community that will be achieved in, say, ten years and then remain little changed for some period. But this image is difficult to sustain. Typically the initial enthusiasm is soon depleted and it becomes necessary to restimulate interest in continued development. This in turn results in higher costs while yielding less mastery and fulfillment.

One example of such an approach is the model town (Heraud

1968). In the United States, the social and recreational facilities of model towns typically are built in scale and kind far in excess of what is available in an urban community of comparable size. Building ideal facilities is part of a strategy for attracting and retaining home buyers to these sites. It generally turns out, however, that the investment in such facilities is not sufficient to animate community life. In fact, the existence of preplanned facilities may act as a *dis*incentive to individual and group initiative. Social change based on a predetermined image leads to the building of programs or facilities for hypothetical general uses and not for the specific activities a specific community might want. The former approach is plausible when the goal is to satisfy everyone in general; but what is acceptable to everyone usually is compelling to no one. As a resident of Columbia, Maryland, told me, "Around here James Rouse [the model town designer] is the only person who has any fun."

By contrast, the Merleau-Pontean seeks excellence by stages, since this fosters mutual learning and allows many projects to be initiated by members of a group without excluding members who enter the group later on. Optimally, this permits each person to invest some of herself in successively refined efforts. Individuals get behind things, influence projects, try to make a difference. Each improvement is taken as evidence of progress, and every initiative tends to beget additional ideas for enhancement. Small achievements increase the motivation of members to engage in larger and more complex actions as evidence of their power to shape a more distinctive identity. In this view a "division," "program," or "community" exists at all stages of development. The social unit has to function appropriately for each particular stage. Perception is thus maintained both of continuing progress and of continuing commitment to the values that informed the project at its inception. Moreover, opportunities remain available for ordinary people to contribute to that progress. "Progress," indeed, becomes not so much an image of the future as an activity in the present.

Excellence by stages is distinguished from Karl Popper's notion of a piecemeal approach to planning in that the latter is technicist, fragmented, and controlled by experts. Because the sociological knowledge necessary for large-scale engineering is simply nonexistent, said Popper, a piecemeal approach is more feasible and moral because it focuses on "the greatest and most urgent evils of society, rather than searching for, and fighting for, its greatest ultimate good." Indeed, Popper insisted that a wholistic or utopian method "simply does not exist: It is impossible" because "it violates the principles of scientific method. [The piecemeal approach is] true . . . while the other is false and liable to lead to mistakes which are both avoidable and grave" (Popper 1972, 69–70).

Popper did not oppose social engineering in principle, nor did he reject the goal of an exhaustive all-knowing science. The essence of such social engineering is not empowerment of citizens but control by experts within the ever-expanding boundaries of positive science. In this view, however, the goals of social engineering, the nature of the evils that it is to correct, and even the belief that reason is up to the task of social reconstruction, have nothing to do with theory, reflection, or reasoned judgment since, for Popper, these originate in the noncognitive realm of interests and action (Dahrendorf 1968, 167).

The positivist formulation of the relation between theory and practice is thus as pretentious as it is modest. It is modest in not wishing to push the technological redesign of society beyond known laws of physical and social motion. It is pretentious, however, in presupposing an ultimate utopia of scientific knowledge as a possible basis for expert social engineering. Popper and Lenin turn out to be brothers under the skin. Their main difference is that Lenin believed that a science of society—Marxism—was already available as a basis for scientific social engineering. Yet Popper and Lenin both held that positive science is the only possible basis for societal guidance and that this conception of rationality and planning is the sole legitimate one. In the ultimate rationalistic utopia, the advancement of positive science would eliminate the need for the piecemeal approach. Indeed, such omniscience would exclude the necessity for planning, management, and decision making entirely. If God knows everything that will occur, he confronts no as yet unmade decisions but has a comprehensive all-encompassing will. Unpredictability and risk invade our project, however, to the precise extent that we differ from God. The positivist project to eliminate unpredictability from the social world thus suggests the celestial pretentions that inform their approach (MacIntyre 1981, 92).

Within the range of available knowledge, positivist planning practice seeks to base itself on analyses of established situations. It thus becomes "a search for an exhaustive inventory of 'ultimate' truths or an insistence upon ultimate truths as the only basis for action. Actions are defended, not with reference to present reality, but in terms of the fiction called 'ultimate truth' " (Boguslaw 1982, 30). Since such truths are few and elusive, life continues to proceed without them. By contrast, excellence by stages might be exemplified by a more wholistic, localized, "bottom-up," inductive approach in which the rationality of planning is part of the process of implementation itself. For example, in parts of the Third World today, shantytowns are characterized by progressive development, by which families build their housing and their community in stages as their resources permit, the more important elements first. The procedures followed by these self-selecting occupant-builder communities, free to act in accordance with their own needs, enable them to synchronize investment in buildings and community facilities with the rhythm of social and economic change. (Turner 1970, 1)

Merleau-Pontean planning does not insist on optional solutions based on expert knowledge. Instead it accepts that the specificity of plans is inversely related to their plausability (Gellner 1975, 73–74). Goals and objectives that are stated in a general, open-ended, unspecified manner are more plausible than those that are precisely and exactly specified. Specific procedures and outcomes are self-defeating if used as criteria of success of the plan since such procedures and outcomes are negotiated and transformed through attempts to implement the initial goals of the plan itself. Hence, the Merleau-Pontean planner sets the inquiry and bargaining in motion with the expectation of continuously developing insights, shifting interests, and emergent consensus. Such an approach is dialectic. As Heraclitus said, "That which is in opposition is in concert. . . . Harmony consists of opposing tension, like that of the bow and lyre" (1954).

Making Decisions versus Negotiating Frameworks

Frameworks define the rules of any interaction, but their existence does not normally become apparent until the framework is contested. An example of this in art is Dada. Only when you are handed a teacup lined with fur on the *inside* do you become aware that "teacupness" is embedded in a framework that includes a number of activities of which the "teacup itself" is but one expression. It is only in terms of its framework that the object or action makes sense. Frameworks thus are sets of rules, usually tacit, as to what is to be considered relevant or irrelevant. For example, it is irrelevant to checkers whether players use old bottle tops on a piece of squared linoleum or gold figurines on inlaid marble. In both cases the pairs of players can start with the same positions, employ the same sequence of strategic moves and countermoves, and generate the same contour of excitement (Goffman 1974).

In settings in which there is wide agreement as to what kind of game is being played and what are its rules, players will focus on strategies for optimizing the use of resources within the given frame.

But to the extent that there is lack of such agreement, players will focus on the negotiation of the definition of the framework, the rules of the game. Indeed, even in normal settings—that is, ones with wide agreement as to the obtaining framework—hipsters, politicos, social dadaists, sewer freaks, and reality brokers of all sorts are aware that to work a situation one must subtly control its definition. If we can get football players to believe the framework is croquet, then (as croquet experts), we innocently give away points without risk of losing what is now our game. An example of such reframing is provided by Mayo (1945), who presented workers' "attributing ills to a hostile world" as a symptom of their pathological obsessions, and then recommended a therapeutic style of management to help them overcome these "disorders."

An emancipatory discourse for planning would not eliminate such political/linguistic struggles, but it would enable citizens to metacommunicate *about* them rather than be manipulated *by* them. These frameworks of meaning generally are built up through subtle cues and clues by which, for example, the job interviewer is made to understand that it is *you* who really are interviewing the company rather than the company interviewing you, or that your army is on a peacekeeping mission rather than taking sides in a civil war. By such renegotiations of framework, Negro becomes black, local racism becomes states' rights, or the War Department becomes the Department of Defense.

Because the present era is characterized by a radical relativization of frameworks, a main job of societal guidance is not to make decisions within such frameworks, but to help design and negotiate the frameworks of meaning themselves. Both positivist and romantic approaches to planning and communication inhibit such negotiations. One-eyed positivism is blind to such problems and possibilities because it assumes that rationality is independent of contexts and cultures. One-eyed romanticism sees every culture as being unique and incommensurable. For one there are only brute data, for the other there are purely hermetic meanings. Yet most of the crises that afflict us cannot be resolved, or even addressed, from within the perspective of a single framework. Pollution, nuclear threats, resource scarcities, recessions, and the like all are interdisciplinary, intercultural, international issues.

Just as the redefinition of frameworks can foster identities for people, movements, and organizations, the failure to modify or at least to review them can lead to the over-planned entropy of a closed system in decline. In business firms, for example, conscious decisions usually represent a choice between options within the frame of "profitability." By contrast, reflection on the frame itself may yield a sensitivity to an alternative range of considerations, say survivability instead of profitability. In this alternative emergent framework the key question would not be "How do we price our widgets?," but "What business should we be in?" As Thomas Watson of IBM said, "The firm began its great period of growth when we understood that our business was not business machines, but information."

One curious aspect of the negotiation of frameworks is that this process often escapes managerial control or even awareness. Put conversely, the few persons who "decide" what the "goals" of the enterprise should be next year are less important than the many persons who determine what is *known by* the company today and, hence, what options will be perceived as available. In sum, the ostensive rationality of elites as they make decisions is assured only by the apparent a-rationality of nonelites as they negotiate the frameworks of such decisions.

Cybernetic theory can itself be used to reveal the limits of cybernetic systems. According to Ashby's law of requisite variety, when a control system insulates an organization from the diversity in its environment, the internal structure of that organization may deteriorate as it loses its complexity and other properties as an open system. "Only variety in the control mechanism can deal successfully with variety in the system controlled" (Beer 1959, 50). "If a system fails to maintain an adequate degree of variety in its internal system, then it becomes impossible to cope with the range of information to which it is exposed, and to develop the strategies necessary for effective response to environmental change" (Morgan 1982, 524). The logic of cybernetic systems theory, if pushed far enough, ironically becomes an implicit recommendation for radically decentralized democratic self-governance, since this ideally would be a control system as complex and various as the "environment" of advanced societies today.

Planning and Politics

Positivists strictly distinguish planning from politics. The decision-maker, systems designer, or social planner is supposed to stand outside the problem on which he works. This extra-systemic planner has agency, but none of the members within the system do. Once the goals of the system have been set—by the politician, the client, or the designer himself—the value-free experts can proceed. Thus subjectivity and objectivity are allocated into discrete compartments—subjectivity is granted to a godlike systems designer, managerial elite or, ultimately, the electorate, whereas the system itself is seen as objective. In liberal reformist versions of rationalistic planning, some subjectivity is given to the individuals who ambulate within the system, and there is the possibility of feedback for redirection or even redesign by the techno-administrative elite that takes into account this new information. However, even this liberal approach to planning obscures the ongoing rationality and creativity of members within the system. Citizens are seen as atomized individuals who can make decisions only within a pregiven framework of rules and constraints to which their decisions contribute nothing. "Statistical decision theory, for instance, assumes that the deciding individual's order of preference is already established and that values are already comparable" (Diesing 1962, 242).

The separation of planning from politics is conceptually arbitrary and empirically incorrect. Instead, planning itself is highly political. Moreover, orthodox planning legitimates a privileged role for experts and their elite clients, and hence is inherently antiegalitarian in method and content. A Merleau-Pontean method of planning would be part of a new kind of politics, a politics of civic prudence that would replace the politics of technical expertise. In this new politics, the role of the planner would be that of wise counselor rather than technical expert (Kettler 1970; Stanley 1978).

As noted in the previous section, the heart of planning as politics is the planners' capacity to shape the framework of public discourse by defining the agenda of issues and the range of reasonable responses to them. Is crime to be considered a problem and, if so, is the solution to be found in increased police protection or decreased unemployment? What are the trade-offs between building more jails, reducing plea bargaining, instituting a guaranteed annual income, or creating full employment? And what are the subsidiary consequences of such alternatives? Would an increase in the minimum wage ultimately create more unemployment and hence increase poverty and then crime? And who but experts in the policy sciences could even begin to understand and discuss such interconnections and render them decisionable by lay citizens? Hence, as issues become more complex and discussed more in technical language, planners and policy experts become key actors in shaping public discourse and decision making.

But this does not mean that an educated public must be left out of the processes of formulating issues and making decisions. On the contrary, practicing planners and analysts know that even highly complex decisions "are made by officials with little technical knowledge of the situation at hand. When information is requested to make the issues intelligible to the power elite, the pertinent information is condensed and presented in a straightforward manner which the public could understand" (Brulle 1984, 24). The key question, then, is not whether planning is political, but what kind of politics and whose political agenda it will serve.

Defenders of positivist planning also assume that what they do is effective. In fact, few government and even private sector plans actually work, at least for the purposes or reasons for which they were conceived and justified. For example, Light and his colleagues (Light, Mosteller, and Winokur 1972, 67) studied some thirty social programs that had been implemented with great care according to a rigorous experimental design. They found that only about 15 percent seemed to do what they were supposed to do. And even if stated goals are matched by measurable program outputs, it is generally impossible to know whether these outputs have anything to do with the overall purposes of the program. For example, the stated goal of providing incentives to firms might increase retraining of workers, but it is usually impossible to measure the impact of such program outputs on broader purposes such as the reduction of overall rates of unemployment.[4] In light of findings such as these, delays that would be entailed through broader public discussion of policy directions and methods are unlikely to adversely affect outcomes. Instead, "a course of action arrived at in open discourse will be more legitimate and more rational. Thus agency performance may actually increase" (Brulle 1984, 25).

A Merleau-Pontean approach thus would not damn the political currents in planning. Instead it would widen and even reverse their flow. More persons and constituencies would be involved in the planning process and, instead of focusing mainly on the humanization of planners and technicians, the focus would be on the enlightenment and empowerment of citizens. Consider, for example, the political role of population projections by planners and demographers concerned with land use and zoning. A high demographic projection will satisfy groups that have a stake in higher growth—developers, investors, and merchants. A low number will please conservationists, traditionalists, and patricians. Since statistical projections involve much practical judgment—there is a wide space for nontechnical political negotiation over numbers.[5]

The Merleau-Pontean does not wish to turn citizens into statisticians nor planners into politicians. But she would seek to empower citizens to see how political issues are embedded in technical discourse and the reverse, and to address each at the appropriate level. By contrast, technicist discourse, partly because it can do certain things so well, easily expands to include more and more social life and experience. It thereby leads us to ignore history and traditions, to turn political and moral questions into technical or instrumental ones, and to treat every "problem" as though it had a "solution" (Rapoport 1964, 30). To discuss the value of high or low growth by negotiating statistical projections, for example, easily become a technicist mystification that excludes lay participation and fosters civic incompetence. The costs for whatever limited consensus that is thereby achieved are paid for by those who are excluded from it.

How can a critique of such pretentions stop short of a total rejection of the very ideal of applied science? One way to avoid rejecting science in the name of emancipation would be to interpret science itself as part of the history of human freedom. Indeed, this equation of knowledge and human liberty has been taken for granted by most thinkers since the Enlightenment. As scientific rationality took the form of *social* technologies, however, and as man became the object of instrumental manipulation, the role of scientific rationality in enhancing freedom came more and more into doubt. To preserve science and technology as well as freedom and dignity, then, requires that we reformulate science and technology to include moral agency and praxis, and that we expand our conceptions of freedom and dignity to include civic competence and communal empowerment.

Of course, reform of administrative procedures or planning methods cannot by themselves bring on an emancipatory society. The success of this project depends on the development of social movements that can successfully press their demands for participation in the governance of society. Moreover, such social movements themselves would have to foster a critical and open discourse in order to avoid the mere reproduction of democratic elitism and interest group politics under the rubric of enhanced "participation." With all this, the transformation of planning into an emancipatory discourse—in administrative agencies, in corporations, and in social movements—is a key requirement in the realization of an emancipatory society (Brulle 1984, 4).

Such a discourse would go beyond conservative and libertarian rejections of societal guidance as well as liberal and technicist exhortations to "use" science for human good (Boguslaw 1965; Gross 1980; Schick 1970). An emancipatory planning discourse would provide a methodological consciousness whose structure is a contemporary version of the classical and Renaissance effort to bridge what are now thought of as the sciences and the humanities, the realm of facts and laws and the realm of purposes and meanings. It would invoke the Renaissance conception of science, art, and politics as *poesis*, as a making of the world through language.

In this vision, the planner or civic leader is more like a sage and artist than an expert. The sage is one whose personal life shows integration, whereas the artist is one whose artifacts display integration. The degenerate forms of these ways of being and making are seen in the sage who plays God and the artist who produces schlock. The social scientist-cum-planner ideally stands between the sage and the artist. She is a person who embodies life-wisdom and crafts practical theories. But the technocratic social scientist of today both plays God *and* makes schlock. "If theorists would presume less about the technocratic translatability of their ideas and would apply to pragmatist activity the criteria of prudential wisdom, then perhaps the pragmatists would show greater receptivity to genuine intellectual wisdom on the part of thinkers" (Stanley 1978, 244). Such a methodological consciousness is desirable, if somewhat luxurious, for practitioners of the natural sciences. It is a necessity for sophistication in the social sciences. And it is morally imperative for those who shape social plans and decisions in the name of other people's interests.

Fantasy and Rationality

In the view of both positivists and romantics, objective reality was defined by reason, and symbols were seen as creations of fancy. Yet through all this, thinkers such as Durkheim, Boas, and others recognized that the most fundamental cultural forms, the collective representations, are not products of isolated reflective intelligence but are born out of intense communal effervescence. Collective representations derive their compelling power from the sense of the sacred they elicit. They are the basic forms or categories of human experience and it is only through their discipline that rational thought becomes possible. In light of these ideas we may speak meaningfully of "symbolic realism" and "rational fantasies." Shared symbols are not mere frills or imperfections in our scientific understanding. Instead, they are the very stuff of human consciousness and being. As constitutive of human experience, symbols are *real* in the fullest sense of the word. From this viewpoint reason and fantasy are not opposites but brothers under the skin: Both are real in the symbolic sense; both are social in that they are expressed and validated intersubjectively; both can properly be modes for social adaptation or revolution.

From this perspective, the notion of "theory" being checked out by "data" also falls away, and the advice to construct more and better plans appears misleading. It is wasteful to spend time trying to anticipate all future contingencies, not only because one can never know how things will turn out, but also because the "future" can be shaped by those who enact it. The great value of "future planning" therefore lies not in its power to preempt the future, but to reveal to us our *current* situations. By generating a "scenario" planners create a utopian (or dystopian) reality—an imagined world, a *u*-top-ia, in no place, at no time, a negative space in which criticism (or validation) of the present can occur. Planning in this sense can purge the present of its bad faith by judging it against an "alternative future." But to the extent that such alternative futures are presumed to be inevitable or scientifically derived, instead of purifying the present they sanctify it, enshrining present actions in trend extrapolations.

All of us carry within us images of many things, such as our immediate setting, the place where we live or work, the town in which we grew up. Such images are different for different persons depending on their social location, interests, and intentions. The image of the town for the person who drives will stress highways and parking lots; the paraplegic's image will stress elevators and access ramps. Strictly speaking, there is no ultimately correct image because images are not merely copies of things. Instead, they are representations that serve some cognitive or practical purpose. Thus, rather than speaking of images as correct or true, it makes more sense to speak of them as more or less helpful in relation to some range of concerns. In these terms, truth becomes a quality of those images that respond to the broadest, most universal settings or interests (Perelman and Olbrechts-Tyteca 1969). In these terms, also, social planning involves the construction of broadly shared images that can lead to more effective and inclusive forms of policy, organization, and action. Planning depends on the creation of fruitful images that are inherently fictive since they specify actions or conditions that do not yet (and may never) exist. Yet such fictive images are logically necessary for the self-direction of any person, society, or cybernetic system (Buckley 1967; Young and Massey n.d., 17).

In this sense planning is a disciplined use of the imagination. It is a way of dreaming with reason. Construed as an oneiric practice, the self-understanding of planning cannot be a positivist philosophy of science but rather a critical depth hermeneutic. A properly reflexive discourse for social planning would see it as akin to psychoanalysis in that both can be understood as practical self-transformations through the creative use of language, the converting of the object (the patient) into the agent (the self-directing personality). Contrary to scientistic conceptions of planning and psychoanalysis, we can view both practices as the acquisition of discursive skills with which persons and peoples author a new self or society. Whereas psychoanalysis offers present cogency as succor for fears from the past, planning does this for fears of the future. Positivist planning goes much further: The future with its irrationalities is preempted, made predictable, and thereby abolished. Indeed, in positivist planning there is no future, only a projected present that has not yet occurred. Conceived as rational dreamwork, however, planning is a language game that can enhance the awareness and self-direction of contemporary agents in their current situations through images of what has not yet come to pass.

Like psychoanalysis, social planning also operates as a kind of narrative discourse, a way of imagining and bringing into being a possible future self. Social planners use descriptions of the past and images of the future to construct a narrative beginning, middle, and end. The planners and their planning are constitued as the beginning, for in the beginning was the Word, and the planners, in the name of their clients, are the ones who announce it. The middle of the narrative takes place in what usually is called the future; this constitutes the duration of the plan. The end arrives when the plan has been fully executed or, more likely, abandoned.

If politics is the art of the possible, planning is the art of the imaginable. It represents as empirically existing what is known to not actually exist. These two arts are interdependent, since the possible is known only in terms of the imaginable; and since a utopia, though fictive, is imagined as empirically possible. An emancipatory use of planning would recognize these ideological and utopian functions. Trial and error, the poor man's form of experimentation, presumes that there is a right answer out there and that our trial missed it. But with plans, images of the future, and simulations, we together can make sense out of, indeed build, a reality by first imagining it and then discovering through civic discourse whether it works. It was for this that Vico recommended rhetoric, which "throughout deals with the audience to which it is addressed." The competent rhetor/planner knows that for truths to have consequences they require a consensus prudently attained. This is the "semblance" of truth in the *sensus communis* of citizens participating in public discussion (Habermas 1974, 44).

As a mode of societal change, fantasy operates in at least three ways: (1) as a form of creating meaning that is directly appreciated in its own right; (2) as a kind of magical trial through which social arrangements must pass before becoming widely adopted; and (3) as a means of ordering and legitimizing a society's ultimate concerns.

1. Fantasy and myth, and their expression in ritual and cult, are the

social equivalents of Freud's alienated inner kingdom: To repossess it is to come home to oneself. Such revolutionary homecomings are an ecstatic destruction of barriers as well as a participatory creation of collective meaning through fantasy and myth (for examples see Hobsbawn 1959; Lyman and Scott 1970; Zolberg 1972). This value of fantasy to an organization or movement can be seen through the negative example of members who are indifferent to having their goals realized. Apparently the achievement of the "goals" would destroy the reason for the members to continue an organizing process that is itself their source of orientation. Thus rehabilitated drug users may "mess up" just before being released in order, apparently, to return to the halfway house. Organizations and social movements also may mess up at the moment their ostensive goals are being realized. Workers appear to do something similar to avoid filling management's quotas; even though messing up may deprive them of bonuses, it also preserves the game that may be their chief source of meaning at the work site. Similarly, suffering can function to cement group solidarity, even to a point that members may regret the loss of their oppression. Indeed, this group feeling may be preferable to the state of despair, or absence of feeling, that might be left in the wake of achieving "realistic" bonuses, trivial social reforms, or other minor gains.

In the industrial world fantasy generally has a bad press, perhaps because it is one means of resisting the totalizing potential of instrumental reason. But is it possible that the very form of thought characteristic of an alienated situation could be transformed into a mode of change and liberation? Put another way, can a mythic structure of affectivity and community be combined with a rational structure of moral responsibility and, can these together be made to replace the amoral and unloving isolation of instrumental reason? Such questions present a terra incognita to social thinkers. Yet some preliminary explorations suggest that "irrationality" at the level of affectivity and community "instead of undermining the rational structures of responsibility, may in fact preserve and expand our capacity to sustain them" (Kavolis 1974a, 118).[6]

Even if such a mode of being in the world is possible, what chances has it of gaining currency? In the early industrial era fantasy was associated with artists, women, and the lower orders, whereas rationality was the preserve of the white male bourgeoisie. But if fantasy is characteristic of people who are not interested in or have little to gain from bourgeois rationality, in postmodern societies such lack of interest is likely to grow (Heilbroner 1975). Processes of organizing, formerly thought of as instrumental, increasingly may be engaged in for their affective and communal rewards. Planning and action for change might be engaged in not to get things changed, but mainly to experience a sense of group cohesion.

2. Also, in a pragmatic sense, cultic fantasy represents a kind of magical trial in which new roles and arrangements may become validated before gaining wider acceptance. The secrecy surrounding group marriages and ritual orgies of swingers, for example, was used to recruit as well as to exclude, and served as a first step in normalizing new conjugal practices. In a Sorelian sense, occult beliefs may be necessary to engender and renew the dissonance from everyday reality upon which the drama of conversion depends. And such dissident organizations, in the very process of creating their innovations by scorning convention, may gather sufficient public exposure and hence membership to demonstrate and legitimize their alternative arrangements.

Fantasy can be the source of new identities as well as new social practices, and it is a form of planning in which anyone can engage. Even in ordinary daydreaming, though the specific vision is experienced individually, the dreamer still finds himself immersed in a commonly shared culture. Fantasies generally are more institutionalized, however, as for example in the American male's dream of flying off with the girl in the airline ads or, more broadly, as in the American Dream itself. In the United States these myths are fairly public, though their mythic quality is rarely acknowledged. In many tribes the dreamer must keep the contents of his vision secret; in still others he may seek advice on how to interpret it (von Grunebaum and Caillois 1966). As Anselm Strauss (1964, 68–69) told us.

> The interpretation of the vision, in some measure at least, affects the future action of the man as a member of the tribe. It may yield him a mandate or a command to act in a generalized way, and it may give or confirm a sense of identity. . . . Viewed in this way, the range of covert processes—variously denoted by the terms "reverie," "fancy," "daydreaming," and "fantasy"—are important for the conservation and change of identities.

The point of course is not only that a mythic underlife exists in advanced societies, but that in accepting the positivist denial of its relevance we abandon care and control of it, and leave the way open to the manipulation of our fantasy lives by persons and groups whose intentions are alien to our own. The Merleau-Pontean planner wishes not to capture the imaginations of constituents or clients, but to help them recapture their imaginations for themselves.

3. At a fundamental level, fantasy and myth are the symbolization of an organization's or society's ultimate concerns. Man's response to values in prehistory was a form of idolatry; his appreciation of the goodness or power of a thing involved that thing's being sacred. This is no less true of such ultimate concepts as efficiency, profit, dignity, or freedom today. These ideas do not take their power from reason or utility, nor from the negation of privation. Unless they preserve the significance rooted in their mythic origins, they become not only trivial but untrue (Horkheimer 1974, 36).

Foundational myths cannot be validated by science because they refer to the nature of Being upon which any science might be built. Thus, faith in the myths is not an act of knowing that has a low degree of evidence. If this is meant, one is speaking of belief rather than faith. Faith is the state of ultimate commitment. This involves respecting the mythic element of our truths, and trusting the truths of our myths. For these reasons, while they can never be justified or calculated into a rational social plan, such foundational myths are presupposed in the expectation of efficacy of any effort at societal direction. By explicitly acknowledging this, we begin to elevate our naive beliefs to the level of faith. To fully do this requires us to bring two features explicitly to consciousness: the "as if" character of our myths, and the existential character of our relation to them. The first feature involves an appreciation of others who do not share our own foundational assumptions; the second calls for an adherence to the ethical requirements of our own commitments.

In their conception of who they are and what they might become, all peoples must deal with certain basic issues. Among them is the status of human as a moral agent, of the polity as legitimate, and of the relation between person and polity within some broader conception of Being. Planning can never respond to these foundational issues if it operates solely at a rationalistic level. But planning can also function as myth. As Albert Hirschman (1967, 13; see Goulet 1973, 31–37) noted in response to the criticisms by rationalist economists of Third World development plans, these plans do not need to be accurate to be effective. We systematically underestimate our own creativity, said Hirschman, but such plans tend correspondingly to underestimate the difficulties to be faced. Thus their explicit errors tend to cancel out their implicit ones. The overstatement of the goals, and the process of national planning itself, are a collective mythmaking through which members of a society can create an ideal image of themselves and mobilize their energies for tasks that otherwise they would not dare tackle. A narrowly rationalist plan would not have this power. In a similar fashion, more general models of social development (Marxism, for example), even where they are no longer compelling as hypotheses for a science of history, can still be important as moral constructs, as a telos to guide intelligent public choice. By establishing alternative contexts of mythical interpretation, they infuse our present situations with an eschatological light that reveals their moral implications. Such myths about the nature of history or society serve a policy function as scenarios of hope and articulations of value, as means for judging, and thence for accepting or transforming, the intolerable scarcities in the actual world of the present.

Extending this point we might say that social planning represents two kinds of truth—the Aristotelian concept of "speaking the truth," or the truth of propositions, as contrasted to truth as an authentic response to reality, a "being in truth" (Wolff 1970, 45–46). The first refers to hypotheses advanced within some disciplinary framework; it is a truth of discourse. The second is mainly an act, a feature of existence; it involves "witnessing" not in the sense of being an uninvolved observer, but in the sense of bearing witness, of being a representative *for* a truth rather than merely re-presenting it.

In this existential or mythic sense of truth, social planning (like social science itself) can be on the side either of piety or of profanation, of order or of renovation. It can sanctify the conventional by formalizing it into occult scientistic language, or it can demystify the sacrosanct by dialectically exposing its contradictions. In opening the sacred to scrutiny, social analysis at once profanes and purifies it. The being in truth of social thought is less a destruction of idols than a revelation of the sacred.

To cope with the falling apart of the world we do not need better techniques or more rationalistic plans. The fragmentation of our experience will not be rectified by fiats or policies, no matter how authorative or energetic their source. Part of the story is always the intrinsic logic and exhistential adequacy of our foundational myths as revealed in the consequences of the plans and policies to which they lead. I am doubtful that science and technology, much less scientized sociology, though they function as myths, are adequate on this existential level. All this suggests that one criteria for a liberating method of social change is that both rationality *and* fantasy be seen as mutually supportive modes of creating a viable future. Such a future will require far-reaching changes in the structures and processes of social science as well as of institutions that for the most part continue to behave as inflexible automatons programmed to only a thin repertoire of actions.

Thus to the empirical meaning of representation must be added the existential mythic meaning, in which planning seeks to make society the representative of a transcendent social truth. The planner, citizen, or leader is an existential representative of an ideal society insofar as she facilitates its articulation through Peitho, through public persuasion (Voegelin 1952, 75). To the extent that the social thinker, planner, or civic leader can become a sage and artist and not merely an expert or technician, the theories and plans through which she manifests her inner experience and social vision become the witness of a new social order. Of course this seems utopian, even foolish. But so did the abolition of slavery or the creation of democracy some centuries ago. An emancipatory discourse for societal self-direction requires such mythic or utopian thought and compels us to join voices with the French students of May 1968: *"Soyons réalistes, demandons l'impossible!"* So let us be realists, and ask for the impossible.

NOTES

Chapter One

1. My use of the term "rhetoric" shifts in accordance with the two-fold conversion process of the book as a whole: first, to humanize social science discourse, then to suggest the deployment of this newly liberated discourse for a reconstituted civic practice. As discussed in *Society as Text* (1987), the term "rhetoric" is itself used rhetorically. Positivists use the term as "mere rhetoric," a device of persuasion and the opposite of fact, logic, or truth. As my treatise develops, this meaning is decentered and "rhetoric" becomes the means by which facts, logic, and truth are themselves created. Finally, I construe *"critical* rhetoric" to be a self-reflective public discourse, with nuances variously of a preachment that reveals its own partisanship, an articulation of the "pre-rational" linguisticality of all truth claims, a pluralistic philosophy of reflective *différance,* and a concerned practice of responsible civic life.

Chapter Two

1. The labels positivism and romanticism are excessively broad and summary, but I have not found better appellations to capture succinctly the main tendencies of modern Western culture. Each of these two terms covers a set of viewpoints whose resemblances distinguish them from their opposites. Of course one could either elaborate the fine distinctions or elide the gross ones. But the first strategy would create a redundant exegesis whereas the second would decontextualize and dehistoricize the rest of the book. Hence I have retained this distinction between positivism and romanticism even while recognizing its limits. Conflicts between these two broad positions are very much alive today, although they may be differently expressed, as in Gidden's objectivism versus subjectivism, Bernstein's objectivism and relativism, Habermas's empiricism and subjective hermeneutics, or Manfred Stanley's survival versus dignity.

2. I am not here assuming a cultural monolithism but rather certain interrelated trends. Fideism, fundamentalism, and other pre- or antimodern beliefs or practices would be easy to note, particularly outside of France, Scotland, and England. For arguments that rationalistic empiricism was the dominant movement see John Nef (1960), W. Warren Wagar (1977), and

Jacques Ellul (1964). Ellul's book, like Nef's, is not about technology or machines, but *la technique*, the historical development of rationalized organization and methods.

3. See Benjamin Nelson (1967) and Edward C. Grant (1962, 612–116).

4. "Technologies of representation are not, as one might expect, an invention of the social sciences. For example, history demonstrates that fourteenth-century inquisitors used a kind of standardized questionnaire by which they interviewed suspected heretics. In the case of the so-called heresy of the Free Spirit, Grundmann has shown that the questionnaire contained literally those eight errors of 'an abominable sect of malignant men known as beghards and faithless women known as beguines in the Kingdom of Germany' condemned by the Pope at the Council of Vienne in 1311" (Knorr-Cetina 1981, 35–73). Nor was a statistical orientation particular to conservatives or liberal reformers. Marx was a half-century ahead of his time in using survey techniques, and he understood even in 1880 the difficulty in getting at subjective feelings. See Robert Blauner (1960, 339). For the entire questionnaire that Marx used see Tom Bottomore and M. Rubel (1956, 204–212).

5. The practical implications of Skinner's work have been explained by Skinner himself in *Walden Two* (1948). The benign conditioning of *Walden Two* was anticipated in Nicolai G. Chernyshevsky's positivist utopia *What Is to Be Done?* (1863). Dostoevsky parodied this vision so effectively in *Notes from the Underground* (1864) that he remains Chernyshevsky's (and Skinner's) most incisive critic. See Hacker (1955) and Kariel (1967) for more on the positivist-romantic debate within psychology and its political implications.

6. The comparisons and questions here are paraphrased from Manfred Stanley's design (1983) for a concentration in Social Foundations of Public Policy at the Maxwell School of the University of Syracuse. See also Stanley's brilliant landmark work *The Technological Conscience: Survival and Dignity in an Age of Expertise* (1978).

Chapter Three

1. Much of this section is drawn from extensive conversations with Manfred Stanley, as well as from his works (esp. 1978).

2. See Peter Winch's *The Idea of a Social Science and its Relation to Philosophy* (1958) and the even more strongly stated arguments for ideographism in A. R. Louch's *Explanation and Human Action* (1966). For criticisms of this position see Robin Horton's "Professor Winch on Safari" (1976); Percy Cohen's "The Very Idea of a Social Science" (1968); Ernest Gellner's "The New Idealism" (1973); and Alasdair MacIntyre's "The Idea of a Social Science" (1978).

3. Schutz (1970, 114), however, was far from a dogmatist on this point: "We . . . are not only centers of spontaneity . . . but also the mere passive recipients of events beyond our control which occur without our interference. Imposed upon us as relevant are situations and events which are not connected with interests chosen by us, which do not originate in acts of our discretion, and which we have to take just as they are, without any power to

modify them. . . . We do not consider the imposed relevances as being connected with our spontaneously chosen goals. Because they are imposed upon us they remain clarified and rather incomprehensible."

4. In his recent and brilliant *Trying to Make Sense*, Winch addresses many of the issues that I raise here, and develops positions that are often compatible with my own. Unfortunately this work came to my attention only as the present volume was going into press.

Chapter Four

1. For attempts to define "dialectic" besides those cited in my text, see Blau (1964, 12), Friedrichs (1970), Gurvitch (1962), Hall (1967, 385), Hook (1939, 378), Kaufmann (1967, 167), Marcuse (1976), Schneider (1971), and Sorokin (1966, 462–525). Somewhat arbitrarily, I restrict my use of the term to a cognitive or methodological procedure. The meaning of dialectic as willed negation in practice, or the relationships between this praxiological meaning and the cognitive meaning, are vital questions, but ones outside my immediate scope. Similarly, I treat structuralism essentially as a method and, for heuristic reasons, thereby suspend consideration of psychobiological structures or macrosocietal structures such as class.

2. The ways soft definitions of dialectic facilitate reductive attempts at "integration" are illustrated by van den Berghe's (1963) argument that functionalist and dialectical thought both are based on essentially similar assumptions. Equally reductive, but in an empiricist direction, is John Turner's suggestion (1974) that a series of propositions be developed and empirically tested to reconcile the differences between functionalism and dialectic. In a similar spirit Piotr Sztompka (1974) argued that the most adequate conflict model is a subtype of the functional model. A tendentious polemic by André G. Frank (1966) argued just the opposite–that functionalism, when it is not metaphysics, is a subspecies of Marxist dialectic. For an important attempt to assimilate structuralist methods into Marxist dialectical materialism, see Seve 1967. For a major statement on the history, forms, and political uses of dialectic, see McKeon 1954.

3. The concept of structure could be developed more fully, since the term may disguise different operations. As one reviewer asked, for example, "are structures necessary and ineluctable (e.g., such that certain artificial languages could not be learned) or do they constitute only a likely or practical constraint (e.g., such that certain languages are more difficult to learn or less manageable)? Or, put differently, are structures something which operate probabilistically (having an aggregate impact) or do structures operate more deterministically (through every individual element)? As often employed, 'structure' could denote (1) the microstructure underlying face-to-face interaction (e.g., the sort of background which Garfinkel's breaching experiments reveal); (2) macrosocial structure which limits or enhances life chances (e.g., economic class) and cultural norms which prescribe/proscribe behavior; or (3) cognitive structures which constitute, organize, and channel mental/cultural creations. What do the structures operative at these apparently different lev-

els (hierarchies?) have in common, if anything? Does structure in effect refer to the results of a single type of analysis which abstracts out a ground or frame? Or is the commonality between micro, macro, and cognitive structures traceable to a common basis (e.g., the structures of the human brain)? In other words, structure may denote the boundaries of different domains but boundaries which have no necessary relation to one another other than their conceptualization as boundaries. Conversely, is there some common source (mind for instance) or some common operative structuring principle at work here?" For example, Piaget (1970) suggests this latter sort of panstructuralism, as does Harré (1978). Lévi-Strauss's structuralism is of type (3), cognitive structuralism, though he claims for it the status of panstructuralism based on universal properties of the human brain. My focus here is mainly on method of logic. From this viewpoint, all forms of structural thinking must deal with problems of boundaries, genesis, and transformation, and all of them tend to be positivist in their denial of a significant role for human agency and meaning creation in their theories. I am grateful to Robert McAnlay and other reviewers for raising these questions.

4. The relationship between existentialism and phenomenology is much debated, with one's position depending mainly on whether the term "phenomenology" refers to the early Husserl or to the late Husserl as interpreted by Heidegger and Sartre. Some ethnomethodologists, for example, inspired by the early Husserl, can be seen as extreme positivists seeking to take the closest possible look at their data. For them Husserl's dictum "Back to the things themselves!" is taken literally. Other phenomenological sociologists, such as Lyman and Scott (1970), stress the existential side, thereby relinquishing any claim or hope of ultimates, either in theory or data or, presumably, in action. Some writers, such as Gillis (1976, 73–76), sharply distinguish existentialism from phenomenology and argue that Sartre was not a phenomenologist. For our purposes, however, in light of Husserl's late work and its elaboration by Heidegger and Sartre, it is appropriate to consider Sartre an existential phenomenologist. Hence, Lévi-Strauss's reference to "Sartrean phenomenology" is consistent and well grounded.

5. Definition by opposition also has been a basic principle in structural linguistics, at least since Saussure (1965, 162): "Concepts are purely differential. They are not defined positively by their content, but negatively by their relationship with other terms of the system. Their most exact characteristic is to be what others are not."

6. The work of Lévi-Strauss itself provides numerous instances of the use of dialectical opposition to define the boundaries of his central interest. Like anthropologists for decades before him, Lévi-Strauss seeks to understand his own society by studying "primitives." Though a technique of *dépaysement* he becomes a "critic at home" and a "conformist elsewhere." By investigating savage cerebrations he illuminates the deeper structures of *mentalité moderne* (see Brown 1989 [1977], 3, esp. n. 13; Geertz 1967).

7. See Aristotle's *Organum and Topica*. As Piaget stated, "Genesis is simply transition from one structure to another, nothing more; but this transition always leads from a 'weaker' to a 'stronger' structure; it is a 'formative'

transition. Structure is simply a system of transformations, but its roots are operational; it depends, therefore, on a prior formation of the instruments of transformation—transformation rules or laws" (1970, 141). Note, however, that what Piaget calls a "formative" transformation can also be used to describe a "de-genesis" or an elaboration "downward" in which an element is discovered to have its own elements and thus becomes a "system". In logical, if not Piaget's biogenetic, terms, the notions of "stronger" and "weaker" structures may work in either direction. Neither has ontological priority over the other, but only a relatively greater appropriateness for the relevant cognitive (or other) purposes.

For elaboration of some of these points see the special numbers devoted to structuralism of the following journals: "La pensée sauvage et le structuralism," *Esprit* 31 (November 1963):322 (on Lévi-Strauss); "Le structuralisme," *Aletheia* (4 May 1966) (on Althusser); "Problèmes de structuralisme," *Les Temps Modernes* 22 (November 1966):246; and "Structuralisme: Ideologie et méthode," *Esprit* 35 (May 1967):360.

Chapter Five

1. The symbolic realist or tension theory has profound implications for the philosophy of science and for logic of method in the human studies. This theory suggests that both the deductive and the inductive models of scientific explanation be reformulated by the view that formal representations, whether in science or in art, be understood as a metaphoric redescription (or creation) of the domain of the explanandum. See Berggren 1962/1963; Black 1962; Brooks 1965; Brown 1989; Haskell 1987; Hesse 1970; McCloskey 1964; MacCormac 1971; Ricoeur 1972; Schon 1963; Turbayne 1962; and Wheelwright 1968, 1962. For criteria by which to distinguish scientifically fruitful metaphors see Brown, 1989 [1977].

Martin Landau (1972, 100, 92) observed, "Where a metaphor is dominant, it is a very powerful instrument. It structures inquiry, establishes relevance, and provides an interpretive system. . . . A change in image is a change in method."

2. Classical speculation on permanence and change may be divided into four aspects or styles: (1) early animistic or mythological accounts; (2) "causal" explanations of the Ionian nature philosophers; (3) "formal" explanations of the Platonic school; and (4) Aristotle's synthesis of the form-cause-telos which continues in contemporary social thought. Modern writers stressing systems maintenance can be seen as being more on the Platonic side of Aristotle; those stressing change and growth are more Ionic. (See Gouldner 1970.) In this formulation I use an evolutionary approach to the history of ideas in order to prepare for a critique of the ideal of evolutionism itself.

3. In its modern incarnation, many crucial aspects of Aristotle's thought have been shed, even though his basic evolutionary ideas remain largely unchanged. Aristotle focused on the polis; hence his evolutionism is a form of political theory with its concomitant insistence on rhetorical realization. Eighteenth- and nineteenth-century thinkers were infatuated with Nature;

hence their evolutionism subsumed politics under an historical science of universal forces to be controlled through knowledge of natural (that is, nonrhetorical) laws. This focus on natural laws also is typical of experimental empiricists, only for them laws are causal rather than teleological and the contents of history are events rather than processes. Some contemporary historians have not recognized these distinctions. E. P. Thompson, for example, having rejected "methodology" and "theory," then unreflectively used evolutionary categories. "This book," he stated of his opus, "can be seen as a biography of the English working class from its adolescence until its early manhood" (Thompson 1963, 11). But elsewhere he equally unreflectively becomes a mechanist: "Sociologists who have stopped the time-machine and . . . have gone down to the engine-room to look, tell us that nowhere at all have they been able to locate and classify a class. . . . Of course they are right, since class is not this or that part of the machine, but *the way the machine works* once it is set in motion—not this interest and that interest, but the friction of interests—the movement itself, the heat, the thundering noise" (Thompson 1965, 357).

4. There is a certain parochialism in the debate between evolutionists and empiricists in historical sociology, since evolutionists invoke an image of biological evolution that is no longer accepted, if it ever was, by biologists, whereas empiricists make use of an old-fashioned positivist epistemology that most philosophers today feel has little to do with the practice of or warrant for science. Before the advent of modernity, there was a public life among educated persons in which "science" and "art" were joined in rhetoric. Since they were separated, however, historical sociologists and others have been confronted with two impoverished choices: to marry a secondhand method of biology or physics that even biologists and physicists no longer employ, or to embrace a secondhand narrative form that few serious writers make use of today.

5. Ironically, these very conundrums are implied by the functionalists. The key principle in their concept of the social system is the interdependence of all phenomena in a bounded unit. Yet if this principle is accepted, the identification of an event then becomes extremely difficult (even for functionalists) except at the system boundary level, where all that takes place inside the system can be treated as one single event. Intersystem events would appear to be unavailable to functionalists, although to my knowledge they never have raised this question. Nisbit's work illustrates this difficulty when he distinguishes between intrasystem and extrasystem events and gives priority to the latter, treating them as catastrophes which can be analyzed historically as causes of change to systems.

6. Of course a future state is different from a future goal in that a goal may be a retrospective construction of members (or historians) but also exist prior to or concurrent with the developing project. As discussed earlier, there is a large literature on the question of intentions, motives, or reasons as opposed to causes. In his classic "Actions, Reasons, and Causes," Donald Davidson argued that reasons are causes, but later, in his essay, "Mental Events," he held that even though reasons are causes, psychological-historical science

will never be in a position to articulate the laws that a proper causal science needs to provide. Causality itself has been variously defined. The predominant views include Leibniz's idea that objects really have causal powers to bring about changes in certain circumstances; Hume's belief that causal relations are attributed to events by people on the basis of observed invariate relations between them, but are not discovered in natural things themselves; and Kant's notion that causal relations have to be assumed as real, though they cannot be observed, if nature is to be understood. In addition, there is what has been called the manipulability theory of causality, espoused by Collingwood and others, that causes are events or conditions by which we can produce or prevent other events or states of affairs. See McCullagh 1984, 1972.

7. There is, however, a problem in the above argument, in that neopositivist historical sociologists, and especially Bock, employ a telic explanation. Perhaps this difficulty can be clarified if we speak of Bock, Nisbet, and others as methodologists of historical sociology, who in their own historical scholarship do not employ their proposed method of logic. Although it is not easy to state exactly what they do employ, it would appear to be evolutionism, using the doctrine of survivals. For example, Bock speaks of the survival of Aristotelian ideas throughout Western history as a "heritage of assumptions." Yet it is unclear how this heritage is made to persist. Rather, through historical examples and analyses of texts, Bock shows the presence of certain assumptions in a variety of thinkers faced with similar problems. It is quite clear, however, that Bock and Nisbet do not use the method of controlled comparative analysis in their own works, though in these very works they advocate that method for others. In the case of Hodgin, and to a lesser extent of Teggart, there is a remarkable self-reflection on this problematic. In both Teggart's *Rome and China* and Hodgin's *Change in History* there are controlled comparisons of events and the argument that the frequency of one type of event is related to the presence of the other. Hodgin, however, candidly admitted that the logico-meaningful relationship between the frequencies is not presented and that it ought to be in order to make the explanation complete. Indeed, Hodgin proposed that some other thinker, a psychologist perhaps, might do this. With Teggart, logico-meaningful explanation is employed only to a minor degree, in the form of economic motives, which appear to operate as explanatory devices in accounting for the Rome-China relationship.

8. One reviewer noted that sophisticated empiricists have a partial response to the criticism that descriptions cannot be objective in the requisite sense because they involve event individuations which must be partly a function of the conceptual presuppositions of the scientist. For instance, see Israel Scheffler, *Science and Subjectivity* (1967), and F. A. Hayek, *The Counter-Revolution in Science: Studies in the Abuse of Reason* (1964, 70): "The human mind indeed can never grasp the 'whole' in the sense of all the different aspects of a real situation. The application of these considerations to the phenomena of human history leads to very important consequences. It means nothing less than that a historical process or period is never a single

definite object of thought but becomes such only by the question we ask. What we are accustomed to regard as a single historical event can become any number of different objects of thought."

Chapter Six

1. Roughly translated:

> Around us is history
> on summits of time,
> And dearest moments
> languish on mountains near to us
> but far apart,
> So give us wings of the mind most faithfully
> to cross over and to return.

2. The affinity between structuralist historians and anthropologists goes back to the days shared by Fernand Braudel and Claude Lévi-Strauss at the University of São Paolo in Brazil in the 1930s and, before that, to their common inspiration drawn from the social and linguistic structuralisms respectively of Emile Durkheim and Ferdinand de Saussure. In this tradition, "observable phenomena and available sources are not the result of specific human intention but rather the fragmentary outcrops of an underlying system" (Aymar 1972, 508).

3. For a comparison of Althusser and Lévi-Strauss as structuralists, see Miriam Glucksmann (1974).

4. Aside from the *Annales* school, much professional history today is written as structural analysis rather than narration. For example, both Peter Laslett's *The World We Have Lost* and Huizinga's *The Waning of the Middle Ages* indicate in their titles a supposed homogeneous linear time, but their respective texts are syncronic accounts of given social structures.

5. Theodor Lessing expressed a similar view of history as "originating in desires and volitions, needs and intentions, . . . a realization of the 'dream visions' of the human race. . . . Meaning of history is solely meaning which I give myself, an historical evolution is a development from myself to myself" (Lessing, quoted in Kahler 1964, 19–20).

Gadamer has shown that to accept Husserl's eidetic ontology is not necessarily to accept the transcendental idealism intended to justify it. Descriptive and transcendental phenomenology operate on different levels.

6. Derrida described an image that captures this notion of history as retrospective construction (Derrida 1980, 14; quoted by Ulmer 1981, 74). He sees a post card on display in a case in Oxford's Bodleian library showing Plato dictating as Socrates serves as his scribe: "Socrates writing, writing before Plato, I always knew it, it remained as a photographic negative to be developed after twenty-five centuries—to me of course. . . . Socrates, the one writing—sitting, bent over, scribe or docile copyist, Plato's secretary. He is in front of Plato, no Plato is behind him, smaller (why smaller?) but standing up. With extended finger he has an air of indicating, designating, showing the way or of giving an order—or of dictating, authoritative, magisterial, imperious."

7. Henry Adams provided an example of a formist procedure in his essay "The Dynamo and the Virgin" (1958). In transcoding other modes of historiography into the phenomenological one, Adams began with a rhetorical demystification of the research subject as constituted from a mechanistic perspective. Adams started by introducing the human agent into the problematic, redefining the subject not merely as forces, but including also their effect on human motive. He then engaged in an experiment, hypothesizing that "one can reason back from human action to its precedent cause in nature because the explanation of the human being lies in the empirical-analytic science of the laws of motion. During his discourse, however, he proves that such reasoning is impossible. We know only our own representations of force as they exist in various systems of intelligibility, systems purporting to explain the structures of empirical, social, and psychological phenomena. These systems, manifested in the verbal, plastic, and mathematical arts, make up the structures of the world and frame the signs and events within which our cultural heritage is inscribed. The subject of the research activity is not nature's forces in their relation to ourselves; it is the human mind in the act of representing force—for it is within this fundamental activity that an individual's and a nation's relations to the world are forged" (Lesser 1982, 389).

8. See Benjamin (1969, 256); Halbwachs (1980, 78); Lewis (1975); Lyman (1978, 90–94); Natanson (1962); and White (1973, 332) for similar conceptions. For example, Bernard Lewis (1975) spoke of *History: Remembered, Recovered, Invented:*

> (1) Remembered history. This consists of statements about the past, rather than history in the strict sense, and ranges from the personal recollections acclaimed by the elders to the living traditions of a civilization, as embodied in its scriptures, its classics, and its inherited historiography. . . .
> (2) Recovered history. This is the history of events and movements, of persons and ideas, that have been forgotten, that is to say, at some stage and for some reason rejected by the communal memory, and then, after a longer or shorter interval, recovered by academic scholarship—by the study of records, the excavation of buried cities, the dicipherment of forgotten scripts and languages, and the consequent reconstruction of a forgotten past.
> (3) Invented history. This is history for a purpose, a new purpose differing from previous purposes. It may be invented in either the Latin or the English sense of the word, devised and interpreted from remembered and recovered history where feasible, and fabricated where not.

9. In a like manner, the formal thought that is archeology, though often seen as a demummification of ancient societies, also can have a practical dimension. By unraveling ancient cultures, archeologists make them visible in a modern light. Yet this light also endangers the very object that it illuminates. To prevent the vaporization of the newly exposed culture, the archeologist must "freeze-dry" it in the formal analytic categories through which the culture was initially brought back to life. This freeze-dried version

then becomes an item in the cultural armory of contemporary claimants of that particular past. In this fashion the histories of Egypt and Iran have been used as a basis of modern Egyptians' and Iranians' claims to past greatness and implied future greatness.

10. What I am saying about history of course also applies to any paradigmatic cultural artifact. For example, French became a paradigmatic civilizational language not only because of the political power of the French throne; it was also necessary that French be codified—out of Burgundian, Latin, Langue d'Oc and other tongues—into the formal grammar, syntax, and rules of speech that define the French of the *Académie française*. A similar formalizing function was performed by Arabic grammarians, thus aiding the ascendency of Arabic as the language of letters and government during the 'Abbasids caliphate and providing a cultural integument for the empire (Hodgson 1974). For a sensitive discussion of the role of language, and particularly poetry, in national liberation and state building, see Peter Green (1980). My observations here, as well as related ones in the text, draw heavily on conversations and correspondence with Paul Creelan.

11. Vico provides an example of this when he says that the Athenian plebes "invented" the historical figure, Solon the law-giver, in order to legitimate their claim to rights formerly reserved for nobles (Vico 1972, pars. 1086–1087).

12. See Hayden White (1973); also see David Levin (1959); Nancy S. Streuver (1970, 1974, 1982). Also see recent numbers of *Clio: An Interdisciplinary Journal of Literature, History, and the Philosophy of History; Literature and History; History and Theory;* and *New Literary History.*

13. I have shifted and partly inverted Pepper's use of the terms organicism and formism. For organicism, Pepper stresses the resolution of inner contradictions within a larger whole, thereby making Hegel a good example of organistic thinking. Conversely, for me Hegel is a formist (see next chapter). For formism, Pepper stresses immanence and transcendence, properties which I see as essential to organicism. Thus for Pepper (1942, 162), Aristotle's metaphor of the oak exemplifies formism, whereas for me it illustrates his organistic thinking. The differences between the ways in which Pepper and I sort these categories suggest that even well-conceived typologies are polysemous and may be judged not only by their conformity to a material or transcendent reality (formism and organicism), but also by their utility in various cognitive settings (mechanism and contextualism). I am thankful to James Klumpp for these observations.

Chapter Seven

1. For example, Weber said that "the 'objective' discharge of business primarily means a discharge of business according to *calculable rules* and 'without regard for persons.' When fully developed, bureaucracy also stands . . . under . . . this principle. . . . Its specific nature, which is welcomed by capitalism, develops the more perfectly the more the bureaucracy is 'dehumanized,' the more completely it succeeds in eliminating from official

business love, hatred, and all purely personal, irrational, and emotional elements which escape calculation" (1978:217–226).

Despite such statements, however, it would be incorrect to view Weber as an order theorist who focused only on the rational aspects of formal organizations. For a reinterpretation that "Marxizes" Weber see Collins 1975. Weber also has been criticized for overlooking the informal aspects of organizations. Yet in 1909, 1910, and 1911, Weber undertook empirical surveys of the micro-situations and interactions of workers in large industries. Like Marx before him, Weber constructed questionnaires, lamented low rates of return, and coded data in order to gain a preliminary indication of the occupational choices and adaptations of blue collar workers. I thank Rudolf Faller for these observations.

2. For further examples of sophisticated, comparative, neo-Weberian analyses of formal organizations see Blau (1965); Burns and Stalker (1961); Fullan (1970); Perrow (1970, 1967); Price (1967); James Thompson (1967); and Udy (1959). The more closely one examines specific cases, however, the less trustworthy such positivist findings come to appear. See, for example Samuel Eilon's (1965, 1971) and Lex Donaldson's (1976) criticisms of Woodard's thesis on the relation of technology and type of control and authority. Whereas their criticisms are reformist, those advanced by ethnomethodologists are more fundamental. For example, Denzin challenged the very conception that there are facts about organizations available to investigators as a basis of comparative analysis. As ethnomethodological studies show, this is because organizations perpetuate themselves by generating fictitious records, comparable organizations may attribute very different meanings to the same events, organizational records are produced through gossip, overheard conversations, rumors, discrepant accounts, and the like, and such piecing together of records that are to be taken as factual relies on open-ended categories in order to classify ambiguous cases, conform to the dominant idology, or advance particular interests (Denzin 1969; Knorr-Cetina 1981, 14).

3. Many ethnomethodological, phenomenological, existential, or neo-symbolic interactionist studies have been conducted within formal organizational settings. For examples concerning the administration of justice by organizations, see Scheff (1968); Garfinkel (1967); and Cicourel (1968); concerning educational organizations see Harré (1978); Mehan (1974); Cicourel and Kitsuse (1963); Leiter (1971); and Scott and Lyman (1970); concerning medical organizations see Donald W. Ball (1967); Scheff (1961); Strauss et al. (1964); Houston Wood (1968); Sudnow (1969); and Szasz (1961, 1970); concerning welfare organizations, see Zimmerman (1970); concerning military organizations, see Emerson (1970). For more general views of organization from similar perspectives see Bittner (1965); Burns (1961); Burke (1969); Cicourel (1974); Douglas and Johnson (1977); Mariner (1971); Pollner (1970); and Silverman (1978). Of particular importance are the essays collected by Ralph L. Blankenship (1977).

4. These paradoxes are of course local instances of the more general difficulties of organistic and mechanistic historical science discussed earlier in chapter 5. For relevant examples and discussion see Chester I. Barnard, *The*

Functions of the Executive (1938); Richard M. Cyert and James G. March, *A Behavioral Theory of the Firm* (1963); Talcott Parsons, "Suggestions for a Sociological Approach to Theory of Organizations" (1956); F. J. Roethlisberger and W. J. Dickson, *Management and the Worker* (1941); Philip Selznick, "Foundations of the Theory of Organization" (1948); Herbert A. Simon, "On the Concept of Organizational Goal" (1964); and James D. Thompson and William J. McEwen, "Organizational Goals and the Environment" (1958).

5. For interesting examples of neo-Weberian studies that have affinities with a Marxian or an ethnomethodological perspective, either unwittingly or by design, see Bendix (1957); Bergerson (1976); Burns (1961); Gamson (1968); Gerstl and Jacobs (1976); Hirschman (1970); Kerr and Siegel (1954); Kuhn (1962); Lammers (1975, 1969); Leeds (1964); Lipsky (1969); McCarthy and Zald (1973); McDonald (1973); Needleman and Needleman (1974); Pettigrerw (1973); Pfeffer and Salanick (1974); Pondy (1964); Selznick (1943); Sjoberg (1966); Zald (1970, 1965); and Zald and Berger (1978).

6. That thought is practical social activity, and that everyday life is a process of world creation, is adumbrated by Marx in his "Notes to the Doctor Dissertation" (1839–1841), "Economic and Philosophic Manuscripts" (1844), and "Theses on Feuerbach" (1845). Relevant passages are reprinted in *Writings of the Yong Marx on Philosophy and Society*, edited and translated by Lloyd D. Easton and Kurt H. Guddat (Garden City: Doubleday, 1967) especially pp. 61–62, 307–308, and 400–402. Also see Joachim Israel, "Alienation and Reification," in *Theories of Alienation* (1978).

7. Husserl, of course, did not draw the revolutionary conclusions entailed by his own analysis, and ended up identifying the crisis as a philosophical one capable of philosophical solution: that is, the new phenomenology (Piccone 1971, 25; see Banfi 1956). At the same time, however, within Marxist discourse itself, the problem of the relationship between general theory and organizational practice has yet to be solved. For example, after a penetrating analysis of reification, social democracy, and instrumental reason, Georg Lukacs closed his *History of Class Consciousness* (1971) with a chapter "Towards a Methodology of the Problem of Organization." There, and also in a booklet written about the same time titled *Lenin,* he virtually repudiated his philosophic formulation in favor of a mechanistic Leninist notion of organizational practice. Theory was thus mediated into organizational practice, but only at the sacrifice of the very theory that required mediation (Piccone 1971, 9).

8. Imersheim and Kaplan (1974) have written a provocative essay on this point with reference to paradigm changes within health services organizations. In justifying their analogical use of the Kuhnian model, they consider possible parallels between scientific change and organizational change. First, "to what extent is the technical knowledge regarding organizational activities similar to the scientific knowledge regarding scientific activities? Second, to what extent is this knowledge embedded in paradigms in the sense that this is the case for scientific knowledge?" Revolutions in paradigms of political philosophy are discussed in Kuhnian terms by Parekh (1968, 153–155); in art by Brown (1974, 169–197; 1987) and in civic culture by Wolin (1968) and Strong (1978).

9. As with most arguments, there are strong and weak positions on this one too. The strong position holds that organizations and polities *are* (or are like) paradigms. The weak position holds that organizations and polities *have* paradigms (or something like paradigms). For the purposes of this essay I have taken a strong position. But I also have been careful to redefine paradigm to include practical and political as well as cognitive aspects. Naturally, a more purely cognitive conception of paradigms would be more consistent with a weak position on their similarity to organizations or polities. A weak usage also is more appropriate to the distinctions that Pocock makes in his essays on political theory (Pocock 1973, 9).

10. For examinations of the political uses of ideology and rhetoric both within organizations and in organizations' relations with external constituencies, see Wildavsky (1964), Burke (1967), and Mariner (1971). Also see Sorel's writings (1961, 1969) on the "myth of revolution." Many of Sorel's ideas, if turned upside down and renamed the "myth of the status quo," could be applied to regnant paradigms in formal organizations. For considerations of the use of rituals and emblems as rhetorical devises (symbols intended to persuade), see Moore (1962, 99–104). For an attempt to develop a general model of "Social Order as Determined by the Communication of Hierarchy," see Duncan (1962, Part 6).

11. Illustrations are provided by Erving Goffman (1961a, 19–26). Given the stability of the game rules, one can win or stalemate only through moves. Also see James MacGregor Burns's *Presidential Government*, where a similar observation is made about the polity as a whole: "In a static or highly stable society the policy makers can rely on technicians to administer the status quo. The goals of the society are not in doubt, and innovation can be undertaken on the narrow basis of greater efficiency. But a society undergoing change in its basic valuations turns to the intellectuals to redefine the valuations and to reshape the Administration's or party's goals and the means of realizing them."

12. One test of these assertions would be whether they held true even for total institutions where the ruling group aimed explicitly at controlling consciousness as well as conduct. For evidence of the limits of elite control see studies of monastic, military, and mental hospital settings, respectively by Adams (1970); Blake (1976); and Goffman (1961a). For evidence suggesting that there is little growth of an inmate subculture that could limit elite control, see studies of thought-reform prisons in China by Whyte (1973, 267). The study by Langer (1970) of a New York telephone company also illustrates the potentials of elites to totalize consciousness through the monopolization of channels of communication.

Chapter Eight

1. This is distinct from the usual approach that assumes the continuity of the system being planned for and extrapolates alternative futures from past and present trends. For example, the dominant assumption of Kahn and Weiner (1967, 116) in *The Year 2000: A Framework for Speculation on the Next*

Thirty-Three Years, was that the "capabilities for and commitment to economic development and control over our external and internal environment are increasingly seeming without foreseeable limit." Similarly, *The Global 2000 Report* (1980, 43) assumed the continuance of "present policies."

2. As Delli Priscoli (1979, 11) argued,

> Study after study of drought shows that the perception of drought— rather than less-than-minimum amounts of cubic feet per second or other technical measurement—determines public reactions. In the Northeast drought some years ago management of just such perception was the key issue. Low flow in Philadelphia raised the risk of salt encroachment in the water supply. Upstream releases raised the spectre of jeopardizing New York City for the sake of Philadelphia. To the degree that drought had been "projected" as serious, this germ of conflict escalated. We have only to look at western water rights "wars" to see how nasty things can become. When such conflict occurs we have to ask ourselves, "what role did our projections or process of projecting play in the outcome?"

Similarly, as Manning (1980) observed,

> Organizational work . . . is the social construction of environment as well as the management of unseen aspects of the environment that nevertheless affect everyday organizational life. The organization [read planning practice] . . . is a processor of signs, not of stimuli; it contains a system for coding of incoming data as signs, and thus constitutes a semiotic system (p. 24). . . . In this sense, the environment is created and *enacted* and then rationalized and cast into organizational rhetorics. (p. 2)

3. The moral dimensions of means-end rationality become most evident when applied to human beings. As Bateson (1972, 163) pointed out, instrumentalists who would establish a blueprinted heaven-on-earth

> ignore the fact that in social manipulation, the tools are not hammers and screwdrivers. A screwdriver is not seriously affected when, in an emergency, we use it as a wedge; and a hammer's outlook on life is not affected because we sometimes use its handle as a simple lever. But in social manipulation our tools are people, and people learn, and they acquire habits which are more subtle and pervasive than the tricks which the blueprinter teaches them. With the best intentions in the world, he may train children to spy upon their parents in order to eradicate some tendency prejudicial to the success of his blueprint, but because the children are people they will do more than learn this simple trick—they will build this experience into their whole philosophy of life; it will color all their future attitudes toward authority.

4. These findings suggest that positivist social planning and the scientific design of social programs have little to do with actual practices and outcomes. Instead of drawing these logical inferences from their data, however, Light and his associates concluded that more research is needed. They thereby eschew consideration of alternative hypotheses, for example, that positivist planning reflects elite political interests such as containment, legitimation,

cooptation, or policing (Rein 1976, 97). My criticisms of positivism therefore are not intended to dismiss social planning as an unreliable discourse for collective self-analysis and guidance. On the contrary, they are meant as criticisms from within, as an *inner* hermeneutic that will issue into a new planning practice and newly practical plans. Critical consciousness of planning as symbolic construction invites not gestures of dismissal, but acts of transformation. Self-reflection on methods of societal guidance is one step in the journey from scientism and social engineering to an emancipatory use of reason and a humanizing political practice.

5. Norton Long, a political scientist, summed up this thought: "The question is not whether planning will reflect politics, but whose politics will it reflect . . . ? Plans are in reality political programs. . . . In the broad sense they represent political philosophies . . . ways of implementing different conceptions of the good life."

6. Irrationality at the level of affectivity is, of course, characteristic of Japanese institutions, both traditional and modern. The feelings of cohesion, as well as the possibilities for manipulation in such an approach to industrial organization, is noted in "*Seishin Kyoiku* in a Japanese Bank," in Spindler (1974). See also Arendt (1969); Collins (1982, 3–19); Tiryakian (1972); and Peacock (1969).

REFERENCES

Abel, Leon. 1966. "Sartre vs. Lévi-Strauss." *Commonweal* 84:364–368.

Adamov, Arthur. 1953. *Théâtre*. Paris: Gallimard.

Adams, Henry. 1958. "The Dynamo and the Virgin." In *Collected Writings*, edited by Elizabeth Stevenson. Garden City, N.Y.: Doubleday.

Adams, Robert L. 1970. "Conflict over Charges of Heresy in American Protestant Seminaries." *Social Compass* 17:243–260.

Adorno, Theodor W. 1973 [1966] *The Jargon of Authenticity*. Evanston: Northwestern University Press.

Adorno, Theodor, Han Albert, Ralf Dehrendorf, Jürgen Habermas, Harold Pilot, and Karl Popper. 1976. *The Positivist Dispute in German Sociology*. London: Heinemann.

Alford, Fred. 1985. "Jürgen Habermas and the Dialectic of Enlightenment: What Is Theoretically Fruitful Knowledge?" *Social Research* 52, no. 1 (Spring): 121–149.

Althusser, Louis. 1970. *For Marx*. Translated by Ben Brewster. New York: Random House.

Anderson, Perry. 1974. *Lineages of the Absolutist State*. London: N.L.B.

Apel, Karl-Otto. 1984. *Understanding and Explanation: A Transcendental-Pragmatic Perspective*. Translated by Georgia Warnke. Cambridge, Mass.: MIT Press.

———. 1967. *Analytical Philosophy of Language and the Geisteswissenschaften*. Dordecht, Holland: D. Reidel.

Arendt, Hannah. 1969. "Introduction, Walter Benjamin: 1892–1940." In *Walter Benjamin, Illuminations*, translated by Harry Zorn. New York: Harcourt, Brace and World.

———. 1965. *On Revolution*. New York: Viking.

Argyris, Chris. 1973. "Some Limits of Rational Man Organizational Theory." *Public Administration Review* (May–June): 253–267.

Aron, Raymond. 1968. "Evolution of Strategic Thought, 1945–1968: The Rise and Decline of Strategic Analysis." *Archives Européennes de Sociologie* 9, no. 2: 151–179.

Augustine, Saint. 1910. *City of God*. Book 10, chap. 14. New York: Random House.

Ayer, A.J. 1946. *Language, Truth, and Logic*. New York: Dover.

Aymard, Maurice. 1972. "The Annales and French Historiography (1929–1971)." *Journal of European Economic History*, no. 2: 491–513.

Bacon, Sir Francis. 1864. "De augmentis scientiarum." P. 62 in vol. 9 of *The Works of Francis Bacon*, edited by Spedding, Ellis, and Heath. New York.

Baillie, J. B. 1967 [1910]. "Translator's Introduction." Pp. 21–66 of Georg W. F. Hegel, *The Phenomonology of Mind*. London: Macmillan.

Ball, Donald W. 1967. "An Abortion Clinic Ethnography." *Social Problems* 14 (Winter): 293–301.

Ball, Richard A. 1979. "The Dialectical Method: Its Application to Social Theory." *Social Forces* 57, no. 3 (March): 785–798.

Banfi, Antonio. 1956. "L'humanisme et la culture contemporaine." *Comprendre* 5.

Bao, Ruo-wang (Jean Pasqualini) and Rudolph Chelminski. 1973. *Prisoner of Mao*. New York: Doward, McCann & Geoghegan.

Baptista, José. 1974. "Bureaucracy, Political System, and Social Dynamic." *Telos* 22 (Winter): 66–84.

Barnard, Chester I. 1938. *The Functions of the Executive*. Cambridge: Harvard University Press.

Barraclough, Geoffrey. 1956. *History in a Changing World*. Norman, Okla.: University of Oklahoma Press.

Bass, B. M. 1960. *Leadership, Psychology, and Organizational Behavior*. New York: Harper.

Bateson, Gregory. 1972. *Steps toward an Ecology of Mind*. New York: Ballantine.

Baynes, Kenneth. 1987. *After Philosophy*. Cambridge, Mass.: MIT Press.

Bazerman, Charles. 1984. "Modern Evolution of the Experimental Report in Physics: Spectroscopic Articles in Physical Review, 1893–1980." *Social Studies of Science* 14, no. 2: 163–196.

Beauvoir, Simone de. 1963. *La force des choses*. Paris: Gallimard.

Beck, Lewis White. 1975. *The Actor and the Spectator*. New Haven, Conn.: Yale University Press.

Becker, Howard. 1940. "Historical Sociology." In *Contemporary Social Theory*, edited by Harry Barnes and Howard Becker. New York.

Beer, Stafford, 1959. *Designing Freedom*. London and New York: Wiley.

Bell, Daniel, and Irving Kristol, eds. 1971. *Capitalism Today*. New York: New American Library.

Bellah, Robert N. 1983. "Social Science as Practical Reason." In *The Social Sciences and Policy Analysis*, edited by Daniel Callahan and Bruce Jennings. New York: Plenum.

Bellah, Robert N., Richard Madsen, William M. Sullivan, Ann Swidler, and Steven M. Tipton. 1985. *Habits of the Heart*. Berkeley: University of California Press.

Bendix, Reinhard. 1959. "Industrialization, Ideologies, and Social Structure." *American Sociological Review* 24, no. 5 (October): 613–623.

——. 1957. "A Study of Managerial Ideologies." *Economic Development and Cultural Change* 5, no. 2:118–128.

Benjamin, Walter. 1969. "Theses on the Philosophy of History." In *Illuminations*, translated by Harry Zohn. New York: Harcourt, Brace and World.

Benthall, Jonathan. 1976. *The Body Electric: Patterns of Western Industrial Culture*. London: Thames and Hudson.

Berger, Peter. 1977. *Facing Up to Modernity.* New York: Basic Books.

———. 1964. *Invitation to Sociology.* Garden City, N.Y.: Doubleday.

Bergerson, Frederick A. 1976. "The Army Gets an Airforce: The Tactics and Process of Insurgent Bureaucratic Politics." Ph.D dissertation, Vanderbilt University, Nashville, Tenn.

Berggren, Douglas, 1962/1963. "The Use and Abuse of Metaphor." *Review of Metaphysics* 16, no. 2 (December 1962): 237–258 and 16, no. 3 (March 1963): 450–472.

Bernstein, Basil. 1972. "Social Class, Language, and Socialization." In *Language and Social Context,* edited by P.O. Giglioli. Hamondsworth: Penguin.

Betti, Emilio. 1980. "Hermeneutics as the General Methodology of the Geisteswissenschaften." Pp. 51–94 in Joseph Bleicher, *Contemporary Hermeneutics: Hermeneutics as Method, Philosophy, and Critique.* London: Routledge and Kegan Paul.

Bhaskar, Roy. 1982. "Emergence, Explanation, and Emancipation." Pp. 275–310 in *Explaining Human Behavior: Consciousness, Human Action, and Social Structure,* edited by Paul F. Secord. Beverly Hills, Calif.: Sage.

Bittner, Egon. 1965. "The Concept of Organization." *Social Research* 32: 239–255.

Black, Max. 1962. *Models and Metaphors: Studies in Language and Philosophy.* Ithaca, N.Y.: Cornell University Press.

Blake, Joseph A. 1976. "A Case Study of Resistance in 'Total Institutions': The American Military during the War in Vietnam." Paper delivered at meeting of the Southern Sociological Society.

Blankenship, Ralph L. 1977. *Colleagues in Organizations: The Social Construction of Professional Work.* New York: Wiley.

Blau, Peter M. 1965. "The Comparative Study of Organizations." *Industrial and Labor Relations Review* 18, no. 3 (April): 323–338.

———. 1964. *Exchange and Power in Social Life.* New York: Wiley.

Blauner, Robert. 1960. "Work Satisfactions and Industrial Trends." In *Labor and Trade Unionism: An Interdisciplinary Reader,* edited by Galenson and Lipset. New York: Wiley.

Bleicher, Joseph. 1980. *Contemporary Hermeneutics: Hermeneutics as Method, Philosophy, and Critique.* London: Routledge and Kegan Paul.

Bock, Kenneth. 1963. "Evolution, Function, and Change." *American Sociological Review* 28:229–237.

Boguslaw, Robert. 1982. *Systems Analysis and Social Planning: Human Problems of Postindustrial Society.* New York: Irvington.

———. 1965. *The New Utopians.* Englewood Cliffs, N.J.: Prentice-Hall.

Bondi, Hermann. 1967. *Assumption and Myth in Physical Theory.* Cambridge: Cambridge University Press.

Bottomore, Tom, and M. Rubel, eds. 1956. *Karl Marx, Selected Writings in Sociology and Social Philosophy.* London: Watts and Co.

Bourdieu, Pierre. 1977. *Outline of a Theory of Practice.* London and New York: Cambridge University Press.

Braudel, Fernand. 1980. *On History.* Chicago: University of Chicago Press.

———. 1977. *Afterthoughts on Material Civilization and Capitalism.* Baltimore, Md.: Johns Hopkins University Press.

Brooks, Cleanth. 1965. "Metaphor, Paradox, and Stereotype." *British Journal of Aesthetics*, 5, no. 4 (October): 315–318.

Brown, Richard Harvey. 1989. "Symbolic Realism and the Dualism of the Human Sciences: A Rhetorical Reformulation of the Debate between Positivism and Romanticism." In *Case Studies in the Rhetoric of the Human Sciences*, edited by Herbert W. Simons. Chicago: University of Chicago Press.

_____. 1989 [1977]. *A Poetic for Sociology: Toward a Logic of Discovery for the Human Sciences*. Reprint. Chicago: University of Chicago Press.

_____. 1987. *Society as Text: Essays on Rhetoric, Reason, and Reality*. Chicago: University of Chicago Press.

_____. 1979. "Bureaucratic Bathos or How to Be a Government Consultant without Really Trying." *Administration and Society* 11, no. 4: 477–492.

_____. 1978. "Symbolic Realism and Sociological Thought: Beyond the Positivist—Romantic Debate." Pp.13–37 in *Structure, Consciousness, and History*, edited by Richard Harvey Brown and Stanford M. Lyman. New York and London: Cambridge University Press.

_____. 1974. "Structurings of Contents, Embodiments of Form: Symbolic Realism and the Aesthetics of the Human Studies." *International Journal of Symbology* 5, no. 3 (November): 1–18.

Brulle, Robert. 1984. "Emancipatory Politics and the Administrative Agency." Mimeographed. Department of Sociology, Georgetown University, Washington, D.C.

Buckley, Walter Frederick. 1967. *Sociology and Modern Systems Theory*. Englewood Cliffs, N.J.: Prentice-Hall.

Bultmann, Rudolph. 1957. *History and Eschatology*. Edinburgh. (For a pungent critique, see Alysdair MacIntyre's review in *Philosphical Quarterly* 10 [1960]:92.)

Burawoy, Michael. 1979. *Manufacturing Consent: Changes in the Labor Process under Monopoly Capitalism*. Chicago: University of Chicago Press.

Burchell, Robert W., and David Listokin. 1982. *Energy and Land Use*. Rutgers—New Brunswick, N.J.: Rutgers—State University.

Burke, Kenneth. 1984. *Permanence and Change: An Anatomy of Purpose*. Berkeley: University of California Press.

_____. 1969. *A Grammar of Motives*. Berkeley: University of California Press.

_____. 1967. " 'Administrative' Rhetoric in Machiavelli." Pp. 158–166 in *A Rhetoric of Motives*. Berkeley: University of California Press.

Burns, Tom. 1961. "Micro-Politics: Mechanisms of Institutional Change." *Administrative Science Quarterly* 6, no. 3: 129–166.

Burns, Tom, and G. M. Stalker. 1961. *The Management of Innovation*. London: Tavistock.

Bush, Douglas. 1950. *Science and English Poetry*. New York: Oxford University Press.

Campbell, John Angus. 1984. "A Rhetorical Interpretation of History." *Rhetorica* 2:227–266.

Carey, Alex. 1969. "The Hawthorne Studies: A Radical Criticism." *American Sociological Review* 32 (June): 403–416.

Carnap, Rudolph. 1963. *The Philosophy of Rudolph Carnap.* Vol. 2 The Library of Living Philosophers.

Carroll, Lewis. 1960. *Alice's Adventures in Wonderland and Through the Looking Glass.* New York: New American Library.

Cartwright, D. 1965. "Influence, Leadership, and Control." In *Handbook of Organizations,* edited by J.G. March. Chicago: Rand McNally.

Cassirer, Ernest. 1969. *The Philosophy of the Enlightenment.* Translated by F.C.A. Koelln and James P. Pettegrove. Princeton, N.J.: Princeton University Press.

Chiodi, Guilio. 1970. *Legge naturale e legge positive nella filosofia politica di Thomas Hobbes.* Milano: A Guiffre.

Churchman, C. West. 1971. *The Design of Inquiring Systems: Basic Concepts of Systems and Organizations.* New York: Basic Books.

Cicourel, Aaron V. 1974. "The Acquisition of Social Structure: Toward a Developmental Sociology of Language and Meaning." In *Cognitive Sociology: Language and Meaning in Social Interaction.* New York: Free Press.

———. 1968. *The Social Organization of Juvenile Justice.* New York: Wiley.

Cicourel, Aaron V., and John I. Kitsuse. 1963. *The Educational Decision Makers.* Indianapolis, Ind.: Bobbs-Merrill.

Clignet, Remi. 1985. *The Structure of Artistic Revolutions.* Philadelphia: University of Pennsylvania Press.

Cohen, M.R. 1949. *Studies in Philosophy and Science.* New York: Henry Holt.

Cohen, Percy. 1968. "The Very Idea of a Social Science." In *Problems in the Philosophy of Science,* edited by Imre Lakatos and Alan Musgrave. Amsterdam.

Cohen, Robert S., and Benjamin Nelson. 1984. *Methodology, Metaphysics, and the History of Science.* Dordrecht: D. Reidel.

Colebatch, Hal K. n.d. "Regulation and Paradigms of Organization: Six Theses." In *Regulation, Power, and Resistance,* edited by R. Tomasi and R. Lukas. Canberra, Australia: Canberra College of Advanced Education.

———. 1986. "Organization and Political Analysis." *Politics* 21, no. 1:1–18.

———. 1984. "Public and Private as a Question of Language." Paper presented to the APROS Colloquium on Language and Organizing, Kuring-gai College of Advanced Education, Linfield, New South Wales, Australia (October).

Coleridge, Samuel Taylor. 1956. *Biographica Literaria.* Edited by George Watson. New York: Everyman's Library.

Collins, Randall. 1982. *Sociological Insight.* New York: Oxford University Press.

———. 1981. *Sociology Since Midcentury: Essays in Theory Cummulation.* New York: Academic Press.

———. 1975. *Conflict Sociology.* New York: Academic Press.

Comte, Auguste. 1877. *Lettres d'Auguste Comte à John Stuart Mill.* Paris: E. Leroux.

Confucious. 1956. *Analects.* In *Chinese Classics,* vol. 1. Translated by James Legge. Oxford: Oxford University Press.

Cope, Jackson I. 1973. "Platonic Prespectives: Structural Metaphor from

Cusa to Ficino." Pp. 14–28 in *The Theatre and the Dream: From Metaphor to Form in Renaissance Drama*, Baltimore, Md.: John Hopkins University Press.

Culler, Jonathan. 1973. "Phenomenology and Structuralism." *The Human Context* 5, no. 1: 35–48.

Cyert, Richard M, and James G. March. 1963. *A Behavioral Theory of the Firm.* Englewood Cliffs, N.J.: Prentice-Hall.

Dahl, Robert. 1970. *After the Revolution?* New Haven, Conn.: Yale University Press.

———. 1961. *Controlling Nuclear Weapons: Democracy versus Guardianship.* Syracuse, N.Y.: Syracuse University Press.

Dahrendorf, Ralf. 1968. *Essays in the Theory of Society.* Stanford, Calif.: Stanford University Press.

———. 1959. *Class and Class Conflict in Industrial Society.* Stanford, Calif.: Stanford University Press.

———. 1958. "Toward a Theory of Social Conflict." *Journal of Conflict Resolution* 2: 170–183.

Dallmayr, Fred. 1981. *Beyond Dogma and Despair: Toward a Critical Phenomonology of Politics.* Notre Dame, Ind.: University of Notre Dame Press.

Daneke, Gregory A., and Jerome Delli Prescoli. 1983. *Public Involvement and Social Impact Assessment.* Boulder, Colo.: Westview Press.

Daniels, Arlene K. 1970. "The Social Construction of Military Psychiatric Diagnoses." In *Recent Sociology,* vol. 2, *Patterns of Communicative Behavior,* edited by Hans Peter Dreitzel. New York: MacMillan.

Danto, Arthur C. 1968. *Analytic Philosophy of History.* New York and London: Cambridge University Press.

Darwin, Charles. 1896. *Origin of Species.* New York: D. Appleton.

Davis, Kinglsey. 1961. "Prostitution." In *Contemporary Social Problems,* edited by Robert Merton and Robert Nisbet. New York: Harcourt, Brace and World.

Davis, Kingsley, and Wilfred Moore. 1945. "Some Principles of Stratification." *American Sociological Review* 10, no. 1:242–249.

Degeling, Pieter. 1984. "Language and Discourse in Presentations of Organisational Life." Paper presented to the APROS Colloquium on Language and Organizing, Kuring-gai College of Advanced Education, Linfield, New South Wales, Australia (October).

Degeling, Pieter, and Hal K. Colebatch. 1984. "Structure and Action as Constructs in the Practice of Public Administration." *Australian Journal of Public Administration* 43, no. 4 (December): 320–331.

———. 1982. "On Talking Dirty: Sacred and Profane in Public Administration." Paper presented to the meetings of the American Society for Public Administration, Honolulu (March).

Delli Priscoli, Jerome. 1982. "The Endearing Myths of Public Involvement." In *Citizen Participation* 3, no. 4 (March–April)

———. 1979. "Future Thinking: Fad or Necessity?" *Water Spectrum* 7 (Spring): 7–32.

de Morgan, A. 1847. *Formal Logic: Or, the Calculus of Inference, Necessary and Probable.* London: Taylor and Walton.

Denzin, Norman K. 1969. "Symbolic Interactionism and Ethnomethodology: A Proposed Synthesis." *American Sociological Review* 34: 922–934.

Derrida, Jacques. 1980. *La carte postale: De Socrate à Freud et au-delà.* Paris: Flammarion.

———. 1978. *Writing and Difference.* Translated by Alan Bass. Chicago: University of Chicago Press.

———. 1974. "White Mythology." *New Literary History* 6, no. 1 (Autumn): 16–17.

———. 1972. "Structure, Sign, and Play in the Discourse of the Human Sciences." Pp. 2–18 in *The Structuralist Controversy: The Languages of Criticism and the Sciences of Man,* edited by Richard Macksey and Eugenio Donato. Baltimore: Johns Hopkins University Press.

Desan, Wilfred. 1965.*The Marxism of Jean-Paul Sartre.* New York: Doubleday.

Descartes, René. 1965 [1637]. *Discourse on Method: Optics, Geometry, and Meterology.* Translated by P.J. Olscamp. Indianapolis, Ind.: Bobbs-Merrill.

Diesing, Paul. 1962. *Reason in Society: Five Types of Decisions and Their Social Conditions.* Westport, Conn.: Greenwood Press.

Dilthey, Wilhelm. 1957. *Gesammelte Schriften.* Stuttgart: B.G. Taubner.

Domhoff, William, and Thomas R. Dye, eds. 1987. *Power Elites and Organizations.* Beverly Hills, Calif.: Sage.

Donaldson, Lex. 1976. "Woodward, Technology, Organizational Structure, and Performance: A Critique of the Universal Generalization." *Journal of Mangement Studies* 13: 255–273.

Douglas, Jack D. 1981. "The Myth of Rationalism versus Human Nature: The Myth of State Planning versus Individual Planning." Mimeographed. Department of Sociology, University of California, La Jolla.

———. 1971. "The Theory of Subjectivity in Sociology." Mimeographed. Department of Sociology, University of California at San Diego.

———. 1970. "The Relevance of Sociology." Pp. 185–233 in *The Relevance of Sociology,* edited by Jack D. Douglas. New York: Appleton.

———. 1967. *The Social Meanings of Suicide.* Princeton, N.J.: Princeton University Press.

Douglas, Jack D., and John Johnson, eds. 1977. *Existential Sociology.* London and New York: Cambridge University Press.

Douglas, Mary. 1975. "Deciphering a Meal." In *Implicit Meanings: Essays in Anthropology.* London: Routledge and Kegan Paul.

Douglas, Mary, and Aaron Wildavsky. 1982. *Risk and Culture: An Essay on the Selection of Technological and Environmental Dangers.* Berkeley: University of California Press.

Dreitzel, Hans Peter, ed. 1970. *Recent Sociology,* vol. 2, *Patterns of Cummunicative Behavior.* New York: Macmillan.

Duncan, Hugh D. 1962. *Communication and the Social Order.* New York: Bedminster Press.

Durkheim, Emile. 1965. *The Elementary Forms of Religious Life.* Translated by John W. Swain. New York: Free Press.

Dye, Thomas R. 1976. *Who's Running America?* Englewood Cliffs, N.J.: Prentice-Hall.

Easton, David. 1953. *The Political System: An Inquiry into the State of Political Science.* New York: Knopf.

Edelman, Murray J. 1964. *The Symbolic Uses of Politics.* Urbana: University of Illinois Press.

Eilon, Samuel. 1971. *Management Control.* London: Macmillon.

———. 1965. "Problems in Studying Management Control." *International Journal of Productive Resources* 1.

Ellul, Jacques. 1964. *The Technological Society.* New York: Vintage.

Emerson, Joan. 1970. *"Behavior in Private Places: Sustaining Definitions of Reality in Gynecological Examination."* In *Recent Sociology,* vol. 2, *Patterns of Communicative Behavior,* edited by Hans Peter Dreitzel. New York: Macmillan.

Etzioni, Amatai. 1965. "Organizational Control Structure." In *Handbook of Organizations,* edited by J.G. March. Chicago: Rand McNally.

———. 1961. *A Comparative Analysis of Complex Organizations.* New York: Free Press.

Evans-Pritchard, E. 1965. *The Position of Women in Primitive Society and Other Essays in Social Anthropology.* London.

Faludi, Andreas. 1973. *Planning Theory.* Oxford and New York: Pergamon Press.

Feigl, Herbert. 1943. "Logical Empiricism." In *Twentieth Century Philosophy,* edited by Dagobert H. Runes. New York: Philosophical Library.

Ferguson, Thomas. 1973. "The Political Economy of Knowledge and the Changing Politics of the Philosophy of Science." *Telos* 15 (Spring): 124–137.

Festugière, A. J. 1950–1954. *La révélation d'Hermès Trismégiste.* 4 vols. Paris.

Feyerabend, Paul. 1978. *Against Method: Outline of an Anarchistic Theory of Knowledge.* London: Verso.

Fite, Warner. 1930. *The Living Mind.* New York: Dial.

Foss, Laurence. 1971. "Art as Cognitive: Beyond Scientific Realism." *Philosphy of Science* 38 (June): 234–250.

Foucault, Michel. 1971. *Order of Things: An Archeology of the Human Sciences.* New York: Pantheon Books.

Frank, André G. 1966. "Functionalism and Dialectics." *Science and Society* 30 (Spring): 62–73.

———. 1957. "The Organization of Economic Activity in the Soviet Union." *Weltwirtschaftliches Archiv* 78, no. 1: 105–156.

Frank III, Arthur W. 1980. "Review of Bourdieu's *Toward a Theory of Praxis.*" *Contemporary Sociology* 9, no. 2 (March): 256–258.

French, J., and B. Raven. 1959. "The Bases of Social Power." In *Studies in Social Power,* edited by D. Cartwright. Ann Arbor: University of Michigan Press.

Freud, Sigmund. 1954. "Project for a Scientific Psychology." In *Complete Works.* London: Hogarth.

Freidmann, John. 1973. *Retracking America.* Garden City, N.Y.: Doubleday.

Friedrichs, R. W. 1970. *A Sociology of Sociology.* New York: Free Press.

Fullan, Michael. 1970. "Industrial Technology and Worker Integration in the Organization." *American Sociological Review* 35 (December): 1028–1039.

Gabaglio, Antonio. 1888. *Teoria generale de la statistica: Parte storica.* Vol. 1. Milan: Hoepli.

Gaboriau, Marc. 1970. "Structural Anthropology and History." Pp. 156–169 in *Structuralism,* edited by M. Lane. London. Translated by Court from *Esprit* 31 (November 1966): 322.

Gadamer, Hans-Georg. 1975. *Truth and Method.* New York: Seabury Press.

———. 1967. *Kleine Schriften.* 3 vols. Tubringen: J. C. B. Mohr.

Gaines, Jerry Allen. 1975. "Philosophy of History in Merleau-Ponty's Inventory of Communist Thought and Behavior." *Comparative Communism* 5, no. 1:4–24.

Gamson, William. 1968. *Power and Discontent.* Homewood, Ill.: Dorsey Press.

Garfinkel, Harold. 1967. *Studies in Ethnomethodology.* Englewood Cliffs, N.J.: Prentice-Hall.

Gay, Peter. 1974. *Style in History.* London: Jonathan Cape.

———. 1971. *Party of Humanity: Essays in French Enlightenment.* New York: W. W. Norton.

Geertz, Clifford. 1967. "The Cerebral Savage: On the Work of Claude Lévi-Strauss." *Encounter* 48, no. 4:24–32.

Geiger, Theodore. 1973. *Tales of Two City-States.* Washington, D.C.: Washington National Planning Association.

Gellner, Ernest. 1975. *Legitimation of Belief.* Cambridge: Cambridge University Press.

———. 1974. *Contemporary Thought and Politics.* London: Routledge and Kegan Paul.

———. 1973. "The New Idealism." In *Cause and Meaning in the Social Sciences,* edited by I. C. Jarvie and J. Agassi. London: Routledge and Kegan Paul.

———. 1965. *Thought and Change.* Chicago: University of Chicago Press.

Gerstl, Joel, and Glenn Jacobs. 1976. *Professions for the People: The Politics of Skill.* New York: Wiley.

Gerth, Hans Heinrich, and C. Wright Mills. 1953. *Character and Social Structure.* New York: Hartcourt, Brace.

Gillis, Richard. 1976. "Phenomenology: A Non-Alternative to Empiricism." In *Phenomonology, Structuralism, Semiology,* edited by Garvin and Raphael. Lewisberg, Pa.: Bucknell University Press.

Gittell, Marilyn. 1980. *Limits to Citizen Participation.* Beverly Hills, Calif.: Sage.

The Global 2000 Report to the President. 1980. Vol. 1, *Entering the Twenty-First Century.* Washington, D.C.: Government Printing Office.

Glucksmann, Miriam. 1974. *Structuralist Analysis in Contemporary Social Thought.* London: Routledge and Kegan Paul.

Gödel, Kurt. 1962. *On Formally Undecidable Propositions.* New York: Basic Books.

Goethe, Johan Wolfgang von. 1954–1955. *Faust.* Boston: Heath.

Goffman, Erving. 1974. *Frame Analysis: An Essay on the Organization of Experience.* New York: Harper Colophon.

———. 1961a. *Asylums: Essays on the Social Situation of Mental Patients and Other Inmates.* Garden City, N.Y.: Doubleday.

———1961b. *Encounters: Two Studies in the Sociology of Interaction.* Indianapolis, Ind.: Bobbs-Merrill.

Goldfarb, Jeffrey C. 1970. "The Scholar as Dissident in American Social Sciences." Paper presented at the meetings of the American Sociological Association, Boston (August).

Goldmann, Lucien. 1973. *The Philosophy of the Enlightenment: The Christian Burgess and the Enlightenment.* Translated by Henry Mans. Cambridge, Mass.: MIT Press.

_____. 1970. *Racine: Essai.* Paris: L'Arche.

_____. 1966. "Structuralisme, marxisme, existentialisme." L'homme et la société 2.

Gombrich, E.H. 1966. *Norm and Form: Studies in the Art of the Renaissance.* New York and London: Phaidon.

Gonseth, Ferdinand. 1948. "Remarque sur l'idée de complémentarité." *Dialectica* 2 (June): 3–4.

Goodman, Nelson. 1978. *Way of Worldmaking.* Indianpolis, Ind.: Hackett.

Goodman, Robert. 1972. *After the Planners.* New York: Simon and Schuster.

Gotesky, Rubin. 1952. "The Nature of Myth and Society." *American Anthropologist* 52: 523–531.

Gouldner, Alvin. 1970. *The Coming Crisis in Western Sociology.* New York: Basic Books.

_____. 1959. "Organizational Analysis." Pp. 400–428 in *Sociology Today,* edited by Robert K. Merton, Leonard Broom, and Leonard S. Cottrell, Jr. New York: Harper.

Goulet, Denis. 1973. *The Cruel Choice: A New Concept in the Theory of Development.* New York: Atheneum.

Graff, Gerald. 1982. "Textual Leftism." *Partisan Review* 49, no. 4: 558–576.

Grant, Edward C. 1962. "Hypotheses in Later and Early Modern Science." *Daedalus:* 612–616.

Green, Brian S. 1988. *Literary Methods and Sociological Theory: Case Studies of Simmel and Weber.* Chicago: University of Chicago Press.

Green, Peter. 1980. "The Poet's Greece." *New York Review of Books* (26 June): 40–44.

Greimas, A. J. 1970. *Du sens.* Paris: Seuil.

_____. 1966. "Structure et histoirie." *Les Temps Modernes* 22 (November): 246.

Gross, Bertrand. 1980. *Friendly Fascism: The New Face of Power in America.* New York: M. Evans.

_____. 1964. *The Managing of Organizations: The Administrative Struggle.* New York: Free Press.

Grossman, Lionel. 1978. "History and Literature: Reproduction or Signification." Pp. 3–40 in *The Writing of History: Literary Form and Historical Understanding,* edited by Robert H. Canary and Henry Kozicki. Madison: University of Wisconsin Press.

Gulick, Luther H., and Urwick, Lydall, eds. 1937. *Papers on the Science of Administration.* Reproduction.

Gurvitch, Georges. 1962. *Dialetique et sociologie.* Paris: Flammarion.

Gusfield, Joseph R. 1988. "Science as a Form of Bureaucratic Discourse: Rhetoric and Style in Formal Organizations." In *Wissenschaftsprache und Gesselschaft,* edited by Theo Bungarten.

Habermas, Jürgen. 1984. *The Theory of Communicative Action.* Vol. 1, *Reason and the Rationalization of Society.* Translated by Thomas McCarthy. Boston: Beacon Press.

_____. 1975. *Legitimation Crisis.* Boston: Beacon Press.

_____. 1974. *Theory and Practice.* Boston: Beacon Press.

_____. 1971. *Theorie der Gesellschaft oder Sozialtechnologie.* Frankfurt am Main: Suhrkamp.

_____. 1970. "Toward a Theory of Communicative Competence." In *Recent Sociology,* vol. 2, *Patterns of Communicative Behavior,* edited by Hans Peter Dreitzel. New York: Macmillan.

_____. 1986a. "Dilthey's Theory of Understanding Expression: Ego Identity and Linguistic Communication." Pp. 140–160 in *Knowledge and Human Interest.* Boston: Beacon Press.

_____. 1968b. *Knowledge and Human Interest.* Boston: Beacon Press.

Hacker, Andrew. 1955. "Dostoevsky's Disciples: Men and Sheep in Political Theory." *Journal of Politics* 17 (November): 590–613.

Hage, Jerald. 1974. "The State of Organizational Theory." Mimeographed. University of Wisconsin, Madison.

Halbwachs, Maurice. 1980. *The Collective Memory.* Translated by Francis J. Ditter and Vida Yazdi Ditter. New York: Harper and Row.

Hall, R. 1967. "Dialectic." *Encyclopedia of Philosophy,* vol. 2. New York: Macmillan.

Hampden-Turner, Charles. 1971. *Radical Man: The Process of Psycho-Social Development.* Garden City, N.Y.: Anchor Books.

Hansen, Norwood. 1958. *Patterns of Discovery.* New York and London: Cambridge University Press.

Harré, Rom. 1978. "Architectonic Man: On the Structuring of Lived Experience." Pp. 140–172 in *Structure, Consciousness, and History,* edited by Richard Harvey Brown and Stanford M. Lyman. London and New York: Cambridge University Press.

Harvey, Edward. 1968. "Technology and the Structure of Organizations." *American Sociological Review* 33 (April): 247–259.

Haskell, Robert E., ed. 1987. *Cognition and Symbolic Structures: The Psychology of Metaphoric Transformation.* Norwood, N.J.: Ablex.

Haskell, Thomas L. 1977. *The Emergence of Professional Social Science: The American Social Science Association and the Nineteenth-Century Crisis of Authority.* Urbana: University of Illinois Press

Hauser, Arnold. 1958. *The Social History of Art.* 4 vols. New York: Vintage.

Hawthrone, Geoffrey. 1976. *Enlightenment and Despair: A History of Sociology.* London: Cambridge University Press.

Hayek, F. A. 1964. *The Counter-Revolution in Science: Studies in the Abuse of Reason.* New York: Free Press.

_____. 1952. *The Road to Serfdom.* Chicago: University of Chicago Press.

Hegel, Georg Friedrich W. 1971. *Encyclopedia of the Philosophical Sciences.* Translated by William Wallace. Oxford: Clarendon Press.

_____. 1956. *The Philosophy of History.* Translated by J. Sibree. New York: Dover.

———. 1952. *Hegel's Philosophy of Right*. Oxford: Oxford University Press.

———. 1930. *Jenenser Realphilosophie*. Edited by Johannes Hoffmeister. Hamburg: F. Meister.

Heilbroner, Robert L. 1975. *Corporate Social Policy*. Reading, Mass.: Addison-Wesley.

Helmer, Olaf. 1964. "The Game-Theoretical Approach to Organization Theory." In *Form and Strategy in Science*, edited by John R. Gregg and F. T. C. Harris. Dordrecht: D. Reidel.

Hempel, Carl. 1965. *Aspects of Scientific Explanation*. New York: Free Press.

———. 1959. "The Function of General Laws in History." In *Theories of History*, edited by Patrick Gardiner. Glencoe, Ill.: Free Press.

———. 1954. "The Logic of Functional Analysis." Pp. 271–307 in *A Symposium on Sociological Theory*, edited by Neal Gross.

———. 1942. "Function of General Laws in History." *Journal of Philosophy* 39:35–48.

Heraclitus. 1954. *The Cosmic Fragments*. Edited by G. S. Kirk. Cambridge: Cambridge University Press.

Heraud, Guy. 1968. *Europe des ethnies*. Paris: Presses d'Europe.

Hesse, Mary B. 1970. *Models and Analogies in Science*. Notre Dame, Ind.: University of Notre Dame Press.

Hewitt, John P. and Randal Stokes. 1975. "Disclaimers." *American Sociological Review* 40:1–11.

Hirsch, Fred. 1976. *The Aims of Interpretation*. Chicago: University of Chicago Press.

Hirschman, Albert O. 1970. *Exit, Voice, Loyalty: Responses to Decline in Firms, Organizations, and States*. Cambridge, Mass.: Harvard University Press.

———. 1967. *Development Projects Observed*. Washington, D.C.: The Brookings Institution.

Hobbes, Thomas. 1979. *De Cive, or The Citizen*. Edited by S. P. Lamprecht. New York.

———. 1957. [1651]. *Leviathan, or the Matter, Form, and Power of a Commonwealth*. Oxford: Basil Blackwell.

Hobsbawm, Eric. 1959. *Social Bandits and Primitive Rebels*. Glencoe, Ill.: Free Press.

Hodgson, Marshall. 1974. *The Venture of Islam: Conscience and History in a World Civilization*. Chicago: University of Chicago Press.

Hoffman, R. R., and R. P. Honech. 1981. *Cognition and Figurative Language*. Hillsdale, N. J.: Erlbaum.

Holbach, Paul-Henri Thiry, Baron d. 1957. *Textes choisis: Préface, commentaire et notes*. Paris: Paulette Charbonnel.

Holz, Hans Heinz. 1961. "Sartre's Kritic der Dialektischen Vernunft." *Merkur* 164 (October): 969–980.

Homans, George. 1945. *The Human Group*. New York: Harcourt, Brace and World.

Hook, Sidney. 1939. "Dialectic in Social and Historical Inquiry." *Journal of Philosophy* 36: 365–378.

Horkheimer, Max. 1974. *The Eclipse of Reason*. New York: Seabury Press.

Horkheimer, Max, and Theodor W. Adorno. 1973. *Dialectics of Enlightenment.* London: Allen Lane.

Horton, Robin. 1976. "Professor Winch on Safari." *Archives Européennes de Sociologie* 27, no. 1.

Hubert, Henri, and Marcel Mauss. 1964. *Sacrifice: Its Nature and Function.* Chicago: University of Chicago Press.

Hull, Clark L. 1952. *A Behavior System: An Introduction to Behavior Theory Concerning the Individual Organism.* New Haven, Conn.: Yale University Press.

Huxley, Aldous. 1937. *Ends and Means.* New York: Harper.

Iggers, George G. 1975. *New Directions in European Historiography.* Middletown, Conn.: Wesleyan University Press.

———. 1965. "The Idea of Progress: A Critical Reassessment." *American Historical Review* 71 (October): 1–17.

Ihde, Don. 1971. *Hermeneutic Phenomenology: The Philosophy of Paul Ricoeur.* Evanston, Ill.: Northwestern University Press.

Imersheim, Allen, W., and Howard M. Kaplan. 1975. "Normative Power and Conflict Potential." *Sociological Methods and Research* 4, no. 2 (November): 237–263.

———. 1974. "Organizational Change as a Paradigm Shift: The Case of Health Care Delivery." Paper presented to the meeting of the American Sociological Association, Montreal.

Israel, Joachim. 1978. "Alienation and Reification." In *Theories of Alienation,* edited by R. Felix Geyer and David R. Schweitzer. The Hague: Martinus Nijhoff.

Jackall, Robert. 1983. "Moral Mazes: Bureaucracy and Managerial Work." *Harvard Business Review* 61, no. 5 (September–October): 118–130.

Jackson, Jay. 1975. "Normative Power and Conflict Potential." *Sociological Methods and Research* 4, no. 2 (November): 237–263.

Jameson, Frederick. 1973. "The Vanishing Mediator: Narrative Structure in Max Weber." *New German Criticism* 1, no. 1 (Winter): 52–89.

———. 1972. *Marxism and Form: Twentieth-Century Dialectical Theories of Literature.* Princeton, N.J.: Princeton University Press.

———. 1971. "Metacriticism." PMLA (Publication of the Modern Language Association) 86, no. 1 (January): 9–18.

———. 1961. *Sartre: The Origins of a Style.* New Haven, Conn.: Yale University Press.

Jehenson, Roger. 1980. "A Phenomenological Approach to the Study of Formal Organization." *American Sociological Review* 45, no. 1 (October): 821–842.

Jung, Hwa Yol. 1982. "Language, Politics, and Technology." *Research in Philosophy and Technology* 5:43–63.

Kafka, Franz. 1971. "The Great Wall of China." In *The Complete Stories.* New York: Schocken.

———. 1946. *Stories and Reflections.* Translated by Willa Muir and Edwin Muir. New York: Schocken.

Kahler, Erich. 1964. *Meaning in History.* New York: George Braziller.

Kahn, Herman, and Anthony J. Weiner. 1967. *The Year 2000: A Framework for Speculation on the Next Thirty-Three Years.* New York: Macmillan.

Kamens, David H. 1977. "Legitimating Myths and Educational Organizations: The Relationship between Organizational Ideology and Formal
Structure." *American Sociological Review* 42: 208–219.

Kant, Immanuel. 1951. *Critique of Judgment*. Translated by J. Bernard. New
York: Hafner Press.

———. 1949a. *Fundamental Principles of the Metaphysics of Morals*. Translated by
T. K. Abbott. Chicago: Regnery.

———. 1949b. *The Philosophy of Kant*. Edited by Carl J. Friedrich. New York:
Modern Library.

———. 1963. *Introduction to Logic*. Translated by T. K. Abbott. London:
Greenwood.

———. 1885. *Kant's Introduction to Logic and His Essay on the Mistaken Subtlety*.
London: Longmans, Green and Co.

Kaplan, Abraham. 1964. *The Conduct of Inquiry*. San Francisco: Chandler.

Kariel, Henry S. 1967. "The Political Relevance of Behavioral and Existential
Psychology." *American Political Science Review* 61 (June): 334–342.

Kaufmann, Walter. 1965. *Hegel*. Garden City, N.Y.: Doubleday.

Kavolis, Vytautas. 1974a. "On the Structure of Consciousness." *Sociological
Analysis* 35, no. 2: 115–118.

———. 1974b. "Post-Modern Man: Psychocultural Responses to Social
Trends." *Social Problems* 17 (Spring): 435–448.

Kearney, Richard, and Paul Ricoeur. 1984. *Dialogues with Contemporary Continental Thinkers*. Manchester, U.K.: Manchester University Press.

Keat, Russell. 1981. *The Politics of Social Theory: Habermas, Freud, and the
Critique of Positivism*. Chicago: University of Chicago Press.

Kerr, Clark, and A. Siegel. 1954. "The Inter-Industry Propensity to Strike: An
International Comparison." Pp. 189–212 in *Industrial Conflict*, edited by P.
K. Edwards et al. New York: McGraw Hill.

Kettler, David. 1970. "The Vocation of Radical Intellectuals." *Politics and
Society*, 1:23–49

Klapp, Orrin E. *Symbolic Leaders*. Chicago: Aldine.

Klee, Paul. 1964. *The Thinking Eye*. New York: Wittemborn.

Knorr-Cetina, Karin D. 1981. "The Micro-Sociological Challenge of Macro-
Sociology: Towards a Reconstruction of Social Theory and Methodology."
In *Advances in Social Theory and Methodology*, edited by Karin D. Knorr-
Cetina and Aaron V. Cicourel. London: Routledge and Kegan Paul.

Kolakowski, Lesak. 1968. *Toward a Marxist Humanism*. New York: Grove
Press.

Kosik, Karl. *Die Dialektik des Konkreten*. Frankfurt am Main: Suhrkamp.

Krieger, Leonard. 1968. "History and Existentialism in Sartre." Pp. 239–266
in *The Critical Spirit: Essays in Honor of Herbert Marcuse*, edited by Kurt H.
Wolff and Barrington Moore, Jr. Boston: Beacon Press.

Kubler, George. 1962. *The Shape of Time: Remarks on the History of Things*. New
Haven, Conn.: Yale University Press.

Kuhn, Thomas. 1972. *The Structure of Scientific Revolutions*. Chicago: University of Chicago Press.

———. 1970. *The Structure of Scientific Revolutions*. Chicago: University of
Chicago Press.

_____. 1962. *Bargaining and the Grievance Process*. New York: Columbia University Press.

Lammers, Cornelius J. 1975. "Tactics and Strategies Adopted by University Authorities to Counter Student Opposition." In *The Dynamics of University Protest*, edited by Donald W. Light. Chicago: Nelson Hall.

_____1969. "Strikes and Mutinies: A Comparative Study of Organizational Conflicts between Rulers and Ruled." *Administrative Science Quarterly* 14, no. 4 (December): 558–572.

Landau, Martin. 1972. *Political Theory and Political Science*. New York: Macmillan.

Langer, Elinor. 1970. "The Women of the Telephone Company." *New York Review of Books* (12 March and 26 March).

Leeds, Ruth. 1964. "The Absorption of Protest: A Working Paper." In *New Perspectives in Organizational Research*, edited by W. W. Cooper, H. J. Leavitt, and M. W. Shelly. New York: Wiley.

Lefebvre, Henri. 1966. "Claude Lévi-Strauss ou le nouvel éléatisme." *L'homme et la Société* 1–2.

_____. 1963. "Réflexions sur le structuralisme et l'histoire." *Cahiers Internationaux de Sociologie* 35: 3–14.

_____. 1961. "Critique de la critique non-critique." *Nouvelle Revue Marxiste* (July).

Lehman, E. W. 1969. "Toward a Macrosociology of Power." *American Sociological Review* 43: 453–465.

Leiter, Kenneth. 1971. "Telling It Like It Is: A Study of Teachers' Accounts." Ph.D. dissertation, University of California, Santa Barbara.

Le Roy Laduire, Emmanuel. 1974. *Peasants of Languedoc*. Urbana: University of Illinois Press.

Lesser, Wayne. 1982. "Criticism, Literary History, and the Paradigm: The Education of Henry Adams." *PMLA* (Publication of the Modern Language Association) 97, no. 3 (May): 378–394.

Levin, David. 1968. "On Lévi-Strauss and Existentialism." *American Scholar* 38 (Winter): 69–82.

_____. 1959. *History as Romantic Art*. Standord, Calif.: Stanford University Press.

Levine, Donald. 1985. *Flight from Ambiguity: Essays in Social and Cultural Theory*. Chicago: University of Chicago Press.

_____. 1983. "Prospectus for Essays on Language and Social Theory." Mimeographed. Department of Social Relations, University of Chicago.

Lévi-Strauss, Claude. 1976. *Structural Anthropology*. Vol. 2. Translated by Monique Layton. New York: Basic Books.

_____. 1970. *The Savage Mind*. Chicago: University of Chicago Press.

_____. 1969. *The Raw and the Cooked*. Translated by J. Weightman and D. Weightman. New York.

_____. 1967. *Structural Anthropology*. Vol. 1, chaps. 1 and 2. Garden City, N.Y.: Doubleday.

_____. 1955. *Tristes Tropiques*. Paris: Plon. Translated under the same title by John Russell. New York: Criterion, 1961 (with chapters 14 through 16 and 39 of the French original omitted).

Lewis, Bernard. 1975. *History: Remembered, Recovered, Invented*. Princeton, N.J.: Princeton University Press.

Leys, Colin. 1972. "A New Theory of Planning?" In *Crisis in Planning*, vol. 1, edited by M. Faber and D. Seers. London: Chatto and Windus.

Lichtheim, George. 1963. "Sartre, Marxism, and History." *History and Theory* 3, no. 2:222–246.

Lienhardt, Godfrey. 1975. *Studies in Social Anthropology*. Oxford: Clarendon Press.

Light, Richard J., Frederick Mosteller, and Herbert S. Winokur. 1972. "Using Controlled Field Studies to Improve Public Policy." In *The President's Commission on Federal Statistics*, vol. 2 Washington, D.C.: Government Printing Office.

Lipsky, Michael. 1969. "Toward A Theory of Street Level Bureaucracy." Mimography. Institute for Research on Poverty, University of Wisconsin, Madison (August).

Louch, A.R. 1966. *Explanation and Human Action*. Berkeley: University of California Press.

Lovejoy, Arthur O. 1917. "On Some Conditions of Progress in Philosophical Inquiry." *Philosophical Review* 26:123–163.

Luban, David. 1979. "Habermas and Arendt on Power." *Philosophy and Social Criticism* 6, no. 1:79–95.

Lukacs, Georg. 1971. *History and Class Consciousness: Studies in Marxist Dialectics*. Cambridge, Mass.: MIT Press.

Lundberg, George, Clarence C. Shrag, and Otto Larsen. 1954. *Sociology*. New York: Harper.

Lyman Stanford M. 1978. *The Seven Deadly Sins: Society and Evil*. New York: St. Martin's.

Lyman, Stanford M., and William A. Douglass. 1973. "Ethnicity: Strategies of Collective and Individual Impression Management." *Social Research* 40, no. 2 (Summer): 344–365.

Lyman, Standford M., and Marvin B. Scott. 1970. *A Sociology of the Absurd*. New York: Appleton-Century-Crofts.

McCarthy, John, and Mayer N. Zald. 1973. *The Trend of Social Movements in America: Professionalization and Resource Mobilization*. Morristown, N.J.: General Learning Press.

McClosky, Mary A. 1964. "Metaphors." *Mind* 73, no. 290 (April) 215–233.

McConnell, Grant. 1966. *Private Power and American Democracy*. New York: Knopf.

MacCormac, Earl. 1976. *Metaphor and Myth in Science and Religion*. Durham, N.C.: Duke University Press.

MacCormac, Earl R. 1971. "Metaphor Revisited." *Journal of Aesthetics and Art Criticism* 30, no. 2 (Winter): 239–250.

McCullagh, C. B. 1984. *Justifying Historical Descriptions*. New York: Cambridge University Press.

McDonald, John. 1973. *The Game of Business*. Garden City, N.Y.: Doubleday.

MacIntyre, Alasdair. 1981. *After Virtue: A Study in Moral Theory*. Notre Dame, Ind.: University of Notre Dame Press.

_____. 1978. "The Idea of a Social Science." Pp. 210–229 in *Against the*

Self-Images of the Age: Essays on Ideology and Philosophy. Notre Dame, Ind.: University of Notre Dame Press.

McKeon, Richard. 1987. *Rhetoric: Essays in Invention and Discovery.* Edited by Mark Backman. Woodbridge, Conn.: Ox Bow Press.

———. 1954. "Dialectic and Political Thought and Action." *Ethics* 65, no. 1 (October): 1–33.

———. 1951. "Philosophy and Method." *Journal of Philosophy* 48: 653–682.

Makkreel, Rudolf A. 1980. "Vico and Some Kantian Reflections on Historical Judgment." *Man and World* 13: 99–120.

Malamud, Bernard. 1966. *The Fixer.* New York: Farrar, Straus and Giroux.

Malinowski, Bronislaw. 1932. *The Sexual Life of Savages in North-Western Melanesia.* New York: Harcourt Brace Jovanovich.

Mandelbaum, Maurice. 1960. "Historical Explanation: The Problem of Covering Laws." *History and Theory* 4: 3–26.

Mangham, Ian L., and Michael A. Overington. 1982. "Performance and Rehearsal: Social Order and Organizational Life. *Symbolic Interaction* 5, no. 2: 205–223.

Mannheim, Karl. 1940. *Man and Society in an Age of Reconstruction.* Translated by Edward Shils. New York: Harcourt, Brace and World.

———. 1936. *Ideology and Utopia: An Introduction to the Sociology of Knowledge.* New York: Harcourt Brace Jovanovich.

Manning, Peter K. 1980. "Organizational Works: Structuration of Environments." Department of Sociology, Michigan State University, East Lansing.

———. 1979. "Semiotics and Loosely Coupled Organizations." Department of Sociology, Michican State University, East Lansing.

March, James G. 1957. "Measurement Concepts in the Theory of Influence." *Journal of Politics* 19, no. 2:202–226.

Marcuse, Herbert. 1978. *The Aesthetic Dimension: Toward a Critique of Marxist Aesthetics.* Boston: Beacon Press.

———. 1976. "On the Problem of the Dialectic." *Telos* 27: 12–40.

Mariner, Dorothy Anderson. 1971. "Ideology and Rhetoric: Their Impact on an Organization and on Professional Aspirations." *Pacific Sociological Review* 14:197–214.

Marsh, James L. 1983. "The Irony and Ambiguity of Freedom." *Poetics Today* 4, no. 3:470–492. Special number on *The Ironic Discourse* edited by Edmond Wright.

Marx, Karl. 1967 [1867]. *Capital: A Critique of Political Economy.* Vol. 1. New York: International Publishers.

———. 1964. *The German Ideology.* Moscow.

———. 1946. *Capital.* New York: Everyman's Library.

Masterman, Margaret. 1970. "The Nature of a Paradigm." Pp. 58–59 in *Criticism and the Growth of Knowledge,* edited by Imre Lakatos and Alan Musgrave. Cambridge: Cambridge University Press.

Mayhew, Bruce E. 1973. "Systems, Size, and Ruling Elites." *American Sociological Review* (August): 468–475.

Mayo, Elton. 1945. *The Social Problems of an Industrial Society.* Cambridge, Mass.: Harvard University Press.

Mehan, Hugh. 1974. "Accomplishing Classroom Lessons." In *Language Use and School Performance*, edited by Aaron V. Cicourel et al. New York: Academic Press.

Memmi, Albert. 1967. *The Colonizer and the Colonized*. Boston: Beacon Press.

Menzel, H. "Meaning—Who Needs It?" In *The Social Context of Method*, edited by M. Brenner et al. London: Croom Helm.

Merton, Robert K. 1957. *Social Theory and Social Structure*. New York: Free Press.

Mill, James. 1878. *Analysis of the Phenomena of the Human Mind*. London: Longmann, Green, Reader, and Dyer.

Mill, John Stuart. 1965 [1843]. *On the Logic of the Moral Sciences*. Indianapolis, Ind.: Bobbs-Merrill.

_____. 1958. *Considerations on Representative Government*. New York: Liberal Arts Press.

Miller, J. C., M. I. Rohn Schooler, and K. A. Miller. 1977. "Women and Work: The Psychological Effects of Occupational Conditions." *American Journal of Sociology* 85:66–94.

Mills, C. Wright. 1974. *Power, Politics, and People: The Collected Essays of C. Wright Mills*. Edited by Irving Louis Horowitz. New York: Oxford University Press.

_____. 1959. *The Sociological Imagination*. New York: Oxford University Press.

Mink, Louis O. 1968. "Philosophical Analysis and Historical Understanding." *Review Metaphysics* 21, no. 4 (June): 667–698.

Mitroff, Ian I. 1974. *The Subjective Side of Science*. Amsterdam: Elsevier.

Moore, Wilbert E. 1962. "Details and Ornaments." Pp. 99–104 in *The Conduct of the Corporation*. New York: Random House.

Morgan, Gareth. 1982. "Cybernetics and Organization Theory: Epistemology Technique?" *Human Relations* 35, no. 7:521–527.

_____. 1980. "Paradigms, Metaphors, and Puzzle-Solving in Organization Theory." *Administrative Sciences Quarterly* 25:605–622.

Moscovici, Serge. 1972. *La société contra nature*. Paris: Union Généralé d'Editions.

_____. 1969. "Le marxisme et la question naturelle." *L'Homme et la Société* (July–September): 59–109.

_____. 1968. *Essai sur l'histoire humaine de la nature*. Paris: Flammarion.

Murdock, George P. 1949. *Social Structure*. New York: Macmillan.

Murphey, Robert F. 1971. *The Dialectics of Social Life*. New York: Basic Books.

Nagel, Thomas. 1986. *The View from Nowhere*. Oxford: Oxford University Press.

Narveson, Jan. 1967. *Morality and Utility*. Baltimore: John Hopkins University Press.

Natanson, Maurice. 1962. "History as a Finite Province of Meaning." In *Literature, Philosophy, and the Social Sciences*, edited by Maurice Natanson. The Hauge: Martinus Nijhoff.

Naville, Pierre. 1943. *Paul Thiry d'Holbach et la philosophie scientifique au XVIIIe siècle*. Paris.

Needham, Joseph, ed. 1955. *Science, Religion, and Reality*. New York: Braziller.

Needleman, Martin, and Carolyn E. Needleman. 1974. Guerrillas in the Bureaucracy: The Community Planning Experiment in the United States. New York: Wiley.

Nef, John. 1960. *Cultural Foundations of Industrial Civilization.* New York: Harper.

Nelson, Benjamin. 1967. "The Early Modern Revolution in Science and Philosophy: Fictionalism, Probabilism, Fideism, and Catholic 'Prophetism'." In Vol. 3, *Boston Studies in the Philosophy of Science*, edited by R. S. Cohen and M. Wartofsky. Dordrecht: D. Reidel.

Nelson, John S. 1983. "Political Theory as Political Rhetoric." Pp. 169–240 in *What Should Political Theory Be Now?*, edited by John S. Nelson. Albany: State University of New York Press.

Newton, Isaac. 1966. *Mathematical Principles of Natural Philosophy and His System of the World.* Translated by Florian Cajori. Berkeley: University of California Press.

Newton, Peter M. 1981. "Who Among Us Still Hopes to Learn about the Nature of Man?" *University Publishing* (Winter): 13–14.

Nichols, Elizabeth. 1985. "Skocpol on Revolution: Comparative Analysis vs. Historical Conjuncture." Paper presented to the meeting of the American Sociological Association, Washington, D.C. (August).

Nietzsche, Friedrich. 1962. *Philosophy in the Tragic Age of the Greeks.* Translated by M. Cowan. Chicago:Regnery.

Nisbet, Robert. 1969. *Social Change and History: Aspects of the Western Theory of Development.* New York: Oxford University Press.

Novalis (F. L. F. von Hardenberg). 1953–1957. *Fragments, Werke.* 5 vols. Edited by E. Wasmuth. Heidelberg.

Ouchi, W. G., and A. M. Price. 1978. "Type Z Organization: Stability in the Midst of Mobility." *Academy of Management Review* 3:305–314.

Overington, Michael A. 1979. "Doing the What Comes Rationally: Some Developments in Metatheory." *American Sociologist* 14 (February):2–11.

Parekh, B. C. 1968. "The Nature of Political Philosophy." Pp. 153–207 in *Politics and Experience*, edited by Preston King and B. C. Parekh. New York and London: Cambridge University Press.

Parsons, Talcott. 1966. *Societies: Evolutionary and Comparative Perspectives.* Englewood Cliffs, N.J.: Prentice-Hall.

_____. 1964. "Evolutionary Universals in Society." *American Sociological Review* 29, no. 3 (June):339–357.

_____. 1956. "Suggestions for a Sociological Approach to the Theory of Organizations." *Administrative Science Quarterly* 1:63–85.

_____. 1951. *The Social System.* Glencoe, Ill.: Free Press.

Passmore, John. 1966. *A Hundred Years of Philosophy.* Baltimore: Penguin.

Patcher, Henry. 1974. "Defining an Event: Prolegomenon to Any Future Philosophy of History." *Social Research* 41 (Autumn):439–466.

Peacock, James L. 1969. "Mystics and Merchants in Fourteenth-Century Germany: A Speculative Reconstruction of Their Psychological Bond and Its Implications for Social Change." *Journal for the Scientific Study of Religion* 8:47–59.

Pears, David. 1986. "The Mysteries of Meaning." *New Republic* (19 May):37–41.

Peel, J. D. Y. 1974. "Spencer and the Neo-Evolutionists." Pp. 188–209 in *Theories and Paradigms in Contemporary Sociology,* edited by R. Serge Denisoff, Orel Callahan, and Mark H. Levine. Itasca, Ill.: F. E. Peacock.

Pennings, Johannes M. 1980. *Interlocking Directorates: Origins and Consequences of Communications among Organizations' Boards of Directors.* San Francisco: Josey-Bass.

Pepper, Stephen. 1942. *World Hypotheses.* Berkeley: University of California Press.

Perelman, Chaim, and Lucie Olbrechts-Tyteca. 1969. *The New Rhetoric: A Treatise on Argumentation.* Notre Dame, Ind.: University of Notre Dame Press.

Perlo, Victor. 1957. *The Empire of High Finance.* New York: International Publishers.

Perrow, Charles. 1970. *Organizational Analysis: A Sociological View.* Belmont, Calif.: Wadsworth.

————. 1967. "A Framework for the Comparative Analysis of Organizations." *American Sociological Review* 32:194–208.

Peters, E. L. 1960. "The Proliferation of Segments in the Lineage of the Bedouin of Cyrenaica." *Journal of the Royal Anthropological Institute* 90:29–53.

Peters, R. S. 1966. *Authority, Responsibility, and Education.* New York: Atherton.

Peters, T. 1978. "Symbols, Patterns, and Settings: An Optimistic Case for Getting Things Done." *Organizational Dynamics* 7:3–23.

Petrovic, Galo. 1967. *Marx in the Mid-Twentieth Century.* Garden City, N.Y.: Doubleday.

Pettigrew, Andrew. 1979. "On Studying Organizational Cultures." *Administrative Science Quarterly* 24, no. 4:570–581.

————. 1973. *The Politics of Organizational Decision Making.* London: Harper and Row.

Pfeffer, J. 1978. "Management as Symbolic Action: The Creation and Maintenance of Organizational Paradigms." In *Research in Organizational Behavior,* vol. 3, edited by L. L. Cummings and B. M. Straw. Greenwich, Conn.: JAI Press.

Pfeffer, Jeffrey, and Gerald Salanick. 1974. "Organizational Decision Making as a Political Process: The Case of the University Budget." *Administrative Science Quarterly* 19:135–151.

Piaget, Jean. 1970. *Structuralism.* New York: Basic Books.

Piccone, Michel. 1971. "Phenomenological Marxism." *Telos* 9 (Fall):3–31.

Piven, Frances Fox, and Richard A. Cloward. 1977. *Poor People's Movements.* New York: Pantheon.

Pocock, J. G. A. 1973. *Politics, Language, and Time: Essays on Political Thought and History.* New York: Atheneum.

————. 1968. "Time, Institutions, and Action: An Essay on Traditions and their Understanding." Pp. 209–238 in *Politics and Experience,* edited by Preston King and B. C. Parekh. Cambridge: Cambridge University Press.

Polanyi, Michael. 1958. *Personal Knowledge: Toward a Post-Critical Philosophy.* Chicago: University of Chicago Press.

Pollner, Melvin. 1970."On the Foundations of Mundane Reasoning." Ph.D. dissertation, University of California, Santa Barbara.

Pondy, Louis R. 1978. "Beyond Open System Models of Organization." In *Research in Organizational Behavior,* edited by B. M. Straw and L. L. Cummings, Greenwich, Conn.: JAI Press.

_____. 1964. "Budgeting and Intergroup Conflict in Organizations." *Pittsburgh Business Review* (April):1–8.

Popper, Karl R. 1972. *Objective Knowledge: An Evolutionary Approach.* Oxford: Oxford University Press.

_____. 1957. *Conjectures and Refutations.* London: Routledge and Kegan Paul.

_____. 1940."What Is Dialectic?" *Mind* 49, no. 196:411.

Poster, Mark. 1975. *Existential Marxism in Postwar France: From Sartre to Althusser.* Princeton, N.J.: Princeton University Press.

Pouillon, Jean. 1966."Sartre et Lévi-Strauss." *L'Arc* 26:55–60.

_____. 1965. "Sartre et Lévi-Strauss: Analyse/dialectique d'une relation dialectique/analytique." *L'Arc* 26:55–60.

Price, James. 2967. *Organizational Effectiveness: An Inventory of Propositions.* Homewood, Ill.: Irwin.

Quine, Willard van Orman. 1960. *Word and Object.* Cambridge, Mass.: MIT Press.

Quinton, A. 1975."Spreading Hegel's Wings." *New York Review of Books,* part 1 (29 May):34–37 and part 2 (12 June):39–42.

Rapaport, Anatol. 1964. *Strategy and Conscience.* New York: Schocken Books.

Reedy, George E. 1970. *The Twilight of the Presidency.* New York: World.

Reichenbach, Hans. 1936. *Experience and Prediction.* Chicago: University of Chicago Press.

Rein, Martin. 1976. *Social Science and Public Policy.* New York: Penguin.

Rescher, Nicholas. 1977. *Dialectics: A Controversy-oriented Approach to the Theory of Knowledge.* Albany: State University of New York.

Ricoeur, Paul. 1983. *Time and Narrative.* Vol. 1 Translated by Kathleen McLaughlin and David Pellauer. Chicago: University of Chicago Press.

_____. 1980. "Existence and Hermeneutics." Translated by Kathleen McLaughlin. In *Contemporary Hermeneutics: Hermeneutics as Method, Philosophy, and Critiques,* edited by Josef Bleicher. London: Routledge and Kegan Paul.

_____. 1975."Phenomenology and Hermeneutics." *Nous* 2, no. 1.

_____. 1973. "Herméneutique et critique des idéologies." In *Idéologie et démythisation,* edited by Enrico Castilli. Paris: Aubier.

_____. 1972. "La métaphore et le problème central de l'herméneutique." *Revue Philosophique de Louvain,* 4th series, 70, no. 5 (February): 93–112.

_____. 1968. "Structure, Word, Event, Robert D. Sweeny." *Philosophy Today* 12, no. 4 (Summer).

_____. 1965a. "Existence et herméneutique." *Dialogue,* 4, no. 1.

_____. 1965b. *History and Truth.* Translated by Charles A. Kelbley. Evanston, Ill.: Northwestern University Press.

Riley, Matilda, John Riley, and Toby Jackson. 1954. *Sociological Studies in Scale Analysis*. New Brunswick, N.J.: Rutgers University Press.

Rivera, Sylvia. 1982. "History and Consciousness in Third World Popular Movements." In *Dialogue about Participation*. Geneva: United Nations Research Institute for Social Development (April).

Roethlisberger, F. J., and W. J. Dickson. 1941. *Management and the Worker*. Cambridge, Mass.: Harvard University Press.

Rommetviet, R. and Joachim Isreal. 1954. "Notes on the Standardization of Experimental Manipulations and Measurements in Cross-National Research." *Journal of Social Issues* 10, no. 4:61–68.

Rorty, Richard. 1979. *Philosophy and the Mirror of Nature*. Princeton, N.J.: Princeton University Press.

Rosen, Lawrence. 1971. "Language, History, and the Logic of Inquiry in Lévi-Strauss and Sartre." *History and Theory* 10, no. 3:269–294.

Ross, Edward A. 1936. *Seventy Years of It: An Autobiography*. New York.

Ruyer, R. 1961. *Revue de métaphysique et de morale*. 1–2:1–34.

Ryle, Gilbert. 1954. *Dilemmas*. London and New York: Cambridge University Press.

Sandel, Michael J. 1982. *Liberalism and the Limits of Justice*. New York and London: Cambridge University Press.

Sartre, Jean-Paul. 1970a. "Déterminisme et liberté." In *Ecrits de Sartre*. Translated as "A Confrontation." *New Left Review* 62 (July–August).

_____. 1970b. "An Interview with Sartre." *New York Review of Books* (26 March): 14–22.

_____. 1969. "Itinerary Of a Thought." *New Left Review* 58 (November–December): 43–66.

_____. 1962. *Existential Psychoanalysis*. Translated by Hazel E. Barnes. Chicago: Regnery.

_____. 1960. *Critique de la raison dialectique*. Bibliothèque des Idées. Paris: Gallimard. Part 1, "Question de méthode," translated by Hazel E. Barnes as *Search for a Method*. New York: Knopf, 1963.

_____. 1956. *Being and Nothingness*. Translated by Hazel Barnes. New York: Washington Square Press.

_____. 1952. "Réponse à Albert Camus." *Les Temps Modernes* 82 (August).

_____. 1951. *Troubled Sleep*. Translated by Gerald Hopkins. New York

_____. 1949. *Mort dans l'âme*. Paris: Gallimard.

_____. 1948. *Psychology of the Imagination*. New York. Translated by Bernard Frechtman from *L'imaginaire: Psychologie phénoménologique de l'imagination*. Paris: 1940.

_____. 1947. *Théâtre*. Paris: Gallimard.

_____. 1943. *L'Être et le néant*. Paris: Gallimard. Translated by Hazel E. Barnes as *Being and Nothingness*. New York: Philosophical Library, 1956.

_____. 1938. *La nausée*. Paris. Translated by Lloyd Alexander. New York: New Directions.

Saussure, Ferdinand de. 1965. *Cours de linguistic générale*. Paris: Presses Universitaires de France.

Schaff, Adam. 1970. *Marxism and the Human Individual*. New York: McGraw-Hill.

Scheff, Thomas J. 1968. *Being Mentally Ill.* Chicago: Aldine.

————. 1961."Control over Policy by Attendants in a Mental Hospital." *Journal of Health and Human Behavior* 2:92–105.

Scheffler, Israel. 1967. *Science and Subjectivity.* Indianapolis, Ind.: Bobbs-Merrill.

Schick, Allan. 1970. "The Cybernetic State." *Transaction* 7, no. 4:14–26.

Schneider, Louis. 1971. "Dialectic in Sociology." *American Sociological Review* 36:667–678.

————. 1964. "Problems in the Sociology of Religion." Pp.770–809 in *Handbook of Modern Sociology,* edited by Robert E. Faris. Chicago: Rand McNally.

Schon, Donald A. 1963. *The Displacement of Concepts.* Also published as *Invention and the Evolution of Ideas.* London: Tavistock Publications.

Schutz, Alfred. 1970. *On Phenomenology and Social Relations.* Chicago: University of Chicago Press.

————. 1962. *Collected Papers.* Vol. 1, *The Problem of Social Reality.* Edited by Maurice Natanson. The Hague: Martinus Nijhoff.

Scott, Marvin B., and Stanford M. Lyman. 1970. *The Revolt of the Students.* Columbus, Ohio: Charles E. Merrill.

Searle, John R. 1983. "The Word Turned Upside Down." *New York Review of Books* (27 October):74–79.

————. 1977. "Reiterating the Differences: A Reply to Derrida." *Glyph* 1:198–208. Johns Hopkins Textual Studies. Baltimore: Johns Hopkins University Press.

————. 1970. *Speech Acts.* Cambridge: Cambridge University Press.

Seider, Maynard S. 1974. "American Big Business Ideology: A Content Analysis of Executive Speeches." *American Sociological Review* 39:802–815.

Sellars, Wilfrid. 1963. *Science, Perception, and Reality.* New York: Humanities Press.

Selznick, Phillip. 1957. *Leadership and Administration.* Evanston, Ill.: Row, Peterson.

————. 1948. "Foundations of the Theory of Organization." *American Sociological Review* 13:25–35.

————. 1943. "An Approach to a Theory of Bureaucracy." *American Sociological Review* 8:47–54.

Seve, Lucien. 1984. "Méthode structurale et méthode dialectique (1967)." In *Structuralisme et dialectique.* Paris: Messidon.

————. 1967. "Méthode structurale et méthode dialectique." *La pensée* 135 (October).

Shils, Edward. 1981. *Tradition.* Chicago: University of Chicago Press.

Shiner, Larry. 1969."A Phenomonological Approach to Historical Knowledge. *History and Theory.*

Silverman, David. 1978. "Accounts of Organizations: Organizational Structures and the Accounting Process." In *Processing People: Case Studies in Organization Behavior,* edited by J. McKinlay. New York: Holt, Rinehart and Winston.

Simmel, Georg. 1977. *The Problems of the Philosophy of History: An Epistemological Essay.* Translated by Guy Oakes. New York: Free Press.

————. 1950. "The Negative Character of Collective Behavior." In *The Sociology of Georg Simmel*, edited by Kurt Wolff. Glencoe, Ill.: Free Press.

Simon, Herbert A. 1964. "On the Concept of Organizational Goal." *Administrative Science Quarterly* (June):1–22.

Simon, J. 1971. "A Conversation with Michel Foucault." *Partisan Review* 2:192–208.

Sjoberg, Gideon. 1959. "Operationalism and Social Research." Pp. 175–210 in *Symposium on Sociological Theory*, edited by Llewellyn Gross. New York: Harper and Row.

Sjoberg, Gideon, Richard A. Brymer, and Buford Farris. 1966. "Bureaucracy and the Lower Class." *Sociology and Social Research* (April): 325–338.

Skillen, Anthony. 1978. *Ruling Illusions: Philosophy and the Social Order.* Atlantic Highlands, N.J.: Humanities Press.

Skinner, B. F. 1971. *Beyond Freedom and Dignity.* New York: Knopf.

————. 1953. *Science and Human Behavior.* New York: Macmillan.

————. 1948. *Walden Two.* New York: Macmillan.

Skinner, Quentin. 1969. "Meaning and Understanding in the History of Ideas." *History and Theory* 8:3–53.

Skocpol, Theodora. 1979. *States and Social Revolutions.* Cambridge: Cambridge University Press.

Small, Albion W. 1916. "Fifty Years of Sociology in the United States (1865–1915)." *American Journal of Sociology* 21:748–766.

Sontag, Susan. 1966."The Anthropologist as Hero." In *Against Interpretation.* New York: Farrar, Straus and Giroux.

Sorel, Georges. 1969. *The Illusions of Progress.* Berkeley: University of California Press.

————. 1961. *Reflections on Violence.* New York: Collier.

Sorokin, Pitirm. 1966. *Sociological Theories of Today.* New York: Harper.

————. 1964. "Comments on Schneider's Observations and Criticisms." Pp. 401–432 in *Explorations in Social Change*, edited by G. K. Zollschan and W. Hirsch. Boston: Houghton Mifflin.

Spengler, Oswald. 1928. *The Decline of the West.* vol. 1 New York: Knopf.

Spindler, George, ed. 1974. *Educational and Cultural Processes.* New York: Holt, Rinehart and Winston.

Stanley, Manfred. 1986. "Can American Pluralism Tolerate Civic Education? An Examination of the Status of Civic Rhetoric in America." Paper delivered to the conference on Case Studies in the Rhetoric of the Human Sciences, Temple University, Philadelphia, Pa. (April).

————. 1983. "Concentration in Social Foundations of Public Policy at Syracuse." Pamphlet. Maxwell School, Syracuse University, Syracuse, N.Y.

————. 1978. *The Technological Conscience: Survival and Dignity in an Age of Expertise.* New York: Free Press.

Steiner, George. 1974. "Orpheus with His Myths: Claude Lévi-Strauss.' In *Language and Silence: Essays on Language, Literature, and the Inhuman.* New York, Atheneum.

————. 1966. "A Conversation with Claude Lévi-Strauss." *Encounter* (26 April).

Stinchcombe, Arthur L. 1978. *Theoretical Methods in Social History.* New York: Academic Press.

_____. 1959. "Bureaucratic and Craft Administration of Production: A Comparative Study." *Administrative Science Quarterly* 4 (September): 168–187.

Stoianovich, Traian. 1976. *French Historical Method: The "Annales" Paradigm,* Ithaca, N.Y.: Cornell University Press.

Stone, Gregory P., and Harvey A. Faberman. 1974.[1970]. *Social Psychology through Symbolic Interaction.* Waltham, Mass.: Xerox College Publishing.

Strasser, Stephen. 1964. *Phenomenology and the Human Sciences.* Pittsburgh, Pa.: Dusquensne University Press.

_____. 1962. *The Soul in Metaphysical and Empirical Psychology.* Pittsburgh, Pa.: Duquesne University Press.

Strauss, Anselm L. 1978. *Negotiations.* San Francisco: Josey-Bass.

_____. 1969. *Mirrors and Masks: The Search for Identity.* San Francisco: Sociology Press.

Strauss, Anselm L., et al. 1964. *Psychiatric Ideologies and Institutions.* New York: Free Press.

Streuver, Nancy S. 1982. "The Pepper Papers." *Journal of Mind and Behavior* 3 and 4, special issue.

_____. 1974. "The Study of Language and The Study of History." *Journal of Interdisciplinary History* 4:401–415.

_____1970. *Language of History in the Renaissance: Rhetoric and Historical Consciousness in Florentine Humanism.* Princeton, N.J.: Princeton University Press.

Strong, Tracy B. 1978. "Dramaturgical Discourse and Political Enactments: Toward an Artistic Foundation for Political Space." Pp. 237–260 in *Structure, Consciousness, and History,* edited by Richard Harvey Brown and Stanford M. Lyman. London and New York: Cambridge University Press.

Sudnow, David. 1969. *Passing On: The Social Organization of Dying.* Englewood Cliffs, N.J.: Prentice Hall.

Sumner, William Graham. 1883. *What the Social Classes Owe to Each Other.* New York.

Swabey, Marie C. 1961. *Comic Laughter.* New Haven, Conn.: Yale University Press.

Symposiasts. 1956. *Symposium on the Changes in Sociology.* Special number of *Sociology and Social Research* (July–August).

Szasz, Thomas S. 1970. *The Manufacture of Madness.* New York: Harper and Row.

_____. 1961. *The Myth of Mental Illness.* New York: Hoeber-Harper.

Sztompka, P. 1974. *System and Function: Toward a Theory of Society.* New York: Academic Press.

Taine, Hippolyte. 1982. *The History of English Literature.* Translated by H. van Laun. New York: Holt.

Taylor, Charles. 1971. "Interpretation and the Science of Man." *Review of Metaphysics* 25, no. 3:1–45.

_____. 1964. *The Explanation of Behavior.* New York: Humanities Press.

Taylor, Frederick W. 1947. *Scientific Management.* New York: Harper.

Taylor, Richard. 1966. *Action and Purpose*. Englewood Cliffs, N.J.: Prentice-Hall.

Thernstrom, Stephan. 1969. *Poverty, Planning, and Politics in the New Boston*. New York: Basic Books.

Thomas, James C. 1968. *Music through the Renaissance*. Dubuque, Ia.: W. C. Brown.

Thomas, Kenneth W., and Louis R. Pondy. 1977."Toward an Intent Model of Conflict Management among Principle Parties." *Human Relations* 30, no. 12:1089–1102.

Thompson, Clarence B. 1914. *Scientific Management*. Cambridge, Mass.: Harvard University Press.

Thompson, E. P. 1965. "Peculiarities of the English." In *The Socialist Register*, edited by Ralph Miliband and J. Savill. London: Merlin Press.

———. 1963. *The Making of the English Working Class*. London: Gallancz.

Thompson, James. 1967. *Organizations in Action*. New York: McGraw Hill.

Thompson, James D., and William J. McEwen. 1958. "Organizational Goals and the Environment." *American Sociological Review* 23:23–31.

Thompson, Victor. 1963. *Modern Organizations*. New York: Knopf.

Thucydides. 1951. *Complete Writings: The Peloponnesian War*. New York: Modern Library.

Thurstone, Louis Leon, and E. J. Chave. 1929. *The Measurement of Attitude*. Chicago: University of Chicago Press.

Tilly, Charles, 1978. *From Mobilization to Revolution*. Reading, Mass.: Addison-Wesley.

———. 1971. *History as Social Science*. Englewood Cliffs, N.J.: Prentice-Hall.

Times Literary Supplement. 1970. "Dialectical Methodology." Vol. 3, no. 550 (12 March): 269–272.

Tiryakian, Edward A. 1972. "Toward the Sociology of Esoteric Cultures." *American Journal of Sociology* 78:491–512.

Todorov, Tsvetan. 1969. *Grammaire du Décaméron*. The Hague: Mouton.

Tönnies, Ferdinand.1974. *On Social Ideas and Ideologies*. Translated by E. G. Jacoby. New York: Harper and Row.

Toulmin, Stephen. 1961. *Foresight and Understanding: An Enquiry into the Aims of Science*. Bloomington: University of Indiana Press.

Turbayne, Colin M. 1962. *The Myth of Metaphor*. New Haven, Conn.: Yale University Press.

Turner, John C. 1970. "Barriers and Channels for Housing Development in Modernizing Countries." In *Peasants in Cities*, edited by William Mangin. Boston: Houghton Mifflin.

Turner, John H. 1974. *The Structure of Sociological Theory*. Homewood, Ill.: Dorsey.

Tyack, David. 1974. *The One Best System: A History of American Urban Education*. Cambridge, Mass.: Harvard University Press.

Tylor, Edward B. 1924. "The Science of Culture." In *Primitive Culture*. London: John Murray.

Udy, Stanley. H. 1959. "The Structure of Authority in Non-Industrial Production Organizations." *American Journal of Sociology* 64: 582–584.

Ulmer, Gregory L. 1981. "The Post-Age." *Diacritics* 11:39–56.

Urmson, J. D. 1956. *Philosophical Analysis*. Oxford: Oxford University Press.

van den Berghe, Pierre. 1963. "Dialectic and Functionalism: Toward a Theoretical Synthesis." *American Sociological Review* 28:695–705.

Vico, Giambattista. 1972 [1744]. *The New Science of Giambattista Vico*. Translated by Thomas Goddard Bergin and Max Harold Frisch. Ithaca, N.Y: Cornell University Press.

———. 1965. *On the Study Methods of Our Time*. Translated by Elio Gianturco. Indianapolis, Ind.: Bobbs-Merrill. See *Opere*, vol. 1, edited by Gentile and Nicolini. Bari: Laterza, 1914.

Vidich, Arthur J. 1975. "Political Legitimacy in Bureaucratic Society: An Analysis of Watergate." *Social Research* 42, no. 4 (Winter): 778–814.

Villarejo, Don. 1980. *Stock Ownership and Control of the Corporations*. Boston: New England Free Press.

Voegelin, Eric. 1952. *The New Science of Politics*. Chicago: University of Chicago Press.

Von Grunebaum, Gustav Edmund. 1966. *The Dream and Human Societies*. Berkeley: University of California Press.

Von Grunebaum, Gustav Edmund, and Roger Caillois. 1966. *The Dream and Human Society*. Berkeley: University of California Press.

Waelens, Alphonse de. 1962. "Sartre et la raison dialectique." *Revue Philosophique de Louvain* 60 (February): 79–99.

Wager, W. Warren. 1977. *World Views: A Study in Comparative History*. Hinsdale, Ill.: Dryden Press.

Wallace, Walter L. 1971. *The Logic of Science in Sociology*. Chicago: Aldine.

Wamsley, Gary, and Mary Zald. 1973. *The Political Economy of Public Organizations*. Lexington, Mass.: Lexington Books.

Warnock, Mary. 1967. *Existentialist Ethics*. London: Macmillan; New York: St. Martin's Press.

Warriner, Charles K. 1980. "The Sociology of Organizations: A Critique and Suggestions." Paper presented to the Annual Meetings of the American Sociological Association, New York (August).

Weber, Max. 1978. "Types of Legitimate Domination." In *Economy and Society: An Outline of Interpretive Sociology*, edited by Guenther Roth and Claus Wittich. Berkeley: University of California Press.

———. 1949. *From Max Weber: Methodology of the Social Sciences*. Edited by Edward Shils and Henry Finch. Glencoe, Ill.: Free Press.

Weick, Karl E. 1969. *The Social Psychology of Organizing*. Reading, Mass.: Adisson-Wesley.

Weil, Frederick. 1978. "Is/Was There a Legitimation Crisis? Evidence from Seven Western Countries." Paper presented at the Annual Meetings of the American Sociological Association, Chicago (August).

Weinberg, Martin S. 1965. "Sexual Modesty, Social Meanings, and the Nudist Camp." *Social Problems* 12:311–318.

Weinshimer, Joel C. 1985. *Gadamer's Hermeneutics: A Reading of "Truth and Method."* New Haven, Conn.: Yale University Press.

Wellmer, Albrecht. 1971. *Critical Theory of Society*. New York: Herder and Herder.

Wheelwright, Phillip Ellis. 1968. *The Burning Fountain: A Study in the Language of Symbolism.* Bloomington: Indiana University Press.

______. 1962. *Metaphor and Reality.* Bloomington: University of Indiana Press.

White, Hayden. 1978. *Tropics of Discourse.* Baltimore: Johns Hopkins University Press.

______. 1973. *Metahistory: The Historical Imagination in the Nineteenth Century.* Baltimore: Johns Hopkins University Press.

Whyte, Martin King. 1973. "Corrective Labor Camps in China." *Asian Survey* 13, no. 3 (March): 253–270.

Wildavsky, Aaron. 1964. *The Politics of the Budgetary Process.* Boston: Little Brown.

Wilden, Anthony. 1972. "The Epistemological and Biosocial Crisis: The Difference That Makes a Difference." Mimeographed. Department of Communications, University of California, San Diego.

Wilson, Thomas. 1969. *Arts of Rhetoric.* Amsterdam: Theatrum Orbis Terrarum; New York: Da Capo Press.

Winch, Peter. 1970. "Understanding a Primitive Society." In *Rationality,* edited by Brian Wilson. London: Oxford University Press.

______. 1958. *The Idea of a Social Science and Its Relation to Philosophy.* London: Routledge and Kegan Paul.

Wisdom, J. O. 1968. "Anti-Dualist Outlook and Social Inquiry." In *Problems in the Philosophy of Science,* edited by Imre Lakatos and Alan Musgrave. Amsterdam: North Holland Publishing Co.

Wittgenstein, Ludwig. 1979. *Notebooks 1914–1916.* Oxford: Basil Blackwell.

______. 1963. *Philosophic Investigations.* Translated by G. E. M. Anscombe. Oxford: Basil Blackwell.

Wolff, Kurt. 1970. "The Sociology of Knowledge and Sociological Theory." In *The Sociology of Sociology,* edited by Larry T. Reynold and Janice M. Reynolds. New York: McKay.

Wolin, Sheldon. 1968. "Paradigms and Political Theories." Pp.125–152 in *Politics and Experience,* edited by Preston King and B. C. Parekh. New York and London: Cambridge University Press.

Wood, Gordon. 1982. *New York Review of Books* (16 December): 59.

Wood, Houston. 1968. "The Labelling Process in a Mental Hospital Ward." M.A. thesis, University of California, Santa Barbara.

Woodmansee, John. 1975. *The World of a Giant Corporation.* Seattle, Wash.: North Country Press.

Woodward, Joan. 1965. *Industrial Organizations: Theory and Practice.* London: Oxford University Press.

Wright, Edmund, ed. 1983. "Introduction." *The Ironic Discourse,* a special issue. *Poetics Today,* 4, no. 3:391–398.

______. 1977a. "Perception: A New Theory." *American Philosphical Quarterly* 14, no. 4:273–286.

______. 1977b. "Words and Intentions." *Philosophy* 52, no. 199:45–62.

Wrong, Denis. 1968. "Some Problems in Defining Social Power." *American Journal of Sociology* 24:183–193.

Yates, Frances. 1964. *Giordano Bruno and the Hermetic Tradition.* Chicago: University of Chicago Press.

Young, T. R., and Garth Massey. n.d. "The Dramaturgical Society: A Macro-Analytic Approach to Dramaturgical Analysis." Boulder, Colo.: Red Feather Institute.

Zald, Mayer N. 1970. *Power in Organizations*. Nashville, Tenn.: Vanderbilt University Press.

———. 1965. "Who Shall Rule: A Political Analysis of Succession in a Large Welfare Organization." *Pacific Sociological Review* 8:52–60.

Zald, Mayer, N., and Michael A. Berger. 1978. "Social Movements in Organizations: Coup d'Etat, Insurgency, and Mass Movements." *American Journal of Sociology* 83:823–861.

Zeitz, Gerald. 1978. "A Labeling Theory of Authority." Draft paper. School of Business, Temple University, Philadelphia, Pa.

Zijderveld, Anton C. 1970. *The Abstract Society: A Cultural Analysis of Our Time.* New York: Doubleday.

Zimmerman, Don H. 1970. "Record Keeping and the Intake Process in a Public Welfare Agency." In *Explorations in Sociology and Counseling,* edited by Stanton Wheeler. Boston: Houghton Mifflin.

Zolberg, Aristide. 1972. "Moments of Madness." *Politics and Society* 2, no. 2:183–207.

Index

Accidents, Aristotle on, 85–86, 88
Adamiecki, Karol, 22–23
Adamov, Arthur, 1
Adams, Henry, 179n.7
Adorno, Theodor W., 36, 39, 45, 132
Advertising, 152
Age of Reason, The (Sartre), 61
Alienation, 5
Althusser, Louis, xiii, 40, 81, 100, 101
American Management Association, 23
Analytical reason, 63–65
Anaximander, 85
Anderson, Perry, 89
Annales school, xiii, 81, 102–4
Anthropology, 4, 52, 63–65. *See also* Lévi-Strauss, Claude; Structuralism
Apel, Karl-Otto, 44, 120
Archeology, 179n.9
Arendt, Hannah, 143
Argyris, Chris, 128
Aristotle, 10, 92, 168, 175n.2; and functional evolutionism, 80, 85–89; on metaphor, 82–83
Army Corps of Engineers, 24
Art, 84; Dadaist, 156; and human sciences, 10; as metaphorical, 94–95; romantic concept of, 30, 40–45; separation of science from, 79–80, 114; and social planning, 161–62

Ashby, W. R., 158
Augustine, St., 86
Authority, 73
Aventures de la dialectique, Les (Merleau-Ponty), 105
Ayer, A. J., ix, 28, 37
Azande, 41–43

Bacon, Sir Francis, 9, 12, 14, 89
Baillie, J. B., 117
Barraclough, Geoffrey, 111
Bateson, Gregory, 184n.3
Baudelaire, Charles, 95
Bazerman, Charles, 20
Beauvoir, Simone de, 61
Becker, Howard, 87
Beckett, Samuel, 3
Becoming, 99
Beer, Stafford, 158
Behaviorism, 19, 29, 60, 116
Being, 99, 167
Being and Nothingness (Sartre), 58–61
Bell, Daniel, 151
Bellah, Robert N., 7
Bellamy, Edward, 20
Benthall, Jonathan, 21
Bentham, Jeremy, 16
Berggren, Douglas, 83
Bernstein, Basil, 76
Betti, Emilio, 121
Bhaskar, Roy, 40
Binary opposition, 68
Binet, Alfred, 18

Vedas, 99
Verein für Sozialpolitik, 17
Vico, Giambattista, 10, 33, 40, 82, 83, 114, 164
Voegelin, Eric, 169
von Grunebaum, Gustav Edmund, 166

Wallace, Walter L., 72
Warriner, Charles K., 152
Watson, John B., 19
Watson, Thomas, 158
Weber, Max, xii–xiv, 6, 7, 56, 111; on causality in history, 90; Garfinkel's demystification of, 127–32; on historical process, 105; organization theory of, 124–27, 140; social action types of, 71
Weick, Karl E., 142, 152
Weinberg, Martin S., 131
Weiner, Anthony J., 144, 183n.1
Wellmer, Albrecht, 41

White, Hayden, 82, 97, 118
White, Martin King, 106, 116
Will, 61, 106
Winch, Peter, 30–31, 35, 41–44, 47, 59
Winokur, Herbert S., 160
Wittgenstein, Ludwig, 33, 43, 59, 70, 134
Wolff, Kurt, 168
Wolin, Sheldon, 135, 137
Wood, Gordon, 20
Woodmansee, John, 138
Woodward, Joan, 19, 126
Work, liberation in, 45
World Hypotheses (Pepper), 96
Wright, Edmund, 29, 31

Yates, Frances, 48
Young, T. R., 163

Zald, Mayer N., 151
Zolberg, Aristide, 165